THE "LOST" TREASURES OF LOUIS COMFORT TIFFANY

THE "LOST" TREASURES OF LOUIS COMFORT TIFFANY

Hugh F. McKean

Photos by Will Rousseau and others

DOUBLEDAY & COMPANY, INC., GARDEN CITY, NEW YORK   1980

Library of Congress Cataloging in Publication Data

McKean, Hugh.
    The "lost" treasures of Louis Comfort Tiffany.

    Bibliography: p. 287
    Includes index.
    1. Tiffany, Louis Comfort, 1848–1933.   I. Title.
N6537.T5M32   709'.2'4
ISBN: 0-385-09585-6
Library of Congress Catalog Card Number 76–2796

ALL RIGHTS RESERVED
PRINTED IN THE UNITED STATES OF AMERICA
FIRST EDITION

My darling wife, Jeannette, deserves more credit for this book than I could ever give her.

Acknowledgments

I am indebted to many members of the Tiffany family who have helped in endless ways in the preparation of this manuscript. These include three of Louis Tiffany's daughters, Mary Tiffany Lusk (Mrs. Graham Lusk), Dorothy Tiffany Burlingham (Mrs. Robert Burlingham), Comfort Tiffany Gilder (Mrs. Rodman Gilder); six grandchildren, Louise Lusk Platt (Mrs. Collier Platt), Louis Tiffany Lusk, Comfort Parker O'Connor (Mrs. Cornelius E. O'Connor), Joy Gilder Treat (Mrs. Asher E. Treat), Helena Gilder Miller (Mrs. A. Amasa Miller), Katrina Burlingham Valenstein (Mrs. Arthur Valenstein); seven grandnephews, Professor Woodbridge Bingham, Hiram Bingham, Alfred M. Bingham, Dr. Charles T. Bingham, the Reverend Brewster Bingham, Mitchell Bingham, and the Honorable Jonathan B. Bingham; and one great grandson, Harry Platt.

I am grateful also to Marilynn Bordes, Associate Curator, Department of American Decorative Arts, the Metropolitan Museum of Art; to Dr. Wilbur Dorsett, Professor of English, Rollins College; to Dr. Edwin P. Granberry, Professor Emeritus of Creative Writing, Rollins College; and to my brother, Dr. Keith F. McKean, Professor of English Language and Literature, the University of Northern Iowa, for all their invaluable assistance and encouragement.

Notes

Unless otherwise noted, all artwork is in the collection of the Morse Gallery of Art, Winter Park, Florida.

Unless otherwise credited, photographs are by Will Rousseau.

Contents

Prologue

Cumulous clouds piling up on the horizon and cool breezes coming in off the Sound gave the day a crisp quality you could feel all the way to your fingertips. The view of Cold Spring Harbor and the land running out to the Sound was still beautiful, but charred timbers and twisted pipes made bizarre patterns against the sky, and jagged holes stared where windows should have been. Laurelton Hall, Louis Tiffany's great summer place was a ruin.

Curiously, the fires had spared some of its finest parts. Glass tesserae flashed in the entablature over the immense columns in the loggia. Wine-red poppies still bloomed on their capitals. The bronze lanterns hanging between them had not lost their delicate leaded panels and iridescent glass. The Daffodil Terrace, with its marble columns and capitals abloom with glass daffodils, was still intact, and the blue glass lining in the opening Mr. Tiffany had left so an old pear tree could live out its days was still there.

Jeannette, my wife, and I walked around what was once a lawn. It was strewn with the lovely gray furniture from the dining room. I shook something muddy leaning against a tree. It rattled. The head of the wrecking company waiting to clear the property was with us. I asked him what it was. "That's one of the old man's windows," he replied. (It turned out to be a section of the famous "Four Seasons" window.)

We walked the little distance to the small building Mr. Tiffany had built for the chapel he had designed for the World's Columbian Exposition in Chicago. The chapel had dazzled more than a million visitors and had made his reputation in Europe. He had treasured it as some of his finest work. The heavy oak door, adorned with a wrought-iron Celtic cross, was standing ajar. The inside reeked with rot and neglect. Bits of broken glass were everywhere. Weeds grew out of the walls. It was littered with the dead butterflies, dried leaves, bird droppings, and old newspapers abandoned buildings always seem to collect.

The leaded-glass windows, saved miraculously from the fires, were stacked against the walls. The electrolier, at least those parts spared by vandals, was still hanging. The "Lily" window designed by Mr. Tiffany as a backdrop for the baptismal font, was still in place, but the altar and font were gone.

I was glad to leave for a quiet walk through what had once been terraces and gardens. Paths I had followed as a young man looking for places to sketch led nowhere now. It was all sadly strange. Before we left we had bought everything the fires had spared. We did not want our new "treasures," any more than anyone else, but we did not want them destroyed.

My visit to Laurelton Hall as a young artist was my father's doing. After high school I had wanted to study art. When we discussed it he suggested, "Why not go to college first?" The year I graduated from Rollins College, he sent two of my paintings to the jury of the Tiffany Foundation, without my knowledge, and I received a surprise and welcome invitation to spend September and October of 1930 at Laurelton Hall.

The Florida boom had collapsed. The stock market had crashed. My father was pressed financially. Even so, he made it possible for me to spend the summer months of that year in New York City so I could take life classes at the Art

Students League. Living in a cheap rooming house on New York's West Side and drawing naked people in crowded hot studios was not glamorous, but I needed the training. I had no money for entertainment, except for an occasional ride on one of the summer street cars. The electric signs in Times Square (an important American art form) and the soap-box orators denouncing the rich, the free enterprise system, and the white race, were a new and fascinating experience which cost nothing.

When September finally arrived I was more aware of the world's problems, better at drawing the human figure, tired of New York, and ready for a change.

I arrived at Oyster Bay on the wrong train, at the wrong time, from the wrong direction because I had not changed trains when I should have. Even so, one of Mr. Tiffany's cars with a driver was there to meet me. We entered the estate by the long, gravel driveway. He was following orders, he explained. Mr. Tiffany wanted all young artists coming to Laurelton Hall to remember "they were his personal guests." "After this," he added, "you can use any drive you choose."

The evening air was spiced with the fragrance of petunias. The pools, fountains, terraces, and gardens were unlike anything I had ever seen, and I was dazzled. There was so much of everything—so many gardens, so many vistas, so many terraces.

We ten or so men residents lived in what had once been the stables and carriage house. Mr. Tiffany had remodeled them all with taste. We had our own servants, kitchen, dining room, art gallery, and studios. The bedrooms were former stalls. Each had a view of lawns and gardens, and each opened onto a courtyard with a fountain in the center. The women lived somewhere else.

I have never been a good correspondent, but I did manage to write my family a few letters which now frustrate me because of what they do not say. I mention the fact that I had "just come back from an organ concert in Mr. Tiffany's house. . . . The organ is in his fountain room and lighted very mysteriously with dim colored lights. In the center of the room, there is a globe hung on a long chain which looks like a moon. . . . There is a fountain made of a big glass vase . . . lighted with hidden lights. The water runs out the top . . . and it changes so

gradually that I didn't notice it changing for half an hour or so. . . . The whole place is the most mysterious layout I ever saw. Poor old Mr. Tiffany is so deaf that he can't hear the music when the fountains play, so he just sits and taps his cane. It seems too good to be true—I feel that I might wake up and find it a pipe dream."

Those months, in contrast to my stay in New York, passed very quickly. I painted, swam in Cold Spring Harbor, played tennis, and bowled. Alan Dunn, the quiet master who made millions of Americans chuckle with his brilliant cartoons in *The New Yorker*, taught me how to play chess.

I am often asked if I "studied" with Mr. Tiffany. No one "studied" in the literal sense. There were no classes. He did bring lecturers from New York to discuss various schools of art. Concerts were arranged for us. But the Tiffany Foundation did not offer instruction. Mr. Tiffany had surrounded us with endless beauty and every luxury, including the one he valued most—freedom.

There was one "rule," and I learned of it in some way I have now forgotten. We were not to "socialize" with the butlers, gardeners, or any of the employees. So when I was invited very quietly to have an Italian dinner at the home of one of the gardeners, I was delighted. I still cannot understand why, but on that night I forgot and ate dinner in our own dining room. The two other men who were also invited wisely only went through the motions.

When we arrived at our host's house, we found a charming Italian family, all in high spirits and ready for a great Italian dinner. I did manage to eat a mountain of spaghetti buried under an avalanche of grated cheese, but I almost foundered on the veal cutlet which followed. It was as big as a dinner plate. If that can be considered a painful experience, and in some pleasant way it was, there were no others in two glorious months.

Walking around the place twenty-seven years later brought back memories, and raised questions. Why was Laurelton Hall in ruins? Why had America forgotten the man who made it? And why had so much of his work been "lost" in our search for new forms and new values? I have talked to many people who knew him. I have examined all the documents I can locate. The results are recorded on these pages, but remember, dear reader, new information will always throw more light on these fascinating matters.

FIGURES 1-7 *"Wisteria." Leaded windows. Tiffany Studios, c. 1910. Unsigned. Made for the dining room of Laurelton Hall. Height 38".*

THE "LOST" TREASURES OF LOUIS COMFORT TIFFANY

And to make things worse, few Americans seemed to care.

Louis Tiffany did care. Such public image as he enjoys today is that of a worldly man, and in many ways he was worldly.

The Tiffanys were descended from Squire Humphrey Tiffany who, on a dark day in 1685, while traveling from Swansey to Boston along with a horse whose name is not known and a lady named Frances Low, departed this life in a "clap of thunder" (according to a contemporary account). His progeny were mostly industrious New England Presbyterians, with a dash of Puritanism thrown in. Louis' grandfather, Comfort Tiffany, was a prosperous textile manufacturer in Killingly, Connecticut. Louis' father, Charles Lewis Tiffany, founder of New York's famous Tiffany & Company, was one of the country's very wealthy men.

Louis, therefore, was used to and loved those amenities the envious malign as luxuries. He moved in the top social strata, entertained like a prince, and traveled in style (the Imperial Suite on the *Berengaria* and a private car on the rails). He enjoyed rare wine, good food, the theater, and the opera.

But there was more to Tiffany than that. He loved the country, the woods, farming, animals, flowers, trees, dragonflies, Queen Anne's lace, dandelions, and toadstools. He liked walks in his gardens early in the morning when spiders' webs sparkled with dew. He liked leaves against the sky, and the patterns in a newly cut onion. He was a devoted husband. He loved his children, grandchildren, and great-grandchildren. He was prompt, well organized, determined, hardworking. And, most important of all, his life was one long effort to add beauty to life in America, not necessarily to the lives of the rich, but to the lives of everyone.

Beauty to Tiffany had a special meaning with broad implications. The formulas taught by art schools had little to do with it. There is, he believed, a different kind of beauty for every artist, and it can be found only when one is free to search the frontiers of the mind. The quest for beauty to Tiffany meant purpose, order, self-discovery. Finding beauty meant sharing it with others. The appreciation of beauty to him was a civilizing experience. He was convinced America needed beauty, and he was right. It did.

Tiffany's thinking was not the result of some college course in art or aesthetics. He attended the Flushing Academy in Long Island, and later Eagleswood Military Academy in Perth Amboy, reluctantly. His father probably agreed to his studying art instead of attending college because Tiffany gave him no choice. Louis did not like school, ever.

Even his training in art was casual. It began with George Inness, the landscape painter, who looked like a bearded eagle and painted like a poet. Inness, no more a teacher than Tiffany was a student, seems to have played a dubious role in the success story. Apparently, all Tiffany did was sit in a corner and watch Inness paint. How rewarding the experience was is difficult to say. Inness had little good to say about his student.

Tiffany's early pictures were painted with the little touches of the brush typical of Inness' paintings of that period. Later, he "studied" with Samuel Colman, the American painter, and with Leon Bailly in Paris. Samuel Colman, who had a deep interest in the decorative arts, and Edward Chandler Moore, the art director of Tiffany & Company from 1868 until his death in 1891, seem to have been major influences.

In 1865, at the age of seventeen Tiffany crossed the Atlantic on the paddle steamer *Scotia*.[1] The fifty or more drawings[2] and watercolors from that happy venture disclose a natural talent and an interest in picturesque churches, streets, harbors, boats, and gardens. He returned to Europe many times to paint and to patronize the theater, the opera, and the better restaurants. He liked the Germans (one of his ponies was named Bismarck), but he spent more time in France, possibly because he spoke fluent French.

He studied the early Christian mosaics in Ravenna, and the twelfth- and thirteenth-century windows in Chartres Cathedral. The mosaics fascinated him. The windows haunted him. Their colors were *in* the glass, not on it. In other words, the colors were due to metallic oxides dissolved in the pot metal (molten glass). By the middle of the nineteenth century no one was making windows that even approached them in quality. The glass was thin, the colors were harsh, and the images were made by applying enamels to them (enamels were powdered colored glass brushed onto the surface of clear glass and heated enough to fuse them in place). This meant the nineteenth-century stained-glass windows were, in effect, pictures applied to glass with a brush. To

Tiffany, this was important. It involved an art principle. He believed an artist should bring out the beauty of his materials. He was convinced the enamels darkened the glass and made it less attractive.

The Chartres windows fascinated Tiffany for another reason. The men who made them were not trying for a natural look. They surrounded their saints with ruby glass if they wanted red in their window, and blue, or another color, if they thought that would be better. That one never sees a saint surrounded by red space presented no problems at all to the medieval masters. The Chartres windows tell a story and convey ideas. They are not pictures of places or people. Because of this they raise a question with many ramifications. Should leaded windows attempt to represent natural scenes? Or should they have a look all their own? If Tiffany's aesthetic had been more complete, he might eventually have been able to resolve this matter, but it seems to have bothered him all his life. He wavered between two points of view. Some of his windows are naturalistic scenes. Some are essentially decorative screens of color.

When he held a brush, no uncertainty clouded Tiffany's mind. His paintings always clearly and intentionally record something he had seen and enjoyed. In 1867 his watercolor "Afternoon" was "hung on the line" (a special nod to its quality) by the National Academy in its Annual Exhibition. He was a nineteen-year-old unknown. One newspaper critic dubbed his picture a copy (another flattering "nod") and lectured the young painter accordingly. Tiffany carefully preserved the clipping.[3] By the time he was thirty, a series of honors and an impressive record of sales indicated that his future as a painter was assured.

But the deep blues and ruby reds in Chartres continued to haunt him and so did the memory of the sparkling colors of the precious stones in his father's "shop." (Pure colors to a conservative painter are a forbidden world. All the colors we see in nature are grayed a little by the atmosphere.) Then, too, Tiffany found contemporary glass dull by comparison. The glass in ordinary bottles, due to impurities left in the sand and to bubbles resulting from haste and casual workmanship, was richer, more attractive.

Early in the 1870s he began to experiment with colored glass both at home and on a larger scale in Thill's Glasshouse in Brooklyn. Soon he was making colored windows for churches. That he had had no training or experience in the field bothered neither Tiffany nor the churches. In 1878 he formed his first company, Louis C. Tiffany & Company, built a glasshouse of his own, and engaged Andrea Boldini, who had "represented himself as one of the workers in the Murano factory under Dr. Salviati," to preside over it. After two disastrous fires that destroyed two successive glasshouses, Tiffany began new experiments in the Heidt Glasshouse in Brooklyn. John LaFarge, who was also to make a name in the field of leaded windows, had been working there for some time. According to his own account, Tiffany as especially interested in finding ways to minimize the use of enamel in representing draperies. After years of attempting to get the kind of glass he wanted from furnaces owned by others, he began to realize that he would never be satisfied with such work. Eventually (in 1893) he built a glasshouse, the Stourbridge Glass Company, in Corona, Long Island, and engaged Arthur J. Nash, an experienced glassmaker from Stourbridge, England, to run it.

Tiffany's first windows, those made in the 1870s, were essentially screens of colored glass—the shapes determined partly by the glass and partly by his imagination. Before long, however, he began to introduce motifs from nature. Plant forms were suggested by the glass itself—a leaf by a section of green glass that happened to look like a leaf; a gourd by a section of yellow glass which varied from light to dark in a way that might suggest a gourd. Tiffany called these "mosaic windows," a term meaning they were made of pieces of unpainted glass set as one arranges the pebbles in an ornamental sidewalk. By the early 1880s, however, he was using the human figure, and that was something else. Hands and feet had to be done in enamels, there was no other way. Or was there? He could not get that goading thought out of his mind.

In the meantime, Tiffany had become involved in another activity. Although he was already an associate member of the National Academy, he joined George Inness, John LaFarge, Augustus Saint-Gaudens, George de Forest Brush, Thomas Eakins, Homer Martin, Albert Ryder, John Singer Sargent, James McNeill Whistler, and other prominent painters and sculptors to form the Society of American Artists, which held its first exhibition in the Kurz Gallery during March and April of 1878. The association was a gentlemanly protest against the conservatism of the National Academy.

He was now painting and working in glass and active in art organizations, but his dream of touching millions of American lives with beauty was still very much a dream. The industrial revolution was gaining momentum. Americans had pressed-glass dishes, cast-iron stoves, scroll saw pergolas, horsehair sofas (with steel springs), and countless other attractive products of steam, sweat, and boredom, but machine-made beauty was not the kind Tiffany had in mind. America had a few museums, which most people were too busy to visit, but he did not think of art as being limited to something one must go to see, anyway.

His friend and former teacher, Samuel Colman, fed Tiffany's discontent by reminding him that the home is one art form that involves nearly everyone, and in 1879 the thirty-year-old painter entered a new field—interior decoration, now called interior design. He, Samuel Colman, Lockwood de Forest (whose passion was carvings from India, which had become far more accessible when the Suez Canal opened in 1869), and Candace Wheeler (who worked in embroidery) established the Associated Artists, and its beginning was not clouded by modesty. Tiffany announced that he and his associates were ready to undertake all kinds of interior decorating, and curiously enough that seems to have been the case.

Fortunately for the Associated Artists, both the new millionaires and their mansions needed help. Americans had abandoned the restrained elegance of the eighteenth-century classic revival. The standard exterior was a fanciful and picturesque complex of unrelated elements: towers, gables, balustrades, balconies, piazzas, columns, and chimneys. The interiors were often a crowded mishmash of statues, oriental rugs, ornate furniture, imported paintings, carvings, palm trees, and fountains. There was a lot of everything except that kind of beauty which feeds the soul. The machine had created a new aristocracy who were pleased with their station in life and not the least bit reticent about enjoying it.

George Kemp was the first client to commission the Associated Artists to decorate a house—his enormous place on Fifth Avenue. All the associates had a hand in the project, and it included hangings and carvings from India, ceramics from China, a painted frieze of fruit and vegetables by Tiffany, and a ceiling set with iridescent seashells. Some doors were topped with leaded-glass transoms done in the mosaic manner. The result was ornate, but it was refreshingly different, and there was an American look about it. Commissions came tumbling in, and Tiffany was successfully launched in another field for which he had no training.

Before they disbanded (in 1883) the Associated Artists had decorated the homes of many prominent Americans. In 1883 Tiffany decorated the public rooms of the White House, and in 1918 he furnished Cuba's new Presidential Palace.

Tiffany, always searching for new ways to reach the public, also designed wallpapers and fabrics.

In 1881 the Associated Artists, prompted undoubtedly by their imaginative leader, ventured into still another field by designing *On the Road to Slumberland, or My Boy and I*, a book of songs and poems for children by Mary D. Brine.

In 1878 the inquisitive young painter had also tried his hand at photography, and made some of the earliest pictures of people and animals in motion.

The Associated Artists disassociated themselves, almost certainly, because of Tiffany's conviction that the best way of doing things was his own. The corporation under which they had functioned, Louis C. Tiffany & Company, continued until 1886, when it was reorganized as the Tiffany Glass Company, a new business geared to offer an even greater variety of services. Sometime in these years another entity called Tiffany and de Forest functioned for a brief period.

Tiffany was now a painter and a designer of interiors and of stained-glass windows, but he was still far from where he wanted to go. Many Americans lived without experiencing good art of any kind. The country grew in size and wealth, and its appetite for the often tasteless products of the machine grew along with it.

It happened that Tiffany loved competition, and especially the kind provided by the international expositions which were exerting an ever-increasing impact on the world's thinking. When he learned that no provisions had been made to exhibit leaded windows in Chicago's forthcoming World's Columbian Exposition scheduled for 1893, he promptly arranged to exhibit some of his own work in part of the space his father's jewelry company had reserved in the Manufactures and Liberal Arts Building, and began immediately to design a display that was to bring him international fame.

The great Exposition was intended to be a showcase of America's progress, and it was; but the planners, in the spirit of L'École des Beaux Arts in Paris, had decreed that all the buildings in the Court of Honor would be "classic," the cornice in each sixty feet from the ground, and all uniformly white. The Romans, who painted their marble gods and public buildings in bright colors, would have gnashed what teeth they had at such restrictions, but Americans were so impressed by "the White City" that during the next decade they poured millions of dollars into dressing up their buildings, public and private, with columns, capitals, cornices, and other classic features.

Louis Tiffany's chapel and the golden door that Louis Sullivan designed for the Transportation Building were two exceptions to all the plaster classicism.

The chapel glowed with mosaics of Favrile glass, mother-of-pearl, and semiprecious stones. An electrolier (as the chandelier was called) hanging in front of the altar featured the emerald-green glass Tiffany loved. The stained-glass windows were spectacular.

Both were imbued with a refreshing independence, and both were greeted with cheers from many critics who saw them as steps toward the development of an architecture with an American flavor. The verdict was not unanimous; Tiffany's chapel was labeled "overrich" by some, and it was ignored by others. Nevertheless, it was viewed and admired by over a million and a half visitors from all over the world, and the warmth of its reception led to Tiffany's becoming a major influence on the decorative arts of Europe as well as on those in America.

It also happened that since 1884 he had been intrigued with blown glass by Émile Gallé, so much so that he had been experimenting in the field himself. In 1895 examples of this new venture were shown in his New York show rooms, and the art critic of the New York *Times* marveled at the "astonishing results" in the "vases, jugs and different attractive and artistic forms of glassware, curious and entirely novel both in color and texture."[4] A demand for the vases developed and Tiffany soon became an interna-

tional leader in yet another field of art for which he had no training.

During the Exposition, Tiffany had revived a friendship with S. Bing,[5] a perceptive man and a dealer in Oriental art, who had a shop in Paris and a showroom on New York's lower Fifth Avenue. Bing had been asked by the French government to report on art in America and especially on that in the Columbian Exposition. The report was most complimentary of Tiffany's work. Before long they were making a plan. Bing would give his Paris gallery, heretofore devoted to prints and art from the Orient, a new direction, a new look, and a new name. He would feature the work of a group of far-out young artists who had made his present shop their informal headquarters. He would also represent Tiffany, who in 1892 had reorganized his decorating business as the Tiffany Glass and Decorating Company, and arrange for some of the advanced French painters to design windows to be executed in Tiffany's brilliant new glass.

Both were men of action. Bing promptly engaged Sir Frank Brangwyn, the English painter and designer, to paint a frieze for the outside of the new gallery and arranged for Tiffany to execute windows from designs by ten French painters including Pierre Bonnard and Toulouse Lautrec. René Lalique was invited to exhibit his jewelry; Auguste Rodin his sculpture; Eugène Carrière, Maurice Denis, and Fernand Khnopff, their paintings. Aubrey Beardsley, the long-faced Englishman, displayed his prints and drawings. Will Bradley, the skillful American "artist-designer" who worked in the Art Nouveau manner, and Charles Rennie Mackintosh, the Scottish artist-designer, were invited to exhibit their posters.

Le Salon de l'Art Nouveau, as it was then called, opened the day after Christmas in 1895. Sales during the first few months included Tiffany vases and a leaded window to the prestigious Musée des Arts Décoratifs of The Louvre. The museum already owned one it had bought in 1894.

In 1897 Tiffany's furnaces and workrooms were mass-producing in the spirit of the time, but everything was made by hand and made well. The furnace in Corona, Long Island, was turning out a kind of glass the world had never seen before and may never see again. An ecclesiastical department, through its mausoleums, was adding a new and impressive dimension to America's cemeteries. An architectural department was designing complete interiors for residences and public buildings. The furniture shops on Second Avenue were making modern as well as traditional furniture. The Tiffany Glass and Decorating Company occupied extensive quarters at 333–341 Fourth Avenue. In its elaborate showrooms one could find antiques, art pottery (including Rookwood and Grueby), Oriental rugs, Favrile glass vases, and furniture. Important customers could see their selections assembled on a trial basis in private showrooms. Tiffany was, as one visitor described him, a "ubiquitous" director of operations. At one point, he employed over two hundred artisans and designers, all of whom knew they were there to execute his designs or his wishes: As a consequence, everything that bears his name reflects his standards and to considerable extent his taste.

In 1900 Tiffany absorbed the Schmitt Brothers Furniture Company and reorganized his New York operations under the name Allied Arts Company. In 1902 he reorganized his growing business as the Tiffany Studios. According to his own statements he was now turning out textiles, fabrics, rugs, hangings, embroideries, upholsteries, furniture, mosaics, leaded glass, lighting fixtures, electroliers, bronzework, ornamental windows, frescoes, altar crosses, sacred vessels, vestments, needlework, memorials in the form of figure windows, mausoleums, tombstones, brasses, mosaic tablets, bronze tablets, crosses, altar furniture, cinerary urns, and endless small artifacts, such as candlesticks, bookends, boxes, mirrors, and toilet articles. In 1902 he also reorganized the Stourbridge Glass Company in Corona as the Tiffany Furnaces. In addition to blown glass, the Furnaces were now making metalwares, pottery, and enamels.

As early as 1894 Louis Tiffany had been made a director of Tiffany & Company. In 1902, the year his father died, he became vice-president and art director. Until 1902 his glass, metalwares, lamps and other art products had been marketed through a few carefully selected dealers, such as Neiman Marcus in Dallas, Shreves in San Francisco, Marshall Field in Chicago, S. Bing in Paris and, of course, his own showrooms. By 1902 almost everything he made was displayed on the sixth floor of the big jewelry company and listed in the *Blue Book*, a small, elegant, but unillus-

trated catalogue covering all items made by or for Tiffany & Company and all the things they carried, including Rookwood and Moorcroft pottery. The *Blue Book* was sent on request to anyone. Prices for Tiffany's pieces ranged from $1 (for bonbon dishes) to figures in the thousands. Prices on Tiffany & Company items ran as high as $35,000. The *Blue Book* made it clear, however, that the intent was to appeal to America's purse as well as its taste, and that pieces were gladly sent on approval to clients known to the company. It was, in fact, a mail-order catalogue, done appropriately in very high style.

The trade name Favrile, registered with the U. S. Patent Office on November 13, 1894, applied to everything Tiffany made except the jewelry. According to Tiffany, the name derived from "fabricate" and was chosen to indicate the object was handmade.

Although Tiffany did not practice architecture, he designed houses for himself and his family. (Working drawings were made by architects who were sympathetic to his wishes.) One was a mansion on Seventy-second Street and Madison Avenue, built in 1885 for his father (Stanford White made the working drawings). He built the Briars (1890) and Laurelton Hall (1903–4), both in Oyster Bay, Long Island. He also designed and built houses for his daughters as they married.

Parts of the Seventy-second Street house were early Art Nouveau, the fashionable turn-of-the-century style, and almost a decade ahead of anything comparable in Europe. Laurelton Hall, the country place he built for himself on nearly 600 acres fronting on Cold Spring Harbor in Oyster Bay, with its gardens, fountains, and court replete with pipe organ, polar-bear rugs, tropical plants, and flowers was, in effect, the only major Art-Nouveau residence built in America. It reached a level of creativity this country has seldom seen. The reported cost was in the millions. This was an exaggeration, but its 1904 taxes were $157,000. This was all made possible by his inheriting one third of his father's $12 million estate, a figure that does not include the real estate.

Tiffany's record of medals and awards both here and abroad is impressive, and the extent of his influence on the decorative arts of Europe has never been equalled by any other American.

In the first decade of the new century, a shift in the country's art preferences was beginning to develop. Tiffany was still receiving commissions for major projects and still winning awards at expositions and world fairs. Some critics continued to refer to him as one of America's leading "colorists." The Tiffany Studios were busy, but much of the cash flow was generated by the ecclesiastical department from sales of memorials and tombstones.

The world that knew and thrilled to his art was growing noticeably smaller, however. New painters, more interested in creating forms derived from nature than in recording the appearance of nature, were getting the attention of the critics. The new painters used colors they *liked*, not those they saw in nature. The images in their pictures were abstractions, which is to say something like the things they saw, but not necessarily very much. Painting was becoming more like the windows in Chartres Cathedral, and curiously, Tiffany did not like the trend at all. He thought pictures of ideas and experiments in new technical effects did not belong in a frame, but he did not put it that way. He denounced the new breed of painters as "modernists." The art world, no longer interested in what he had to say, plunged right on in its new direction. Before long it discovered sexual hangups and social comment and made the most of them. That was almost too much. Tiffany, with his commitment to beauty and good taste, was more unhappy about it than ever.

Not being a quitter, he turned to other art forms to make his point. One especially, the social gathering, is usually ripe for improvement and he designed some spectacular new kinds. The first, the Egyptian Fete, staged by his friend, J. Lindon Smith, was held on February 4, 1913. Music was written for the occasion by Theodore Steinway, and played by musicians from the New York Philharmonic Orchestra. The guests, chosen from New York's famous and wealthy, included the Rockefellers and the Havemeyers. The event was written about, talked about, and misinterpreted for years.

Two others followed. One, in May 1914, was a dinner for 150 guests who were taken from New York to Laurelton Hall by a special train and met at the station by a fleet of cars. An elaborate birthday masque called the "Quest of Beauty," given two years later, spelled out in detail his views on beauty. All were covered by the press and enjoyed by the guests, but in 1917 the coun-

try went to war, and Tiffany's thoughts on "beauty" and "good taste" seemed less relevant than ever.

During these same years he had decided to try another tack, one that led to his commissioning an old friend, the art critic of the New York *Times*, Charles deKay, to write *The Art Work of Louis C. Tiffany*. It was published anonymously in 1914 by Doubleday, Page and Company. Four hundred ninety-two copies were printed on heavy rice paper, and ten on vellum bound in a handsome cover designed by Tiffany himself. The posh book stated in words what he had said in line, shape, color, texture, mass, and space for years. The chapter headings alone—"Tiffany the Painter," "Tiffany the Maker of Stained Glass," "Favrile Glass," "Enamels and Jewelry," "Textiles and Hand Stuffs, "A Decorator of Interiors," "A Builder of Homes," and "As Landscape Architect"—make one of its points. Even so, the book could obviously reach only a few.

Tiffany had, of course, continued to paint and also to undertake special projects that attracted him because of their challenge. In 1911 he had made the massive mosaic fire curtain for the National Theater of the Palace of Fine Arts in Mexico City. The spectacular lighting system is also from his agile mind. In 1914 he made "The Bathers," a naturalistic window containing several nude figures. It was a technical tour de force, for no enamels were used in the flesh tones. All its colors were due to the metallic oxides melted in the glass.

In 1915 he made a mosaic from Maxfield Parrish's painting "The Dream Garden" which is still in the building formerly used by the Curtis Publishing Company in Philadelphia. By 1920 he had reorganized the Furnaces once again. He continued on as president and art director but Douglas Nash, a son of Arthur Nash, became active in management. In 1928 Tiffany bowed out altogether. Douglas Nash continued to operate the Furnaces, but under a new name, which made it clear Tiffany was no longer involved. They went out of business in 1932. The New York operations were also reorganized. The uptown showrooms were moved to more modest quarters on Madison Avenue. The ecclesiastical department was moved to 46 West Twenty-third Street.

Tiffany continued to design windows, and to

FIGURE 9   The Art Work of Louis C. Tiffany. *Cover design by Louis C. Tiffany. Inscribed on fly leaf: "No. 1—To Mr. and Mrs. Charles L. Tiffany, my dear son and daughter, Merry Xmas 1914."*

paint pictures, and as president to run the Tiffany Studios. The ecclesiastical department kept them in the black for a while, but they filed for bankruptcy in 1932 and were liquidated in 1938.

Tiffany was too well organized not to have planned that his efforts in the cause of beauty and good taste would continue after his death. His conviction that beauty leads to a better life never waned, or that Laurelton Hall and his chapel were endowed with true beauty. He planned, therefore, that they would remain on their hill overlooking Cold Spring Harbor, and around them he created a Foundation. The board members were his personal friends. He was confident they would carry out his plans. But to make doubly certain nothing could possibly go wrong, Tiffany provided that the president would always be an artist. He then entrusted the Foundation with his house, his chapel, his finest leaded windows, his paintings, and the vast number of works of art he had collected from all over the world. In addition, he endowed it with $1,500,000 (the equivalent of ten times that amount today). He also spelled his plan out very clearly to the directors: It was founded on Laurelton Hall, its gardens, and its collections. Young artists would be invited to live there for periods of a month or two. They would paint, sculpt, make prints, vases, or jewelry; walk in the gardens, swim in the Sound; read in the library; watch the fountains; listen to the organ; study the works of masters; or, as he often did himself, sit on the terrace overlooking the harbor and reflect on the beauty of the world. They would

see for themselves how an environment filled with beauty can nourish the human spirit. If he could not reach everyone, he would at least reach a few, and he planned that it would be an *important* few.

After Tiffany's death in 1933, everything seemed to come apart. In July, 1946, with permission of the courts, the Foundation was reorganized into an institution quite different from the one he had planned, and everything was sold. In 1948 all the real estate, including Laurelton Hall, went on the market.[6] Later, the home burned, and the chapel he had loved so dearly was left open to the weather and to vandals.

His Foundation now quietly gives about $100,000 each year to help young artists on their difficult way. They learn little about their benefactor, however. Most of his personal work is stored away in warehouses, and Laurelton Hall is gone.

NOTES

[1] See his sketchbook made on the trip.
[2] Encyclopaedia Britannica, XV ed., Macropaedia, Vol. 18, p. 666.
[3] The clipping, without source, is carefully preserved in his scrapbook.
[4] The New York *Times*, Thursday, October 17, 1895—"Arts Notes."
[5] It cannot be said with certainty what the "S" stands for, and Bing may have preferred it that way.
[6] The collections brought $84,468.31; the real estate brought a total of $91,981.82.

Chapter 2

WHAT WAS LOUIS TIFFANY REALLY LIKE?

My Dear Sister:
I received your letter this afternoon and was very glad to hear from you. On Friday evenings we all have a letter to write which for me is rather difficult because I am such a miserable writer and speller and when they examine them they are so full of mistakes that I feel quite ashamed of myself.

I study a number of lessons but I like philosphy [sic.] ever so much better than any other for our teacher is so kind and explains so nicely that you understand all about what you are learning and that is not the case in all studies.

I want to come home and see you very much but I console myself by thinking that it will soon be Christmas. . . . It is very much like West Point. You have to keep your gloves in one corner of your closet, your umbrella in another, your overcoat hung up on a nail in the back part of it, everything has a place for it, and everything has to be put in its place or you are marked and have to go on guard duty which is not very pleasant. . . .

With much love to all, I am your affecionate brother Louis.

From a letter to his sister Annie, written by Louis Tiffany, age fourteen, from Eagleswood Military Academy, Perth Amboy, N.Y., November 14, 1862.

Until one bright Saturday morning early in the fall of 1930, to me Louis Tiffany was a name associated in some vague way with glamour and glass. I had arrived at Laurelton Hall two days before to join fourteen other young artists who were living and working there as guests of the Tiffany Foundation.

We were all happily gathered in the courtyard of our quarters waiting for Mr. Tiffany. It was his custom to visit the gallery every Saturday morning to see what his protégés had accomplished the preceding week. Our assembling ahead of schedule was not due to instructions. At Laurelton Hall the atmosphere itself let you know that to be early was to be prudent.

Time did seem to be moving slowly, and someone suggested that since I had never seen the drama that was soon to unfold, perhaps they should prepare me. All agreed with bubbly enthusiasm. Instantly, one of the young painters bent over and began to trot around like a little old man. A little English butler standing nearby picked up a chair, hunched his shoulders, shoved his false teeth forward in his mouth (he had two plates) and became an amusing facsimile of Stanley Lothrop, the resident director. Mr. Lothrop was an odd little man once accurately described in the press as "keen, kinetic, and gnome-like." One of the sculptors and a painter got down on all fours and scrambled around like dogs. A woman designer announced she would be Miss Hanley, "even though you can't see through my dress." (Miss Hanley, they explained, was Mr. Tiffany's nurse-companion and Mr. Lothrop's fiancée.)

The little group then clustered as though they

were in a car with "Miss Hanley" at the wheel, "Mr. Tiffany" beside her, and "Mr. Lothrop" and "the dogs" in back. They shuffled around the fountain and pulled to a stop in front of the rest of us. "Mr. Tiffany" was smiling; "the dogs" barked; "Miss Hanley," waving her fingers like the comedian in a silent movie, called, "Good morning boys and girls." When they had got out of their imaginary car, "Mr. Tiffany" headed for the gallery and "Mr. Lothrop" followed so closely with a chair that "Mr. Tiffany" could sit down with no warning at all. They were talented, lively young people, performing with a flair, in a spirit of creative good fun, and it was very amusing.

Of course, in the midst of it all, a beautiful old automobile with the brocade elegance and sensible lines of a sedan chair, rolled into the courtyard and stopped with a crunch. There, in the front seat, was the real Mr. Tiffany, smiling and benign, dressed in a white suit and wearing an orchid in his buttonhole. Miss Hanley, a handsome woman in her forties, dressed in yellow and a little on the fluttery side, wiggled her fingers and called, "Good morning boys and girls." It was all remarkably like the charade (which had reconstituted itself instantly into a group of beaming young people).

The car, a Crane, made in 1912, was in mint condition. Cranes were built by hand and each was numbered. Mr. Tiffany owned numbers 11 and 12. He preferred Cranes to the new cars because Cranes "had quality." When he had got down to the running board and then to the ground, the relative accuracy of the impersonations was obvious. He was perhaps 5'6" tall. He walked at a decided angle. Mr. Lothrop followed him so closely with a chair that he could, and did, sit down without ever bothering to make certain the chair was there. The dogs barked and jumped so much it seemed certain they would topple him over, but they did not. Miss Hanley's yellow dress *was* diaphanous when she stood against the light.

The impromptu charade had captured most of it except an air about Mr. Tiffany which kept the amusing aspects of the situation all in their proper place. His eyes were deep set, blue, and kindly. His gaze was searching. He had an aura of Edwardian elegance and along with it the self-assurance of a man who knows what is important and what is not.

We followed him into the gallery. He studied the pictures on the lower levels, gazed helplessly at those hung higher, and said he wished he could see them all. That was as planned. Mr. Lothrop hung the kind Mr. Tiffany did not like (there were a good many) out of his range of vision (my own were usually hung pretty high). Mr. Tiffany's voice was low. He chose his words carefully and spoke with a beautiful "upper strata of New York" accent. What he said was punctuated with friendly glances at us and frequent gestures with his hands.

It was all very touching. He had provided us with acres of parks, gardens, and natural woods, rolling fields and meadows, arbors, and vistas of beaches with blue water and boats with bright sails. Containers of flowers were brought to the studio every morning in the hope they would tempt someone to paint them. This rarely happened. I think he saw very little art that he cared for. (One morning, weeks later, after studying a painting I had made of a rather tumbled down house in the less attractive part of Oyster Bay, he turned to me and said, "Mr. McKean, paintings should not hurt the eyes." He said it with a twinkle in his eye and he gave the "r" the elegant fluid effect characteristic of his way of talking.)

Mr. Tiffany handled the situation with grace and tact. He did not believe in rules for art. He had not come to tell us which way to go. There were no teachers or classes at Laurelton Hall. He commented only on what he liked in the pictures he could see, which was not a great deal. After he had been around the gallery, he sat down on one of the benches and talked for a little while about the importance of beauty and the tragedy of those forced to live without art. To see Mr. Tiffany was an impressive experience. He was as one granddaughter described him to me, "A nice bright old man." After a little while, he got up and went out into the court followed by Miss Hanley, the dogs, Mr. Lothrop, and the chair. When they were all back in the Crane, there was a genteel whirring, a little smoke from the exhaust. A mild jolt put his hat askew. Then with a smile and a wave, the quaint little party wheeled away as suddenly as it had come. The preview had not even hinted at the real charm of it all.

The next evening, after the usual dinner served by the two butlers in our own dining room (a screened breezeway with views of the gardens), we assembled, as was the custom, scrubbed and brushed to wait for a telephone call. It came right on schedule, at eight o'clock. Would we care to join Mr. Tiffany, who was listening to some music on the organ? Our spokeswoman, familiar with the routine, acted pleasantly and appropriately surprised, "Why, Miss Hanley, we would be delighted. Yes, we will come right up." We hurried up the steps through the gardens past the Daffodil Terrace, through the magnificent loggia and into the Fountain Court. There he was, seated on one of the divans, which the family called "The Throne." Music was rolling down from the organ loft in one of the upper stories of the court. Miss Hanley was playing (rolls) as loud as possible because Mr. Tiffany did not hear well. The air was filled with the scent of flowers.

The fountains, terraces, glass walls, organ music, marble floors, colored lights, bearskin rugs —snarling heads and all—potted palms and flowering plants were more than anyone could be prepared for. It was a dimly lit fantasy that could not be, and there it was!

We listened to the music for a while. Then Mr. Tiffany decided to make his way through the polar-bear rugs and other picturesque hazards to the terrace. I followed because no one was behind him with a chair and I thought he might trip over something. It was a warm summer night. The stars were out. Lights twinkled around the harbor. A jet of water, which built slowly from a trickle to a geyser, splashed over immense crystals in the fountain. The crystals, lighted from below, changed colors slowly. He said nothing for quite a while, and I seemed to have forgotten every word I had ever known. Then he observed quietly, "Mr. McKean, we can hear that music any time. This night has a beauty that will never come again."

He sat silently, tapping his cane and looking out over Cold Spring Harbor. I sat beside him full of wonder at it all. I have wished many times that I had told him what I was thinking.

At 8:30 every morning Mr. Tiffany was off to work, and at 5:30 he was back. It was good to see him flying along his gravel drive, smiling and waving, in all the vertical elegance of his handsome old automobile, with a chauffeur at the wheel and the vases on the doorposts filled with flowers. We called his car, "Mr. Tiffany's jewel box."

Curiously, during my two months' stay at Laurelton Hall, no one ever told us anything about Mr. Tiffany or his work. One visiting lecturer discussed Michelangelo's sculpture. At other times, there was discussion of other kinds of art, but no one ever mentioned Mr. Tiffany. And what may be equally curious, I never wondered why. Mr. Lothrop did take me into the library one day and pointing to the furniture remarked, "Look at this—and remember he designed it in 1904." But that is all he said.

One view of a man at one time in his life tells a little about him, but only a little. How did others see him? What was the handsome young Tiffany like when his moustache and hair were a reddish brown and his energy was near the explosive point? How would it be to travel with someone who would, as he did, cancel his reservations on the *Titanic* because he had learned the first-class dining salon was *table d'hôte* and "no one was going to tell him what to eat." What was he like as a son? A husband? A father? A friend? What was he like to work for? What in his makeup made it possible for him, with no formal training, to exert a major influence on the arts of his time? What prompted him to dedicate a major part of his fortune to helping young artists and artisans?

The relationship between the smaller Louis, who spent fortunes on daring ventures and a search for excellence in the arts, and his taller businesslike father who was always on course toward the dollar, tells much about both. Charles Lewis began with a little fancy goods store on Lower Broadway which handled such things as papier maché, stationery, and hair brushes. The first day's sales were $4.98. He married one partner's sister, bought out both partners, introduced a line of jewelry, treated his customers graciously and well, saw to it that his establishment got more than its share of publicity. He wound up with the most famous jewelry store in the world, with a reputation for integrity beyond compare—jeweler to nearly all the crowned heads in the world. He walked to work, wore long black coats, enjoyed waiting on customers, marched his family to the Presbyterian Church every Sunday, and featured gold rings in which simple prongs held round diamonds up to the light in a way so spectacular that even his competitors were forced to imitate it. When the French Royal jewels came on the market, he bought them and made the most of all the attendant publicity. The world famous "Tiffany Diamond," which he acquired and named, is still an attraction in the New York store. When General Tom Thumb and Lavinia Warren, P. T. Barnum's famous midgets, were married in New York's Grace Episcopal Church, the little couple received an exquisite silver horse and carriage from Tiffany's, which, out of consideration for their clientele, was displayed in their windows several weeks before the wedding. When Charles died on February 18, 1902, at the age of ninety-two, it was not by chance that he left behind one of the great fortunes of America.

That the relationship between independent non-conforming Louis and his more conservative father was laced with differences, there is no doubt.

As a boy Louis was sent to military school because he was difficult to handle. Warm and beautifully written letters let us see him as a loving and homesick little boy who did not care for military routine. His preference for art rather than college was a disappointment to his father, who had hoped Louis would join him in his business. Louis spent a good part of the year 1865 (he was seventeen) in Europe sketching and visiting cathedrals. Soon he moved into the Y.M.C.A. and never returned to live at home again.

As the years went by, Louis' art became more and more a reaction against the commercialism of his father. The jewelry company carried the finest (and most costly) of whatever field it entered. Louis' jewelry featured inexpensive stones in imaginative settings. All his life he sought ways of creating forms of beauty the average American could afford.

That close ties of affection and respect did exist between Louis and his father is equally obvious. When Louis entertained, his parents were always among the guests. Every Sunday Louis and his family joined his parents for dinner at noon. When Louis made his "Entombment" window (Figure 44) for the Columbian Exposition, his father was the model for St. Joseph of Arimathea, the kindly rich man who buried Jesus in the new tomb he had prepared for himself. When his chapel was reconstructed at Oyster Bay, Louis dedicated the "Entombment" window as a memorial to his father. In the 1890s his father lent Louis large sums when they were greatly needed. He made Louis a director of Tiffany & Company

in 1894, left him one third of his estate, and appointed him executor of his will and trustee for trusts created for other members of the family.

But when the enormous home Charles had Louis build for all the Tiffany families on Seventy-second Street was finished, Louis, as was planned, moved in, but Charles did not, why we do not know. It might have been a disinclination to live in such propinquity with his bustling son. It may have been Charles' preference for walking to work rather than depending on cabs. (The new house *was* pretty far uptown.) It may have been nothing more than a change of mind because Charles preferred his more modest house at 255 Madison Avenue.

Working with and for Louis Tiffany must have been a mixed joy. He was a fountainhead of ideas and a ramrod as an organizer. How satisfactory he was as a partner is open to question. Candace Wheeler, one of the Associated Artists, wrote in pleasant terms of their work together on the Madison Square Theater Curtain, but the partnership lasted only a few years (from 1879 to 1883). His formal partnership with his friend Lockwood de Forest was even more brief. A lack of objectivity about himself, the fertility of his creative processes, and his determined nature may have made give-and-take with Louis Tiffany difficult.

His workmen declared him to be a "good boss," but there was a universal feeling among them that he was looking over their shoulder, and they often commented, *sotto voce*, on seeing him approach, "Here comes trouble." Mr. Tiffany was headstrong and a perfectionist. He abhorred carelessness of any kind, and he nearly exploded when a careless worker dropped a cigar in a pot of molten glass. This combination of traits can mean trouble of a certain kind. Many "completed" projects had to be done over again because what satisfied others did not always satisfy him. Many "finished" things were discarded for the same reason, and this was all costly.

A combination of amusement and affection that appears often in the eyes of Tiffany's children and grandchildren as they talk of him tells a great deal about family relationships, but in addition to being a loving parent, he was a tyrannical head of the family.

His relations with the town of Oyster Bay were not always cordial. He resorted to the courts to have electric power lines run to Laurelton Hall, and there was such feeling about his sea wall that one summer night some hotheads blew it up.

He was a kind and loving husband to Mary Woodbridge Goddard, whom he married in 1872. Julia Goddard Piatt, Mary's sister, in a letter dated September 24, 1883, to her cousin, Kate M. Trott, described Tiffany's gentle care of his beloved wife in her last illness:

. . . and Louis—his care and patience and tenderness—it is beyond anything I ever saw—or hoped for—it seems as if May must live—but only God knows.

and in a second letter, dated January 28, 1884, after Mary's death, also to Kate:

. . . dear Louis, it would break your heart to see him. I shall always love him because he made Mary so entirely happy—she had nearly twelve years of rare happiness on earth. The only drawback she ever had—was her ill health and even with that she would not have exchanged her lot for any on earth.

In 1886 Louise Wakeman Knox became his second wife, and he loved her dearly. It is rather safe to assume, however, that creative, headstrong Louis was a difficult husband at times.

His children were Mary, Hilda, and Charles Lewis II, from the first marriage; and twins, Julia and Comfort, and Dorothy, from the second. An infant son from his first marriage, also named Charles, lived only a few days and is buried in Menton, France.

It is not easy for an outsider to give a balanced account of relationships within a family riddled with intelligence, talent, and strong personalities. The Tiffanys were and are a remarkable family. Tiffany loved his daughters, and they loved him. He opposed all their marriages, and all married against his will. He resented Dorothy's wanting to go to boarding school and did his best to dissuade her. After attending school only a few months, she wanted to return home. Not at all! She spent five years in a school she did not like.

One daughter, while away from home, wrote Papa to ask permission to drink tea and coffee. The reply was a four page letter saying "no" in every possible way. "Tea and coffee were not good for one's health."

During the great influenza epidemic in 1917, Tiffany was determined to gather his entire fam-

ily—adults, children, and grandchildren—on a private train and head West to escape the germs, until somehow the futility of the plan became apparent to him.

Warmth and love sparkle out in endless ways when his family discuss Papa and Grandpa. Grandchildren describe the "spider-web game" with enthusiasm. On birthdays especially, brightly colored yarn was laid out like a giant web and each child given a color which led off to a hidden present.

Grandchildren chuckle (with a touch of irritation) at having had to undress and splash in a pool when Grandpa wanted to paint nude children at play. They smile at the necessity of being at breakfast at 7:30 sharp for hearty meals of such things as pancakes, or steamers, or waffles. A mixture of humor and frustration still shows at their not having been free to pick the flowers in Laurelton Hall or even *one* from a *field* of daffodils. His daughters loved the early walks with him in the gardens before the sun was up. They speak happily of the exciting times when Papa brought home a new kind of glass, and of trips to the glass furnaces at Corona, "a terrifying place where men walked around with white-hot glass on blowing rods." Children and grandchildren still talk with amusement at the profusion of flowers and plants in Laurelton Hall, which often resembled a greenhouse.

Sarah Hanley (whom the family called "Patsie"), played an important role in Tiffany's life. About 1910, when he became ill, she came as a nurse, and stayed on. It may have been love and it may have been nothing more than a needed companionship. Whichever it was, it was a blessing to a sensitive man facing years of living alone —his second wife had died in 1904—and to an attractive young Irishwoman who longed for a way of life the fates had placed beyond her reach. Miss Hanley's education was not excessive. Tiffany taught her to paint landscapes, and tried with moderate success to soften her Irish brogue. She helped him run Laurelton Hall and create his Foundation, and drove his car in and around Oyster Bay (always carefully giving a warning on the horn when they approached a railroad crossing, and always wearing his favorite color, yellow).

Mr. Tiffany offered to marry Miss Hanley, but she declined out of consideration for family feelings. At the suggestion of one of Tiffany's daughters, I called on her in the last year of her life. She was living in the house Tiffany had built for her on a hill near Laurelton Hall and had become a round little bedridden invalid. We spoke happily of past times. I got a distinct impression that she was surprised and pleased that one of "his own" artists was interested in Mr. Tiffany and his work. We discussed with sadness what had happened to his Foundation. She told me of her pain at seeing the fires that took three days to destroy Laurelton Hall. We spoke of all the things Mr. Tiffany had done for art, for young people, and for each of us. I asked her what she had called him, and her answer was immediate—"Padre." When I asked what he was like, her voice took on a curious impassioned quality, "He was a god on earth." It was an interesting observation from a devout Roman Catholic.

I asked about her financial situation. She assured me that Mr. Tiffany had made ample provisions for her.

I did not see Mr. Tiffany as an exacting father, nor as an aggressive competitor nor as a demanding employer. The Tiffany I saw was gentle, shy,

remote, lonely, but very impressive, partly because of his bearing, partly because of the way he was handling rejection and advancing years, and partly because of the brilliance and imaginative planning of his Foundation. It was natural that I should admire him, and it is possible that anything I write is biased in his favor, although I hope not. That would be a disservice.

One source of information about Mr. Tiffany *is* objective, and that is his work. It says a great deal about him to those who understand and can "read" it. This is particularly true of his personal work, the things he designed and, in some instances, made himself. Many of these are unknown today, partly because they were not seen by the public in his own time (many of those works he considered his finest were built into Laurelton Hall) and partly because some have not been out of packing cases for three quarters of a century.

Through this book I will try to let the reader become acquainted not only with some of the "lost" treasures but also with the man who made them.

Chapter 3

THE FORGOTTEN PAINTINGS

*To whatever delightful other labors Mr. Tiffany later turned his hand he was from the first,
and remains today, a painter.*

CHARLES DEKAY, 1911

Louis Tiffany's early success was the kind young painters dream about but very few experience. While he was still an unknown nineteen-year-old one of his paintings was hung "on the line" in a National Academy Show. At the age of twenty-two he became the youngest man ever elected to membership in New York's prestigious Century Association. At twenty-three he was made an Associate National Academician, which must have established a record of some sort. The press notices about his paintings tell the story quite well.[1] He was recognized as one of America's important painters before he was thirty. It sounds a little unreal, but that is the way it was.

The sketches made by the seventeen-year-old on his first trip to Europe (November 1, 1865–March 21, 1866) make it seem more plausible. These little pictures (Figures 11, 12) date from the pre-Inness days. They reveal, however, that Tiffany had studied paintings of the Hudson River School and was sympathetic with their aim of elevating the viewer's mind by calling his attention to the beauty of the countryside. Tiffany's sketches have the same aura of peace, the same suggestion that God is in his heaven and that everything is all right here below; and, more important, they reveal genuine talent.

Tiffany studied with Inness while Inness was still making pictures with delicate touches of a camel-hair brush held in a hand steadied by a mall stick. ("Land of Arcadia," Figure 13, painted in 1848, is an early example of the style.) "Fuller's Country Store," an oil Tiffany painted in 1872, illustrates the Inness influence, but in some ways it suggests the work of Edward Lamson Henry, who painted meticulous and objective reports on America's trains, horse-drawn vehicles, people, and houses. Henry's pictures carefully

FIGURE 10   *Christmas greeting card made by Louis C. Tiffany for his sister Annie, 1864. Watercolor and pencil.*

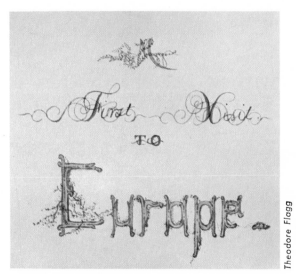

FIGURE 11   *Frontispiece of a book of sketches by Louis C. Tiffany, 1865. Watercolor and pencil, 9¼" x 12⅛".*

FIGURE 12   *Sketch from preceding. Watercolor and pencil, 9¼" x 12⅛".*

Theodore Flagg

FIGURE 13 *"Land of Arcadia." Signed, "George Inness/1848." Oil on canvas, 24¼" x 36¼".*

Theodore Flagg

FIGURE 14 *"House by the Weeping Willows." Signed, "E.L. Henry/1865." Oil on canvas, 14" x 20½".*

FIGURE 15   *"On the Hudson River at Dobbs Ferry." Signed, "Louis C. Tiffany," c. 1880. Oil on canvas, 12½″ x 27½″.*

FIGURE 16   *"Dobbs Ferry." By Samuel Colman, c. 1880. Unsigned. Oil on canvas, 16⅜″ x 40″.*

omit what he thought about anything. "House by the Weeping Willows" (Figure 14), painted in 1865, makes no reference to God. It contains no subtle implications that man should be better than he is. And yet it is so complete in its detail that not only could carpenters build a replica of the "American bracketed" house today, a carriage maker could reproduce the carriage.

"On the Hudson River at Dobbs Ferry" by Tiffany (Figure 15) and "Dobbs Ferry," by Samuel Colman (Figure 16) are very likely the results of a joint sketching trip. Here, Tiffany is squinting his eyes in order to blur details and thereby to reduce the landscape to broad planes of color. The picture is built of large areas of low-keyed color laid on with a bristle brush. The painting intentionally makes the viewer feel he is standing on the riverbank on a cloudy fall day. Both the camera (a new development that fascinated Tiffany) and his teacher-friend Colman encouraged Tiffany to see in broader terms rather than focus his eyes point by point over the surface of his subject matter.

"Duane Street, New York," an oil painted in 1875 (Figure 17), leaves the poetry of the Hudson River School even further behind. "Duane Street" is more than a brilliant record of some grubby buildings. It is a statement about the importance of formal values, about the fact that good art is more than a record of something the artist sees, that it is an order imposed on what he sees. Tiffany has grown as a painter.

"Duane Street" may also be an echo from Tiffany's visit to France in the summer of 1874. In the spring of that year, a group of painters, including Renoir, Monet, Sisley, Cezanne, and Pissarro, rented Nadar's Gallery in Paris to show their pictures, which had been consistently rejected from the official salons. Juries ignored their work, partly because they painted such subjects as haystacks and whores, and partly because they were searching for new ways to suggest light. This quest led eventually to such techniques as brushstrokes of unmixed color laid side by side so they would blend into brilliant effects when seen from a distance. Tiffany may not have been in Paris during their historic exhibition, but he must have seen their paintings somewhere.

Tiffany worked in a variety of mediums including watercolor, tempera (opaque colors mixed with egg yolk or its equivalent), and oils. For supports, he chose anything readily at hand—canvas, paper, wood. Many oil sketches are on miniature wood panels cut from a piece of mahogany furniture.

Among these is one of his family at Somesville, Maine, done in 1888 (Figure 18). To paint this charming little oil sketch, Tiffany stood in a daisy field watching his wife, Louise, his son Charles, his daughter Mary, and the twins, Comfort and Julia (who look like sunbonnet babies), and the latter's nurse enjoy the fresh air, the sunlight, the view, and the company of a docile cow. The whole picture is only a few strokes of a bristle brush. It is a spontaneous record of figures splashed with sunlight and of Tiffany's pleasure in it all. There are no details, no poetic overtones. It records one instant in time, a fragment of a happy day, nothing more. But that is quite a bit.

The large oil painting, "My Family at Somesville" (Figure 19), was painted from this sketch and possibly also from photographs. Here the distant hills of Maine are blurred blues and grays to suggest the intervening atmosphere, but the figures are clearly defined areas of color related to each other in a way reminiscent of a Japanese print. The picture has the same pleasure in the day, but it is more structured and more detailed. The cow and the baby are nearer the vertical axis, the two figures on either side somehow make the formal balance more obvious. Details such as the daisies in the grass give it charm but make it less spontaneous.

Tiffany never parted with these two pictures. The sketch hung in the small gallery off his bedroom in Laurelton Hall, a treasure house seldom seen by guests. The larger painting which was never finished and, consequently, never signed, hung in the painting gallery at Laurelton Hall at the time of his death.

Cartoons for stained-glass windows are another important phase of Tiffany's painting. A good example is that done c. 1888 for the "Education" window in the Yale Library which was commissioned by Simeon B. Chittenden (Figure 20). Such cartoons, usually on a large scale, often reveal Tiffany's difficulty with the human figure. They also show that even in planning windows he tended to think as a painter. Members of his family or maids served as models, and some faces in this cartoon are highly sensitive portraits.

The later watercolors (Figure 21) were broader, freer, closer to Impressionism, but even so, a pencil drawing usually came first and re-

FIGURE 17   *"Duane Street, New York." Signed, "Louis C. Tiffany," c. 1875. Oil on canvas, 27″ x 30″. The Brooklyn Museum, Brooklyn, New York.*

FIGURE 18 *"My Family at Somesville," by Louis C. Tiffany, c. 1888. Unsigned. Oil sketch on wood, 4¼" x 7¼".*

FIGURE 19 *"My Family at Somesville," by Louis C. Tiffany, c. 1888. Unsigned. Oil on canvas, 24" x36".*

Theodore Flagg

FIGURE 20 *Cartoon (one of five sections) for the "Education" window in the Chittenden Library at Yale University, c. 1888. One section signed, "Louis C. Tiffany." Tempera and other mediums on paper mounted on canvas. Height 66".*

FIGURE 21 *"Old Mill at Frieburg." Signed, "Louis C. Tiffany, 1877." Watercolor on textured paper, 13½″ x 19½″.*

FIGURE 22 *"Spring." Signed, "Louis C. Tiffany," c. 1898. Oil on canvas. 58½″ x 94½″.*

Theodore Flagg

FIGURE 23   *"Arab Facing Right." Sketch by Louis C. Tiffany, c. 1895. Unsigned. Oil on canvas, 14" x 7½".*

mained an important part of the finished work. Winslow Homer, by contrast, applied his watercolors with such freedom and such confidence that pencil guidelines were either overlooked or covered up.

Tiffany used watercolors constantly on his travels. They offered an easy way to jot down observations on the mosques, streets, gardens, palaces, and slums of Spain and North Africa, which, because their imaginative use of color and ornament, triggered deep-seated reactions in Tiffany.

"Spring" (Figure 22), a romantic allegory for which younger members of his family were pressed into service as models, illustrates Tiffany's justifiable pride in his offspring as well as his longing to paint the figure in the Renaissance tradition. The composition has the flow and rhythm of a procession on a classic urn. There is, however, an uncertainty in the way some heads and necks connect, and in the way some arms attach to shoulders. Tiffany's figures are usually more satisfying when they are clothed. (See the sketch of an Arab, Figure 23.)

"Sow with Piglets," possibly done before 1900 in tempera (Figure 24), is closer in spirit to "Duane Street." Instead of dreaming of classic art as seen through the eyes of the Renaissance, Tiffany is looking at a fragment of America with the eyes of an American. The sow is content. Her family is busy. The tempera colors sing. If there is anything unusual about the way the legs attach to the balloonlike bodies, it is of no consequence.

"Peonies and Iris" (Figure 25), dated 1915, is Impressionism, but there is something of the Japanese printmaker's interest in the picture plane, an influence often seen in impressionists' paintings. The picture does not invite the eye to move over the surface of the flowers because there are no surfaces. This picture records the light reflected from surfaces.

Tiffany's success as a painter was not limited to the early years. Election to full membership in the National Academy came in 1880, when he was thirty-two. Five of his watercolors were shown in the Columbian Exposition in 1893. Critics continued to praise his new canvasses. Sadakichi Hartmann in *A History of American Art* (1901),[2] includes Chase, Colman, Eakins, Inness, Sargent, Whistler, and Tiffany in a "marvellous list of names, embracing nearly all those who, by their lofty standard, have helped to raise the standard of Modern American Art." His mind, however, always churned with ideas, and his experiments in new mediums had begun by the time he was twenty-five.

Tiffany was not the only painter in the mid '70s who was chafing at the limitations of the brush. In 1865 (the year of Tiffany's first visit to England) William Morris, the renowned and wealthy English poet, designer, painter, and printer, whose calls for more art for the people had caused many an elegant "artist" to squirm in his frock coat, had formed Morris, Marshall,

Theodore Flagg

FIGURE 24   *"Sow with Piglets." Signed, "Louis C. Tiffany," c. 1900. Watercolor and tempera on paper, 18¹¹/₁₆" x 24⅝".*

Faulkner & Company, and was designing wallpapers, furniture, and stained-glass windows. Tiffany respected Morris' views on art, and the two did correspond at some time.[3]

Tiffany was also influenced by Oscar Wilde, the English poet and playwright. Wilde had toured America proclaiming that art is "the secret of life," and had made an impression on Tiffany. Many of their statements are similar in thought and purpose.

The Belle Époque had its share of critics who sensed the shallowness as well as the charm of its glittering ways. The very poor, as usual, grumbled. Anarchists were busily making bombs in basements. But some members of the Carriage Class, even though they dressed in high style, sipped champagne, and dined in candlelight, were dreaming of a world in which more good things were within reach of more people. Louis Tiffany was one of these.

Tiffany's paintings are a more important phase of his work than has been generally recognized. They reveal him as a sensitive person with great talent. They also show he was more aware of the world as it is than many have realized. His success as a painter helps explain how he could move into other fields of art for which he had no formal preparation, and make a success of them. The changes in his style, the development from the roving point of view of his early work to the Impressionism in his later work, throw light on a parallel development in his windows and in the decorative arts. And his commitment to realism in painting helps account for his inability to decide whether windows should be realistic or whether they should be decorative screens of glass, an indecision that was to bother him all his life.

NOTES

1 The following excerpts from Louis Comfort Tiffany's scrapbook are undated, but the National Academy records show "on the way between old and new Cairo, Citadel Mosque of Mohammed Ali and Tombs of the Mamelucks" was shown in 1872 when the twenty-four-year-old Tiffany was living at the Y.M.C.A.:
(a) "Mr. Tiffany also exhibits a large watercolor drawing Bazaar (*sic*) in Cairo which is a very attractive picture, and when exhibited at the Academy of Design in New York, a few weeks ago, probably received more praise than any other work in the collection."

(b) "Lake Dunmore, Vt., Mr. Louis C. Tiffany, who is beyond question taking the lead of the young men and is consequently in great danger of being spoiled by flattery, is represented by a large picture which is accorded the post of honor in the South Gallery. It represents the Citadel Mosque of Mohammed Ali between Old and New Cairo with a procession of Arabs and camels."
2 L. C. Page & Company.
3 William J. Fielding, who served Tiffany as secretary from 1909-33, stated this was the case.

FIGURE 25 *"Peonies and Iris." Signed, "Louis C. Tiffany, '15." Oil on canvas, 37¼" x 25¼".*

Chapter 4

A NEW KIND OF GLASS

I then perceived that the glass used for claret bottles and preserve jars was richer, finer, had a more beautiful quality in color-vibrations than any glass I could buy. So I set to puzzling out this curious matter. . . .

I took up chemistry, built furnaces—two of them were destroyed by fire—and for some time my experiments met with no success. . . . Year by year, the experiments that baffled hope gave way to better results.

LOUIS C. TIFFANY, 1917

Tiffany's selection of glass as a second medium was not solely by chance. As a child he loved those colored chips which brighten every street. The flashes from the jewels in his father's store fascinated him as a boy. As a teenager, he thrilled at the ruby reds, emerald greens, and deep blues in Chartres Cathedral's early windows. All his long life he admired the rainbow tints reflected from the disintegrating surfaces of ancient glass. It is significant that these early and formative memories were of pleasure in the color itself, not in the images.

Nor were these the only reasons for Tiffany's taking up glass. This country has always been staunchly middle class. Much of its thinking is inherited from the Puritans, and from the frontier. Glass in some cultures has been identified with art and wealth. In America it has guarded

"spirits and cures," sparkled on bosoms, brightened sideboards, shut out the cold, and performed so many other services in American hovels, chikees, houses, and tepees that it has become an integral part of American life.

Not only that, but in spite of all the dedicated souls who have sweated over glowing pots for the past six thousand years, glass still guards many secrets, and Tiffany loved to discover things.

In its simplest form, glass is melted sand. The glass we use has many additives, the principal one being an alkali—either potash or soda ash. Hot glass is liquid. It cools, and therefore solidifies, gradually, with no sudden drop in temperature and attendant release of energy, as is usually the case when a molten mass crystallizes. Different parts of a mass of glass, however, cool at different rates (the outside from the inside, for example), thereby setting up internal stresses that, unless released, can cause it to fly apart.

Because molten glass cools gradually the molecules become motionless in the irregular patterns of a liquid. It is therefore a liquid that freezes at a high temperature. This is not the complete story, however. Other characteristics indicate that in its solid state glass is composed of minute crystallites, which have no crystalline outline but are the first steps toward crystallization.

All in all, it is easier to discuss glassmaking than to tell what glass is. It has greater tensile strength and more flexibility than steel. The slightest scratch on its surface will flow under pressure to result in a clean break. While molten, it can be gathered up on the end of a blow pipe (a hollow rod with a wide part on one end and a mouth piece on the other) and blown, twisted, folded, whirled, bent, squeezed, spun, stretched, or pressed into almost any shape. After it has cooled and hardened, it can be cut, polished, or engraved. The ways to make, color, and use glass are endless.

By 1872 Tiffany was making glass in his own studio, a practice he continued until "there was some kind of explosion" after which, according to members of the family, "mother put a stop to it." In 1875 he was experimenting at Thill's Glasshouse in Brooklyn, where he made his first drapery glass, which was folded while it was still fairly soft. In 1878 he established the first glasshouse of his own with Andrea Boldini in charge. This house burned, as did its successor, and Boldini left the scene. From 1880–93 Tiffany used glass made for him, or under his supervision, by the Heidt Glasshouse in Brooklyn. He learned, however, "to his cost that it would be useless to expect to make really beautiful windows unless he could control furnaces of his own where his ideas would be carried out without interference from those who either could not or would not understand." This decision led him to bring Arthur J. Nash, a "practical glass manufacturer,"[1] from Stourbridge, England, and to build a glass factory (in Corona, Long Island). He also engaged a full-time chemist, Dr. Parker McIlhenny, who helped with his research for over twenty years. The Corona factory burned once, but Nash's record was better than Boldini's, who seems to have burned one glasshouse a year.

The Corona furnace contained sixteen of the smaller pots most suitable for colored glass. They were about two feet in diameter and four feet tall. Pots are made of fire clay which remains stable under intense heat. The furnace was heated with crude oil and steam. It was equipped with the standard "glory holes," an opening where a workman can reheat a "gather of glass" when it becomes too stiff to work. Tiffany's workers were organized into the traditional "shops" headed by a gaffer who was assisted by a blower, a decorator, a gatherer, a dip boy, and a carrying-in boy. At the peak of their production, the Tiffany Furnaces had five shops.

The glass in Tiffany's windows and lamps is the traditional "lime glass," about 70 per cent silica, 15 per cent soda, and 10 per cent lime. The rest of the "batch," as the mixed ingredients are called, included small amounts of such things as arsenic, borax, potash, and metallic oxides, all depending on the color and kind of glass desired.[2] Soda (sodium oxide) is a flux, which means it lowers the melting point (from about 2,900° F. to about 1,700° F.). Lime makes glass resistant to water. Metallic oxides are coloring agents.

Tiffany's vases are lead glass, about 50 per cent silica, 30 per cent red lead (a lead oxide), and 15 per cent pearl ash (a form of potash). Such "crystal" rings when thumped. It is heavier, softer, more brilliant, and more costly than lime glass. It, too, contains a wide variety of additional ingredients, all of which serve a special purpose.

When a pot of glass is started, the pot is brought to a white heat and cullet (broken bits of glass) is shoveled in. Cullet liquifies easily and therefore speeds up the melting process. The batch is added gradually to let it condense as it liquifies. When the pot is full, the pot metal, as the liquid glass is called, is held in melt, often at a temperature in excess of 2,700° F., sometimes for as long as two days. (The time depends, among other things, on the color desired.) At this temperature, glass has the consistency of honey, and the pot and the pot metal both glow with a white heat. When the metal is ready to use, the temperature is reduced to about 1,700° F., at which point it handles about like honey on a cold day.

It would seem logical to assume that colored glass has colors in it, but that is not the case. The glass in a green bottle for example, contains no green pigment, only oxide of iron, which transmits light selectively. What we call white light is a blend of the violet, blue, green, yellow, orange, and red in the rainbow. Glass that transmits them all is sometimes called "white glass." That which blocks out the violet, blue, yellow, orange, and red (by turning them into heat) and transmits only the green is called "green glass." If glass blocks out violet, blue, green, yellow, and orange, it is "red glass."

Glassmakers preparing a batch must consider many factors including how the glass will be used, whether they want bubbles in it, which metallic oxides and other agents are necessary to produce the desired color, what must be added to neutralize unwanted oxides already in the raw material, how long the pot metal must be held in melt, what chemicals in the atmosphere might affect the color of the molten glass adversely, what gases may get to it by mistake from the oven itself, and the number of times the cullet has already been used. Copper, for example, makes one shade of blue in lead glass, another in soda glass, and still another in potash glass.

Each color calls for a special formula and special handling. The ingredients in Tiffany's opalescent glass, a multicolored glass that is translucent but not transparent, include saltpeter, bone ash, arsenic, salt, black antimony, and manganese. For some shades of green, he used both copper scales and red ochre; for deep blues, he used cobalt oxide; for light blue, copper oxide; for lavender, manganese.

Reds presented problems for Tiffany, and do for most glassmakers. Gold, copper, and selenium all produce red glass, each a hue of its own. Molten red glass is clear or a pale honey or even a light green color until it is heated a second time. When it has been cooled and reheated, the color will "strike"—meaning the metal (gold, copper, or selenium) has been freed from its bonds to the other elements and has become submicroscopic crystals. The glass is red because these crystals absorb violet, blue, green, yellow, and orange rays and permit the red to pass on through. If the glass is held in melt too long, however, or if an article (such as a goblet with an applied stem) is reheated too many times while being worked, the color may darken to an unattractive liverish hue.

One of the "secrets" of Tiffany's success is that he loved glass and did things with it no one had ever done before. He used traditional methods when they suited him. He revived old ways that had been forgotten. He invented new ones. Some Tiffany sheet glass was rolled in the commercial

manner (poured out on a sheet of iron and flattened with a roller). Some was made in the traditional "crown" and "muff" methods. These two methods involve the blowpipe, a tool used in the same form for two thousand years. Once he has his gather, the worker turns the blowpipe continually to keep it from sagging into the wrong shape.

In making "crown" glass, the worker blows enough air into his gather to form a bubble. This bubble is transferred to a pontil rod (a solid iron rod) with enough hot glass on the end to make it adhere. When the bubble is punctured (with a wooden stick or a metal tool), the centrifugal force of the spinning rod opens it into a disc. When this disc is reheated in a glory hole, the centrifugal force extends it farther. Discs may vary from twenty inches to several feet in diameter, depending on the size of the original gather. When the disc has cooled to a solid, the pontil rod is snapped off, leaving a circular sheet of glass, thin at the edges and thick near the knob in the center.

This disc, and this is true of all glass, must be annealed (reheated almost to its softening point and cooled slowly enough to allow the molecules to realign themselves), a process that reduces the inner stresses. The annealing is done in a special oven which heats the glass to about 50° F. lower than its softening point. The cooling process can take as long as a week for large pieces.

The "muff" method (an innovation of the nineteenth century) calls for blowing a sausage-shaped balloon of glass and cutting off the ends to form a cylinder or muff. The muff is cut the long way and heated until it can be opened and flattened out. The result is a sheet of glass up to three feet across and fairly uniform in thickness.

Some of Tiffany's finest glass resulted from his revival of one of the oldest methods of all: ladling pools of molten glass onto a sheet of iron. When this glass cooled, its surface was naturally indented with crevices, ripples, ridges, small folds, and overlaps of layers of glass.

Some pools were treated manually with rollers to give the surface a variety of ripples and other effects. Some were rolled so parts of the surface would pile up here and thin out there, a technique possible because glass is such a poor conductor of heat that the part touching the iron cools quicker than that near the surface. Other methods called for sheets to be picked up with pincers to let the warmer and softer surface sag into decorative folds.

Drapery glass, one of Tiffany's early innovations, called for workers (using asbestos gloves and tongs) to seize the opposite ends of a soft pool of glass and to push, twist, and turn it until it resembled rumpled fabric itself. Since the thicker the glass the less light it transmits, drapery glass, even at a distance, gives the illusion of a fabric turning toward and away from the source of light.

Tiffany's innovations went on and on. He scattered fragments of colored glass on an iron table and poured molten glass over them. Flakes of colored glass were sprinkled over the surface of sheets of molten glass. Pools of molten glass were stirred with tools to induce swirls and other chance patterns. Hot glass was sprayed with iron and tin salts to give it an iridescent surface. Metallic oxides were sprayed into the air of the annealing ovens to permit the hot glass to attract them to its surface and thereby become iridescent. Threads of dark glass were embedded in clear glass. Hot molten glass of one color was splattered, splashed, and dripped on sheets of another color. Several different colors were stirred together in a way that mixed but did not blend them. Often as many as seven different colors were poured into one pool and let cool in chance effects. Sheets of molten glass were covered with drops of molten glass of another color to achieve mottled effects. Layers of translucent glass were applied to layers of opaque glass. Pools of molten glass were jostled and folded to induce accidental effects. Many innovations were planned; many were the result of Tiffany's seeing a workman make what the workman considered a mistake, but which Tiffany welcomed as a discovery.

The happy result of Tiffany's imaginative experiments was thousands of sheets of beautiful glass full of the kind of lovely flaws the other glassmakers were trying to avoid. Some of his glass looked like onyx, some like amber, some like marble. Other kinds suggested flowing water, or white clouds on a summer day, or masses of foliage. Some had the lustered beauty of dragonfly wings; others flashed with hues of the peacock, the hummingbird, and the butterfly. Some, because he had introduced minute crystals of both gold and silver, had a dichroic effect (red in transmitted light, green in reflected light). Flakes of colored glass floating in a clear matrix gave

some the beauty of a kaleidoscope without the symmetry.

It was as though he had cut up the sky, melted down a flower garden, tossed in some jewels, and made it into glass. Expense and trouble were brushed aside as the trivial things they are. The result was acres of glass, so diverse in surface, texture, color combinations, striation, and overall effect that he could be certain somewhere in the thousands of sheets stored away in his bins a part could be found that would suggest anything he wanted, whether it was a tomato, daffodil petals, or a butterfly wing. The only problem was to find it.

This is not to imply that Tiffany developed, or claimed to develop, an entirely new material. He was always careful to give credit to Gallé, the French master in decorative art and especially glass, for turning his attention to the importance of blown and molded glass. Then, too, in his travels Tiffany surely saw the iridescent glass Ludwig Lobmeyr exhibited in Vienna as early as 1873.

The popular story that Tiffany took secret formulas to his grave is intriguing and durable and more or less true, but not in the sense it implies. All glass craftsmen, including Tiffany, have secrets they try to guard from competitors, usually without success. Tiffany was by nature secretive. No one was allowed in the room when he was mixing a batch. Cecilia Waern, the English critic and writer, observed that "no profane eye is allowed to penetrate"[3] his Corona glasshouse. He did invent new methods for making and working glass, some of which he patented. It is also true that glass workers declared that Tiffany's glass cuts easier and better than other glass. But eventually others knew many and perhaps all of his processes and formulas.

In 1913 Tiffany sued Frederic Carder, the skilled English glassworker and founder of Steuben Glass Works of Corning, New York, in an attempt to protect his patents on methods of making iridescent glass. The suit was settled out of court a year later and there was no personal animosity. Carder made "Aurene" glass from 1904–32. It had an iridescence that is almost indistinguishable from Tiffany's.

Actually it is impossible to protect a glass formula or, for that matter to prove that any innovation really is a discovery. Tiffany might have had bottles of secret mixtures stored and coded with instructions that for a given color a certain amount was to be added to so many hundred pounds of batch but his chemist, at least, would have known the formulas.

Then, too, there were Tom Johnson, the blower, and Martin Bach, Sr., the batch mixer who left Tiffany's employ and by 1902 had set up a glasshouse in Brooklyn where they were making "Quezal" glass which looks very much like Favrile glass even though the pieces were not as well designed. And in 1924 Bach's son Martin Bach, Jr., started an art-glass shop in Victor Durand's factory in Vineland, New Jersey, and made "Durand" glass until Durand was killed in an automobile accident in 1931. It is pertinent also that a chemical analysis will reveal every ingredient of any glass.

There were, however, two secrets of another kind to Tiffany's success. One he could not have taken to the grave, the other he could not have left behind. The first was his father's wealth which placed any material in the world within his reach. Because of it he could travel, study, collect, ignore cost, and defy rules. It gave him freedom, and he made the most of it.

The second was his personality, his sense of order, his curiosity, his capacity for work, his insistence of quality. His orderliness made it possible for him to establish priorities, to organize, to accomplish. His curiosity led him to new knowledge and this kept his work fresh and innovative. His capacity for work let him achieve his goals. His insistence on good workmanship gave everything he made a quality all craftsmen respect.

NOTES

1 DeKay, Charles, *The Art Work of Louis C. Tiffany*. Garden City, N.Y.: Doubleday, Page & Co., 1914, p. 25.
2 The list of possible ingredients also includes dolomite, feldspar, antimony, potassium oxide, barium carbonate, zinc oxide, sodium bicarbonate, saltpeter, uranium, titanium, and steel.
3 Waern, Cecilia, "The Industrial Arts of America; The Tiffany Glass and Decorating Co." *The Studio*, Vol. 11 of Vol. 11–12, 1897, pp. 156–65.

Chapter 5

FROM SHEETS OF GLASS TO WINDOWS

There are still men of force in the arts who are imitated by pupils and others. Such are Claude Monet, landscape and flower painter, Whistler and Sargent, Rodin the sculptor.

Art for the people, if we may judge by the past, is sure to be freer from tradition than that of the bygone schools and is likely to have a larger element of the useful. In other words, the arts and crafts will gain, relatively speaking, on the fine arts.

As to those who cling to the view that art lies only in the hands of the painters and sculptors, their patrons are tending to become relatively fewer as time goes on. No profession is more overcrowded. Clients do not keep increasing; it is rather the other way.

CHARLES DEKAY, *The Art Work of Louis C. Tiffany*

America's love affair with Tiffany's windows may not have been made in heaven, but heaven had something to do with it. By the mid 1870s, when he began his own experiments in leaded glass, the charismatic furor of the second great awakening (a sweeping religious revival that rocked America during its early and romantic decades) had subsided, but Americans were still building and attending churches. Moreover, the high church movement and its handmaiden, the Gothic revival, had crossed the ocean and shaken even some hard-shell Protestants loose from their prejudice against ritual and symbols. The unwritten rule against paintings and statues remained in force, but, curiously, many stalwarts, who would have blown their doctrinal stacks at even the suggestion of a painting of Jesus in the sanctuary of their church, were asking for his likeness in leaded windows.

The mansions of the period were reflecting change of another kind. The symmetrical restraint of the colonial tradition with its prim doorways and regularly spaced rows of windows had fallen out of favor. Americans had developed a taste for turrets, towers, arches, and ornament. As a result, styles were imported and mixed with high-spirited abandon. The Civil War was over. The future was bright. Americans were going to enjoy life! God had showered so many good things on them!

Tiffany saw the situation from several points of view. As an American, he shared his country's buoyancy; as an artist, he was bothered by the vagaries of its taste. As a businessman, he was fired by the dimensions of the economic opportunity.

In 1870 the field of glass was wide open. Several glass studios were making attractive leaded windows (the J. V. R. Lamb Studios of New York, among them). But aside from Page, McDonald and McPherson, who were making good pot metal in Boston,[1] the eighteen or twenty American glassmakers were not producing much good glass.

The churches wanted the image of our Lord and His saints in their leaded windows. Tiffany saw the way to go. They would have their saints, but Tiffany's windows would be more than a skin of enamel painted on thin, poorly colored glass. (A commentator in the New York *Times*, Saturday, November 13, 1880, dubbed the windows in St. Patrick's Cathedral on Fifth Avenue as "beneath contempt.") His windows would be brilliant, glassy, rich in texture and color, different from anything anyone had ever seen, and the brush would be used only as a last resort. The churches would have art as well as glass pictures.

The American dwelling also offered opportunities as Tiffany saw it. Too many of the big houses especially were becoming gaudy displays of bad taste. He would offer the country an alternative. So the furnace was coming in! The fireplace was still a part of the American tradition. In cold weather Americans liked to sit in front of flames, even those fed by gas. Gathering around a hearth is an attractive alternative to going out on a winter night, as everyone knows who has shivered in a carriage and heard a cold horse whinny. Beauty around a fireplace might get to a lot of people.

By 1880 Tiffany was making a variety of glass tiles for mantels and hearths (Figure 26). Some, in a yellow opalescent backed with a metallic coating, glowed like Mexican opals. Some were iridescent. Some had flakes buried in their surfaces, while others had patterns in relief. The sizes varied from one to four inches. A few were oblong; all were made in molds. Projections on the back held some securely in the cement. His tiles called attention to the importance of materials, to the potentials of glass, and to the value of beauty, all at the same time.

Windows, which played a different role from today's windows, called for a different strategy. In addition to keeping out the weather, controlling the light, relating the inside to the outside, and making life a little easier for anyone with claustrophobia, Victorian windows were often seized on as an excuse to display yards of silks, lace, velvets, fringes, and tassels. Socialites, wealthy grandparents, and maiden aunts especially loved to make a great thing of them, and this complicated matters. Still, a screen of colored glass, which glows in the morning, flashes in the sun, flickers in the shadows of a moving branch, and fades slowly with the day, is attractive. And Tiffany approached the matter sensibly. Some of his first domestic windows were in the form of transoms, which glowed quietly if perhaps a little strangely above all the fuss below. These caught on, and by the end of the century many families had come under his vitreous spell. It was a happy circumstance. America was prosperous, full of hope, and looking for ways to express itself, and there was Tiffany with his wonderful glass.

Tiffany's role in making the windows varied according to circumstances. All began with a sketch, possibly by Tiffany but most often by a staff artist. The sketch was usually followed by a painting (cartoon) in color, the exact size of the projected window. Next came the "cut line" and a duplicate. The cut line was executed in heavy black lines on thin paper (or architect's linen) while it was superimposed on the cartoon. The duplicate was cut into templates to serve as patterns for the glass cutters. The cut line was necessarily executed by someone with great knowledge. Careful consideration had to be given to the type of glass needed in each part of the design and to the shape and size of each piece.

Another factor to consider was the limitations of the glass. Some cuts are relatively easy and some are impossible. Some kinds of glass, notably drapery glass, are difficult to cut. It was also important to Tiffany that the design of the pieces of glass have a rhythm and flow. When the cut line and templates were ready, the selection of the glass came next. Sometimes a rough color sketch was made using glass fragments already on hand. These were secured by beeswax to a sheet of clear glass (a glass easel) and while they did not look like the finished window, they did show how the colors would work together. Few laymen realize that pieces of colored glass affect each other in surprising ways; that in some instances one will almost negate the effect of another.

When a basic plan had been decided on, the search for the glass began. As many as two hundred tons of glass in the form of ovals about three feet long were stored in the bins of the Tiffany Studios. Five thousand colors and hues were identified by code. When a large window

FIGURE 26 *Press-molded Tiffany tiles, from 1881–1925. Sizes range from 1" x 1" to 4" x 4". The opalescent pale blue tile with floral design and gold backing (left of center) was patented in 1881.*

Theodore Flagg

FIGURE 27   *Cross-sections of layered Favrile glass fragments.*

was in preparation, the templates were attached to a glass easel and each was removed one at a time so trial pieces could be held over the opening. Some places might call for folds in the glass moving in a particular direction; others for "grain" (streaks of color) of a special kind. Others might require special colors and textures. Some areas might demand pieces that were light in specific areas and dark in others (so they would suggest a round fruit, for example). Finding the glass was a slow process. The right part might be in the center of a large sheet. Irrelevant! It was cut out, regardless of what had to be discarded.

As each piece was cut it was secured to the glass easel, and the result did show what the completed window would look like, without the leading. This could be corrected by painting the exposed glass black. Usually, when all were in place some pieces were found to be wrong for one reason or another. The striations might go in the right direction, but the color might be off. The color might be right, but the folds wrong. This could mean substituting new glass, or possibly leading one piece over the existing one (a process called plating), thereby adjusting its value (lightness or darkness), its hue, or its intensity (the strength of that particular hue).

When all pieces were adjudged satisfactory, they were "leaded up." This called for tacking the cut line to a tabletop so it could serve as a guide in fitting the pieces of the puzzle together. The worker started in a corner first with a strip of lead called a "came." Cames[2] are shaped like an "H" lying on its side. The pieces of glass slide into the openings. Tacks held the glass in place as the work progressed. The joints of the cames were then mitered and soldered, and a puttylike cement worked into any space left between the glass and the lead. This gave the window strength and made it watertight. The outside came is "U" shaped.

Cames (which vary in size) are not all things to all glass however. Bending them around complicated shapes, such as flower forms, or long narrow strips, presents problems. Wrapping them around very small fragments of glass is difficult. Fitting them around a large chunk of chipped glass is impossible. Since the glass in Tiffany's windows (especially those made before 1900) often included all these kinds, he revived old methods of leading and evolved new ones that met his needs. One method called for opening up the cames and using them as lead strips.

The "copper foil" technique, used first in the leaded lamp shades and later in the windows, involves wrapping the edges of each piece of glass with tissue-thin copper foil, treated on the inside with beeswax (to make it adhere) and on the outside with muriatic acid (to make it bond with solder). The pieces thus wrapped are laid on the cut line and melted solder is run between them. This method permitted more freedom in designing the individual pieces, which could be large or minute, thick or thin, and as long, slender, and complicated as even Tiffany could want.

In early windows (before 1900) Tiffany used still another method consisting of setting chunks of glass in masses of solder. The results are reminiscent of medieval jewelry.

Leading gives small windows sufficient strength, but iron "saddle bars" were run across the larger windows and the leading was tied to them by copper wires. These bars, when anchored in the frame or in the walls of a building helped the window withstand high winds. When, as in "Feeding the Flamingoes" (Figure 54), Tiffany did not want a dark line cutting across a face or a hand, he displayed his ingenuity by running thin ribbons of iron around the edges of the pattern. These ribbons gave the window strength and are almost invisible.

The last step was Tiffany's final inspection. The completed window was scanned with the blue eyes of a perfectionist. If each piece suited him, all was well. If one piece was not quite right, no matter how large or how small, he punched it out with a stick he carried for that purpose. Sheet after sheet of new glass was then scanned until a satisfactory part was found.

Sometimes it turned out that the new glass was satisfactory in most respects, but not all. Then more sheets were searched and a second piece tried over the first, and possibly a third over the second and a fourth over the third! When the effect was exactly what he wanted, all pieces were leaded in place, one on top of the other, and the window sent on its way.

Most Tiffany windows were obviously produced by an assembly line of hands, a fact that raises the question what does the term "Tiffany window" mean? And how does one tell them from others made in the same period?

FIGURE 28 *Photograph of a window workshop in the Tiffany Studios. Dan Lauril, right, is grouting a glazed window. Above is an unfinished "Wreath" window.*

FIGURE 29 *A leaded window shop, Tiffany Studios. (This and the other photographs on this page are from damaged glass plates.)*

FIGURE 30 *Grouting a lead came window in a Tiffany Studios workshop, c. 1905. (The enameled pieces depicting the face and hands are not in place.)*

FIGURE 31 *Photograph of a Tiffany workshop showing a cartoon for a window of a knight in armor.*

The answer is that all windows made by the Tiffany Studios are "Tiffany" windows, and that it is not always easy to distinguish his windows from windows made by his contemporaries, for a number of reasons.

John LaFarge, Frederick Stymetz Lamb, and David Lang made superb windows. LaFarge and Tiffany were friendly competitors. They experimented with glass at the same time (the 1880s) in the Heidt Glasshouse in Brooklyn. LaFarge's windows in the Samuel J. Tilden house in New York contain molded leaves, but to the uninitiated they look very much like Tiffany windows. The glass in his handsome "Peony" and "Hollyhock" windows is as rich and beautiful as is Tiffany's. But LaFarge and Tiffany disagreed on many points, and LaFarge's style was his own. In 1893, he took public issue with Tiffany's stand against the restraints of tradition in a booklet, "The American Art of Glass: To be read in connection with Mr. Louis C. Tiffany's paper in the July Number of *The Forum*."

Lamb, whose father and uncle founded the J. & R. Lamb Studios in 1857, made many distinguished windows including "The Arts"[3] which was awarded a gold medal at the Cotton States and International Exposition in Atlanta, Georgia, in 1895, and was later shown at Turin, Italy, in 1902. The magazine *Deutsch Kunst und Decoration*, Vol. XI, 1902–3, attributed the window to Tiffany, even though it contains an enameled landscape which would not be found in a Tiffany window. Lamb later did all the windows in the chapel of Stanford University in California.

Lang, a former employee of the Tiffany Studios, did many fine landscape windows in the Tiffany style for the firm Greene & Greene in Los Angeles.

Neither LaFarge nor the Lambs seem to have had glasshouses of their own, but much of the glass in their windows has a rich Tiffany look. The statements in Tiffany Studios publications that Favrile glass was not sold to any other studios create a mystery, which students will eventually resolve.

Within the broad classification "Tiffany windows" are two categories, the studio pieces and the personal work. The former are made from designs by artists on his staff, the latter from paintings or cartoons by Tiffany himself. Regardless of the extent of Tiffany's involvement, all were made under his supervision, and all have

characteristics in common. Whereas windows by some of his contemporaries might contain hundreds of pieces of glass, some Tiffany windows (and some LaFarge windows) will contain thousands. The contours of the individual pieces of glass in Tiffany windows flow with a rhythm not found in the work of many of his contemporaries. The intricate cutting is another characteristic: Cutting a "U" shape from a larger piece requires great skill because glass tends to break in a straight line. Tiffany's windows have many such cuts. Windows made before 1900 have chipped "jewels" and plating. After 1900 there is less plating, more copper-foil leading, and the jewels and chunks are discontinued.

A Tiffany window has a way of involving the observer in the viewing experience. With each change in position, ever so slight, the light in iridescent glass will shift, the color in the drapery glass will ebb or flow, and the lights in the chipped jewels will go on and off. The brush was never used in a Tiffany window unless there was no alternative. This means they are relatively free of dark smudges to suggest shadows.

Plating, sometimes as many as four or five layers deep, which often makes the weight unbelievable, is a Tiffany characteristic. An air space left intentionally between two of the layers to add brilliance to the colors, a technique he patented in 1881, is another. The copper-foil technique, although used by others, is one of the marks of Tiffany windows made after 1900. Often cames are used where they would serve best (in verticals and horizontals), while copper foil is used in other parts. Heavy leads molded to suggest the limbs of a tree are another feature. Reinforcing ribbons of iron bent around the contours of the glass is yet another characteristic, as is a tendency to bend the saddle bars to avoid crossing a face.

The personal windows have no common denominator except perhaps their diversity. The "studio" windows, those designed by his staff, tend toward formulas: saints surrounded by a glowing light, or arbors with peacocks and fountains, or memorial windows with crosses and doves, or gardens with cultivated flowers, or forests with streams, maidens, and waterfalls. This is not to imply that such windows are not important. They all in some way reflect his taste.

The personal windows are usually the result of

searching for a new way, a new theme, a new approach. Must a leaded window contain recognizable figures to be of interest? Need it be all glass? All translucent? Can abalone shell, broken bottles, ancient glass be used effectively? Can a written message be integrated successfully into the design? Are leads a necessary evil, or can they become a factor in themselves? Will a design be effective if it is also pictorial? Can the effects achieved in impressionist painting be transferred to glass? Must leaded windows transmit light, or can they be effective in reflected light? Must they be used in an outside wall, or will they serve as room dividers? Is Tiffany glass suitable for windows in the thirteenth-century style?

Tiffany wanted to find answers to such questions, and the fascinating result is a group of Tiffany windows that do not look like Tiffany windows. The question then arises, how does one tell a personal window from the studio pieces? Are they all signed? And the answer is that only a few are signed and one must rely on documentary as well as internal evidence.

As we take a closer look at Tiffany's windows it is well to remember they were made for his time, not for ours. Had he been able to look ahead to see our decaying cities with battered mansions staring blankly at nothing and old churches standing tall in threadbare districts, he might have thought differently. Who can know? It is interesting to see, however, that the more footloose this country becomes and the more obsolescence it builds into its housing, the more Tiffany lamps it seems to want, and the more fascinated it becomes with his wonderful windows.

NOTES

1 Riordan, Roger, "American Stained Glass," *American Art Review*, Vol. 2, 1881, p. 229.
2 About 60 per cent tin; 40 per cent lead.
3 Now in La Belle Verriere Restaurant, Winter Park, Florida.

Chapter 6

THE WINDOWS

Naturally I was attracted to the old glass in windows of the Twelfth and Thirteenth Centuries which have always seemed to me the finest ever. Their rich tones are due in part to the use of pot metal full of impurities, and in part to the uneven thickness of the glass, but still more because the glassmakers of that day abstained from the use of paint.

LOUIS C. TIFFANY, *1917*

Tiffany's personal windows—those he designed himself—reveal a long struggle with an aesthetic problem. Should a window be made of untreated glass exclusively, or should enamels be used to achieve effects not possible any other way?

For the others making leaded windows in the latter half of the nineteenth century the answer was easy. When a brush is easier or less expensive use a brush. But Tiffany had an arts-and-crafts conscience. He believed the artist should respect his material, should not ask it to simulate another material, should not apologize for it in any way.

To be more specific, Tiffany loved glass, which he considered "the most beautiful of all the jewels." He was especially fond of molded or chipped chunks of strong reds, greens, blues, and amethyst. He wanted his windows all to say clearly, "glass is beautiful." But he also wanted to use the figure in his windows, and he was a tra-

ditional painter. The problem arose from the fact there is no way the human figure can be treated realistically in a window without using a brush. The brushwork bothered him because an artist brushing powdered glass on a sheet of clear glass to describe a face is resorting to a painter's technique; he is saying, in effect, his glass cannot do all he wants it to. And to make the problem more complex, big chunks of glass (his jewels) have no place in a realistic window wherein all pieces must work together to create the desired illusion.

The young Tiffany met the conflict by marching bravely off in two directions. Some of his early windows glow with chipped jewels, and figures so abstract they called for only a few touches of a brush to suggest an eye, a nose, or a finger. The results are glowing screens of color done in the spirit, if not the style, of the early windows at Chartres. (See "Christ, Ruler of the

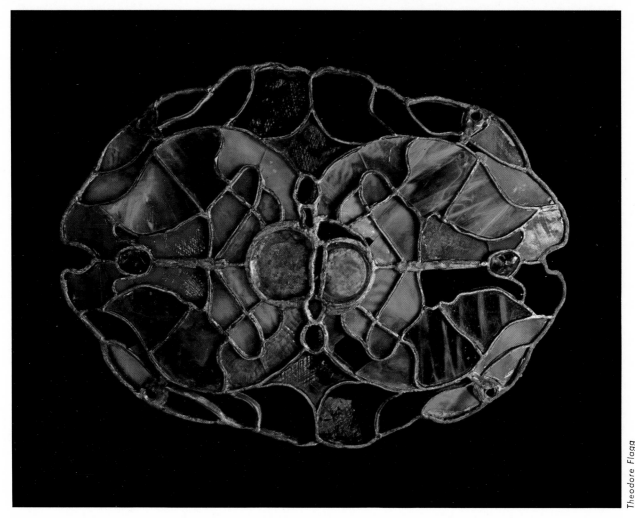

FIGURE 32 *Ornamental leaded panel by Louis C. Tiffany. Possibly as early as 1878. Unsigned. The central pieces are ancient glass backed by metallic foil. Length 14¾".*

Universe," Figure 49, and the angels in the "Medallion" window, Figure 52.)

Others of the early windows are copies of paintings containing naturalistic figures, and even though parts are a mosaic of beautiful glass, all exposed parts of the body are enamels applied with a brush and fired sufficiently to fuse the enamels to the surface of the glass. (See "The Seven Gifts of the Holy Spirit," Figure 47.) In these, the viewer's attention is intentionally directed away from the glass to the image it represents.

Tiffany's wrestling with this conflict led to many beautiful attempts to resolve it. Eventually, he was convinced he had succeeded, but that is a moot question.

Among his first efforts were small hanging panels with a stylized, butterfly theme. They are about fourteen inches across and leaded with cames. They turned up in the ruins of Laurelton Hall, but may have come from either the Bella apartment or the Seventy-second Street house. The pattern in all is similar. Two butterfly shapes face each other on either side of a fragment of ancient glass that he admired and wanted to simulate (Figure 32). The attention is on the glass, not the images. A few pieces of his own glass have a definite luster and may be his first attempts at that effect.

In 1878 Tiffany made windows from opalescent glass bulls' eyes for the Church of the Sacred

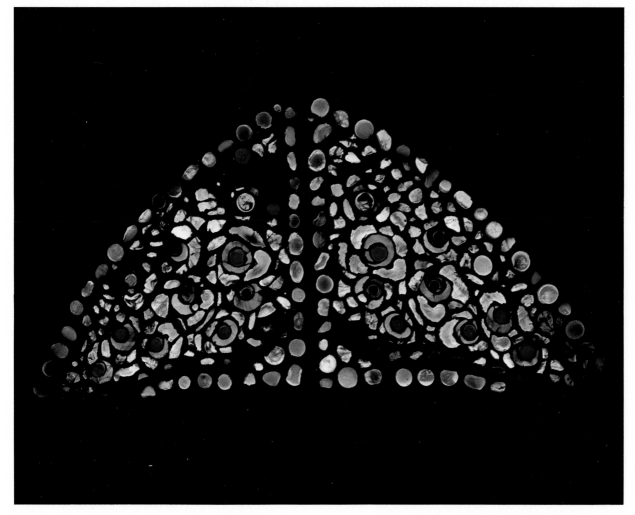

FIGURE 33 *Jeweled Gothic window. The Tiffany Glass Company, 1880–90. Unsigned. Originally was two separate panels from a larger window. Height 31".*

Heart on New York's West Fifty-first Street, which were translucent colored screens serving to soften the light while admitting it. They relied on no images for their appeal.

Another early window was an abstraction made for his Bella apartment, which he occupied from 1878 to 1885. This window consists of panes of colored glass arranged in a handsome, rhythmic pattern. There is no suggestion of pictorial depth, no intentional allusion to nature. The colored shapes are organized on and confined to a single plane. The interest is on form, on how the shapes and colors relate to each other. The window anticipated by thirty years the movement Tiffany denounced as "modernism." Tif-

fany was thinking in glass.

Not long afterward, however, a new direction appears in a window made for an Episcopal church in Islip, Long Island.[1] Here, a figure of St. Mark sits in a bank of clouds shaped like potato chips. The Saint himself, as flat as a pancake, relates nicely to his two-dimensional surroundings. But, as unlikely as it sounds, he turns his head to the right, his knees to the left, and crosses his feet in a pose reminiscent of the Jeremiah in Michelangelo's Sistine Chapel frescoes. Furthermore, details in the eye, eyebrow, and hand, are done with a brush.

Tiffany, although working in glass, is thinking as a painter, influenced by the Renaissance and

FIGURE 34 *The "Wreath" window. Signed, "Tiffany Favrile Glass," on paper label. 1900–10. Scale model for a window later installed in a residence in Dubuque, Iowa. Height 7¼".*

FIGURE 35 *Symbolic window. Tiffany Glass and Decorating Company, 1892–1900. Unsigned. Height 31½".*

its fascination with the world we see. The conflict is beginning to surface.

Also, among Tiffany's early windows were the two made in 1879 for the George Kemp house on New York's Fifth Avenue (where Saks Fifth Avenue stands today). These he not only designed but may have cut and leaded himself. The motifs were the modest eggplant and squash, which seldom enjoy more than a nod from either artists or gourmets. The windows were mosaics of untreated glass ranging from dark purply-browns through strong yellows and vibrant greens to the clear glass in the background. The glass, made in his own glasshouse and rich with bubbles, was cut and placed so the swirls of the crown glass suggest the receding planes of the vegetables and foliage. These windows rely partly on simulating

nature for their effect, but they represent no confusion, no indecision. There is no brushwork. Tiffany was thinking in glass.

The "Eggplant" (Figure 42) and "Squash" (Figure 43) windows illustrated here may or may not be those made for the Kemp house. The critic, Roger Riordan, referring to the Kemp windows commented, "The stained glass window screen represented in Fig. 5 [window screen in pure mosaic glass] is a good example of the mode in which Mr. Tiffany handles his splendid material. . . . The modeling of the leaves and fruit is given by the inequalities of the glass itself, and the play and gradation of color in its substance."[2] His article was illustrated by a drawing of the "Eggplant" window. Minor differences in the leading could be due to liberties Riordan took as

FIGURE 36 *Classic window. Tiffany Studios, 1900–10. Unsigned. Made for a residence in Newcastle, Pennsylvania. Height 92". La Belle Verriere Restaurant, Winter Park, Florida.*

FIGURE 37   *"Pebble" window. Tiffany Studios, after 1902. Unsigned. From the residence of Joseph Briggs.*
Height 61".

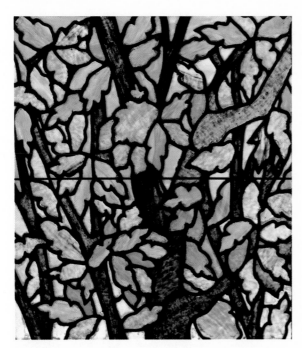

FIGURE 38   *"Leaf" window. Tiffany Glass and Decorating Company, 1890–1900. Unsigned. From the residence of Joseph Briggs. Height 23".*

FIGURE 39   *"Purple Rose" window. Tiffany Glass and Decorating Company, 1890–1900. Unsigned. From the residence of Joseph Briggs. Height 25½".*

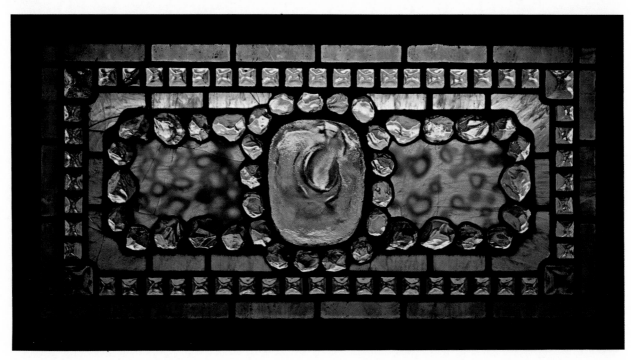

FIGURE 40   *Geometric window. Tiffany Glass and Decorating Company, 1892–1900. Unsigned. Height 13".*

FIGURE 41 *Three-dimensional window with peacock-feather motif. Tiffany Glass and Decorating Company,*
1890–1900. Unsigned. From Laurelton Hall art gallery. Height 48".

FIGURE 42   *"Eggplants." Leaded transom. Possibly from the Kemp residence, which was decorated by Louis C. Tiffany in 1879. Unsigned. Height 32".*

a draftsman, but in the text he states that "the striae and corrugations of the pieces of opalescent glass which form the background are so disposed as to help to bind the whole thing together."[3] The background in these windows is clear and colorless. Unless Riordan erred in his description, these are another version. One set of these windows was made for an exhibition in the Grafton Galleries held in London in 1899, one of which was reproduced in *The Studio*.[4] The fact that Tiffany made at least two versions, and exhibited one set twenty years later, indicates the importance he attached to them.

The windows in the World's Columbian Exposition in 1893 varied greatly, partly because of Tiffany's indecision as an artist, and partly be-

cause of his decisiveness as a businessman. He had visited and was greatly impressed with the International Fairs held in Philadelphia in 1876 and in Paris in 1889. He knew that millions from all over the world would amble, push, and shove through Chicago's Columbian Exposition (by count over 27 million). He realized his glass windows had qualities not equaled by his contemporaries. He was planning to reorganize his business and build a glasshouse in Corona, Long Island. The Chicago Exposition offered an opportunity to give his achievements additional exposure, and he was never one to ignore an opportunity.

But it so happened that the neoclassical planners of the World's Columbian Exposition had

FIGURE 43 *"Squash." Leaded transom. Possibly from the Kemp residence. Unsigned. Height 32".*

set aside no space for exhibiting leaded windows. The situation caused the business and promotion section of Tiffany's mind to go right to work. He arranged with his father to use some of the space reserved by the Tiffany Jewelry Company in the Manufactures and Liberal Arts Building for his newly formed Tiffany Glass and Decorating Company, and planned an exhibit that would include a chapel interior, a "Light Room," and a "Dark Room." All featured windows as well as mosaics, vestments, and lighting fixtures.

In the chapel the "Entombment" (Figure 44) was (according to contemporary accounts) flanked by two circular windows, one, "Jesus Blessing St. John" (Figure 48), and one taken

from a painting by the fifteenth-century Italian master, Sandro Botticelli (Figure 47).

In the "Entombment" five of the faithful have grouped themselves thoughtfully on the far side of Jesus, thus providing the observer an unobstructed view of His body. St. Joseph of Arimathea (a portrait of Louis Tiffany's father) supports Jesus tenderly. St. Mary Magdalene kneels in prayer. The others recede into the shadows. Tiffany's psychological insight was less than Rembrandt's, but he invested his figures with a quiet dignity. Restless trees reach up into a sky shot through with ominous lights but the emphasis is not on the suffering, it is on the peace that has come at last.

A decade has passed since the "St. Mark's"

FIGURE 45 *Detail, "Entombment," head of St. Joseph of Arimathea. Tiffany's father served as the model.*

FIGURE 46 *Preliminary sketch for cartoon for the "Entombment" window by Louis C. Tiffany, c. 1892. Unsigned. Oil on wood panel, 5¾" x 8".*

Theodore Flagg

window, and Tiffany is more sure of his treatment of the human figure. The "Entombment" is reminiscent of the Renaissance painters of the Netherlands. The light falls with theatrical selectivity on the dead Christ, on St. Joseph, and St. Mary. The deep space is heavy with atmosphere. The figure of Jesus is well constructed, and so detailed that it invites the eye to move from point to point over its surface. The window, which began as a small sketch in oil (eight by six inches) (Figure 46), grew into a full-scale painting and was then translated into glass. All exposed parts of the bodies are executed in enamels. The sheet bearing the figure of Jesus is plated between a top layer of opalescent white and a layer of mossy green.

The "Entombment" conveys several messages clearly. It tells the observer that Jesus had a mortal body and great dignity; that He died and was mourned by a remarkably small band of the faithful and that the event had cosmic overtones. But there is more. It also points out that the Tiffany Glass and Decorating Company could and would make windows in the tradition of the oil paintings of the seventeenth century; and that while untreated glass would be used wherever possible, the brush would be employed when necessary. The chipped jewels which give the other chapel windows such brilliance are absent. They would have been a distraction. Tiffany has used glass not to call attention to the picture plane, but to suggest that none exists.

Has he forgotten the mosaic approach? Not at all. Many parts of the "Entombment"—the

FIGURE 44 *"Entombment." Leaded window. Tiffany Glass and Decorating Company, c. 1892. Unsigned. Made for the World's Columbian Exposition. Height 104".*

Theodore Flagg

FIGURE 47 *"The Seven Gifts of the Holy Spirit." Leaded window, after a painting by Botticelli. The Tiffany Glass Company, c. 1885. Unsigned. Exhibited at the World's Columbian Exposition. Diameter 84".*

trees, the hills, the sky, and all the robes—constitute a glorious display of untreated glass. Even so, the emphasis is on the story, not the formal values. He is thinking as a painter, and he is proud of the way his wonderful glass can serve as strokes of a painter's brush. The struggle is very evident.

"The Seven Gifts of the Holy Spirit" (Figure 47), after a painting by Botticelli, was made years before the Columbian Exposition. Here glass is used to simulate a painting by the Florentine Master so admired by the Pre-Raphaelites in England. (The fact that Botticelli's name was misspelled "Bocatelli" in many contemporary accounts indicated the extent to which the great Italian was not known in America.) Instead of the somber colors in the "Entombment" its hues are the jelly-bean colors of fifteenth century tempera paintings. The ladies (who represent the gifts of the Holy Spirit) are endowed with Botticelli's droopy-eyed beauty, and all heads are attached to the neckbone as though something is askew in the skeleton, a characteristic of Botticelli. They also have enough of the naïveté of Kate Greenaway's decorative drawings of children to place them firmly in the nineteenth century.

Unlike the other circular windows in the Columbian Exposition, the Botticelli window is made in one piece—eight feet in diameter. Ribbons of iron, bent around the figures, give the window the structural support it needs and, at the same time, spare it the distraction of saddle bars. All flesh tones are enamel applied by a knowledgeable hand. The rest is a glowing assembly of several thousand pieces of pot metal, all of it presumably made in the Heidt Glasshouse in Brooklyn, which makes present day glassworkers shake their head in wonder and admiration. Curiously, the gray-green dress worn by the figure on the left is cold painted (unfired) and, very likely, an afterthought.

In "Jesus Blessing St. John" the flesh in the figures in the central medallion is enamel, but the symbols of the evangelists are mosaics of untreated glass in which Tiffany stresses the beauty of the material. The rest of the window is a vibrant screen of color alive with his beloved chipped jewels, which flash like a tray of gems in a jewelry store. In this window, Tiffany is thinking in glass.

"Feeding the Flamingoes" (Figure 54), a feature of the "Light Room," is of especial interest.

It uses a theme he had treated in his paintings, and he very likely applied the enameling in the head and arms himself. The feet are carefully covered. The subject is a young woman, draped in a classical robe, extending her hand to a puzzled flamingo whose companion looks on with understandable reservations. The observer is told little about the maiden, except that she is well-groomed and does not know the first thing about feeding a flamingo (who eats with his head upside down and prefers his food in water). The window is poetically unclear about other things as well: Is this a visit to ancient Rome, or to a tropical island, where maidens dress in a timeless fashion and live on friendly terms with aquatic birds? Is she a bird lover, or is she involved in something of a theatrical nature?

The window answers no irrelevant questions. (It is, in fact a study of two stuffed flamingoes set up in front of the fountain, columns, and fishbowl in the studio in Tiffany's Seventy-second Street house.) Tiffany has treated it all as a fantasy of lovely surfaces, a description in detail of something that never was, a happy land where things that please the eye need not make sense. The window offers an escape from the strain of reality. But there is something else: The maiden and the birds are constructed in an equilateral triangle with a fishbowl at its apex. They also form a band parallel to the picture plane, as do the columns behind them. The window is a surprising reflection of the Classical tradition as practiced by the French Academy. The shadows in the maiden's arms and those under her chin are additional indications of a French influence. These are not the dark tones of the "Entombment," but rather the blues and greens found in the shadows of Edouard Manet's paintings.

"Feeding the Flamingoes" is a brilliant work. The maiden, except for her robe (which is drapery glass), is executed in enamels, but the rest, including the birds, is a mosaic of Tiffany's finest glass. The bowl with fish is a disc almost an inch thick. Several pieces near the flamingoes' heads are cased with the top layer cut away to reveal the colors underneath. In the fractured glass, confetti-like flakes float in a rich amber.

Here too, ribbons of iron eliminate the need for distracting saddle bars. The window demonstrates Tiffany's prowess as a glassmaker, his ingenuity in creating images with pieces of untreated pot metal, and in all likelihood, his ex-

FIGURE 48 *"Jesus Blessing St. John." Leaded window. Tiffany Glass and Decorating Company, c. 1892. Unsigned. Made for the World's Columbian Exposition, Diameter 104".*

traordinary ability in painting with enamels. It also shows that he was wrestling with his problem.

Tiffany's Columbian exhibit achieved his objectives. It was the talk of the art world in this country. It created great interest in his work among the critics, museums, curators, and dealers of Europe. It led to his productive association with S. Bing in Paris, which, in turn, led to the Musée des Arts Décoratifs of The Louvre buying a Favrile glass vase in 1894. On the day after Christmas, 1895, ten of his windows from designs by leading French artists (including Toulouse-Lautrec and Bonnard), along with some of his blown glass, went on view at S. Bing's Salon de l'Art Nouveau. The windows were later shown in the Paris Salon, and within a short time, examples had been bought by museums, including the Musée des Arts Décoratifs of The Louvre. The leading art publications in France, Germany, Austria, and England were carrying stories about the tributes to Louis Comfort Tiffany and his "American Glass." For the first time, an American had assumed world leadership in an important branch of the arts.

Tiffany, never inclined to rest on laurels, went right on.

In "Girl Picking Gourds" (Figure 56), made in 1897–98 from a design by the English painter Sir Frank Brangwyn, a maiden, draped from head to below the toes, picks a gourd from a vine on a trellis. She, the trellis, and the foliage are silhouetted against cumulous clouds rolling up in the sky beyond. The pieces of glass are larger than those in most of the windows Tiffany designed himself, and the heavy leading gives it the quality of a drawing. This window, which was exhibited in the Grafton Galleries in London in 1899, is a good and rare example of the few Tiffany windows made from designs by leading European artists.

Of particular significance, however, is the fact that it was a "breakthrough." The flesh tones are *in* the glass, not enamels applied with a brush. The face and hands are two layers. A very few lines applied to the underside of the uppermost layer suggest the eyebrow, nose, lips, and fingers. The flesh tones are due to metallic oxides in the sheet of flesh-colored pot metal underneath. The effect is not quite naturalism, but rather a kind of decorative realism. The light and carefree colors are Art Nouveau. The lines have the swing of Art

Nouveau sobered by England's intellectual climate. The window achieves the realism of a summer afternoon pressed between the pages of a book as a keepsake.

The "Girl Picking Gourds" did not satisfy the part of Tiffany that wanted the realism of the Renaissance. The maiden's body, totally concealed by her robe, has none of the flourish of those figures by the seventeenth-century masters which flaunt their skeletons by turning their head in one direction, their rib cage in another, and their pelvis in another. The window was an important step, but he continued to dream of a nude executed in untreated glass, which would have the sense of mass and anatomical completeness of those by the Renaissance masters.

As the end of the nineteenth century drew near, many thoughtful people began to reflect on the "progress" made during the century.

Are machines, trade, speed, and comforts all the world needs? Does it make sense to live in a Greek temple and drive an auto-car?—to look back in the arts while looking ahead in other fields? Does a new century not call for progress in the arts as well as in technology?

S. Bing, Louis Sullivan, Alphonse Mucha, Gustave Stickley, Victor Horta, Émile Gallé, Louis Májorelle, Paul Gauguin, Toulouse-Lautrec, Pablo Picasso, Auguste Renoir, Charles Rennie Mackintosh, and Louis Tiffany were among those who thought the new century called for new art forms as well new techniques.

The Exposition Universelle held in Paris in 1900 had its roots in that kind of thinking, and Louis Tiffany, at the height of his fame and power, was ready for it. One of his displays was the "Four Seasons" window, with its four intimate views of the growing things he loved, which told of his joy in the drama of the seasons. In "Spring" (Figure 58), purple and orange tulips push up into a cold silvery day. "Summer" (Figure 59) is Oriental poppies under a cobalt blue sky. "Autumn" (Figure 60) has the crackly browns of ripe field corn, and the frosty purple of Concord grapes. In "Winter" (Figure 61), a pine bough is heavy with the silent beauty of wet snow. All are plated several layers deep with Favrile glass made in Corona; it has the beauty of sliced gem stones. In addition, the window was the first to use a new technique adopted from the leaded lamps: that of copper foil in the leading.

The great window was more than a statement

FIGURE 49 "Christ, Ruler of the Universe." Leaded window. Tiffany Glass and Decorating Company, c. 1892. Unsigned. Possibly made for the World's Columbian Exposition. Diameter 104".

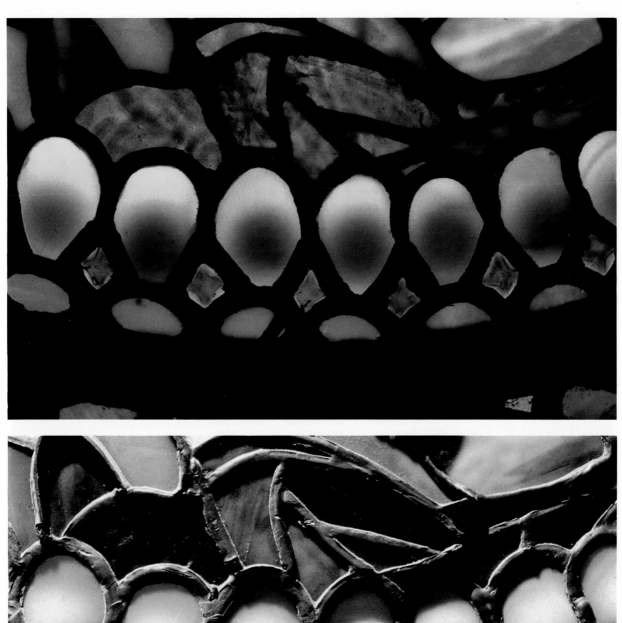

FIGURES 50, 51 *Details, "Christ, Ruler of the Universe," the same section back-lighted and front-lighted*

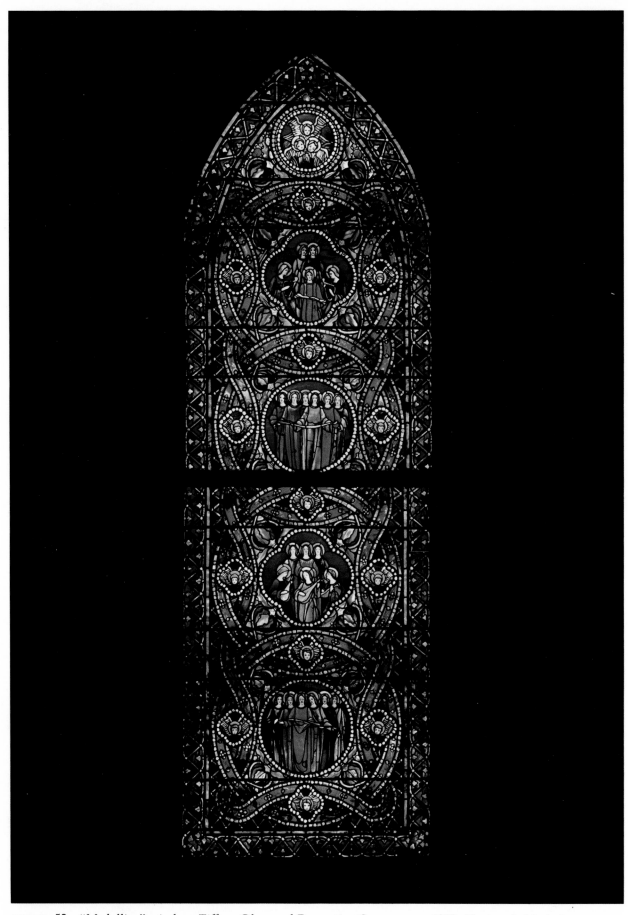

FIGURE 52 *"Medallion" window. Tiffany Glass and Decorating Company, c. 1892. Unsigned. Made for exhibition purposes. Height 146".*

FIGURE 53 *"Adoration." Leaded window, filigree of gilded cames. Tiffany Studios, 1900–16. Unsigned. From the Columbian Exposition Chapel as installed at Laurelton Hall. Height 111¾".*

about art. Under a resolute American Eagle, who spread his wings protectively over it all at the top (Figure 58), a legend read: "Abundance, and Peace and Prosperity." Tiffany was proclaiming his confidence both in his glass and in his country's future.

The "Four Seasons" had other interesting features. The word "Favrile" is worked into a circular device under the eagle's left wing. The initials "L.C.T." form a familiar circle under the other. Vines growing up and around the sides from five massive jars serve as a leafy and appropriate border. The date "ANNO MDCCCC,"[5] was clearly worked into the design in the lower center.

No surface treatment, no paint, no enamels apologize for what glass cannot do in the "Four Seasons." The window is all untreated pot metal, each piece chosen because its color or configuration, or both, would suggest a desired image. It is a superb display of the virtuosity of Tiffany's wonderful glass.

There is something else which even Tiffany may not have realized. The viewer does not see the tulips, the poppies, or the pine boughs in the same way he sees the birds in "Feeding the Flamingoes." He sees light reflected from colored surfaces and affected by the atmosphere. At close range the images are little more than touches of color. Tiffany has seen and admired the impressionist paintings of Monet and Sisley in which broken colors and blurred edges reveal the

FIGURE 54   *"Feeding the Flamingoes." Leaded window from painting by Louis C. Tiffany, c. 1892. Signed, "Tiffany Glass & Dec. Co., 333–341 4th Ave. N.Y." Made for the World's Columbian Exposition. Height 62".*

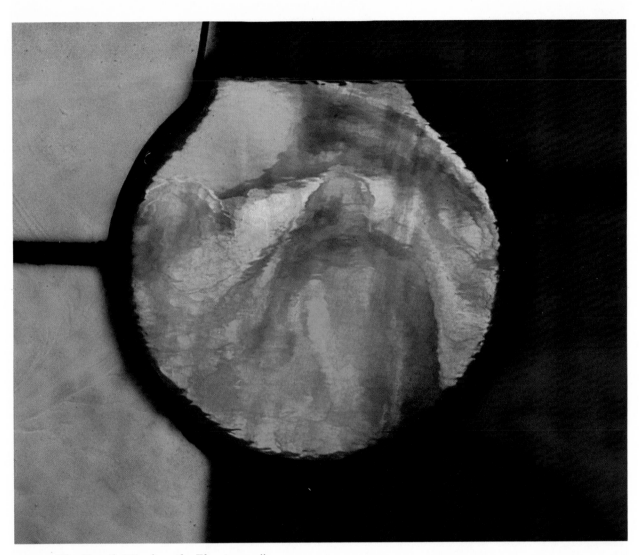

FIGURE 55 *Detail, "Feeding the Flamingoes."*

FIGURE 56 *"Girl Picking Gourds." Leaded window. Tiffany Glass and Decorating Company, c. 1897. Unsigned. From a design by Sir Frank Brangwyn. Height 60".*

FIGURE 57 *detail, "Girl Picking Gourds."*

72

THE "LOST" TREASURES

FIGURE 58 *"Spring" from "Four Seasons." Leaded window. Tiffany Glass and Decorating Company. Signed, "L.C.T." and "Favrile" in monograms. Made for the 1900 Paris Exposition. Height 39".*

FIGURE 59 *"Summer" from Four Seasons." Height 39".*

FIGURE 60   *"Autumn" from Four Seasons." Height 39"*

FIGURE 61   *"Winter" from "Four Seasons." Height 39"*

FIGURE 62   *Detail, "Spring."*

FIGURE 63   *Detail from the top of "Four Seasons." Height 17".*

FIGURE 64   *"Lily" window. Designed by Louis C. Tiffany for the Columbian Exposition Chapel as installed at Laurelton Hall, c. 1916. Unsigned. Height 139".*

FIGURE 65 *"Grape Arbor." Leaded window. Tiffany Studios, after 1908. Unsigned. From a private residence. Height 28". La Belle Verriere Restaurant, Winter Park, Florida.*

FIGURE 66 *"The Scholar." Leaded window. Tiffany Glass and Decorating Company, c. 1892. Signed at a later date, "Tiffany Studios/New York." Height 29".*

FIGURE 67 *"Parrots." Leaded window. Tiffany Studios, c. 1905. Unsigned. From the Watts-Sherman Cottage, Newport, Rhode Island. Height 16½".*

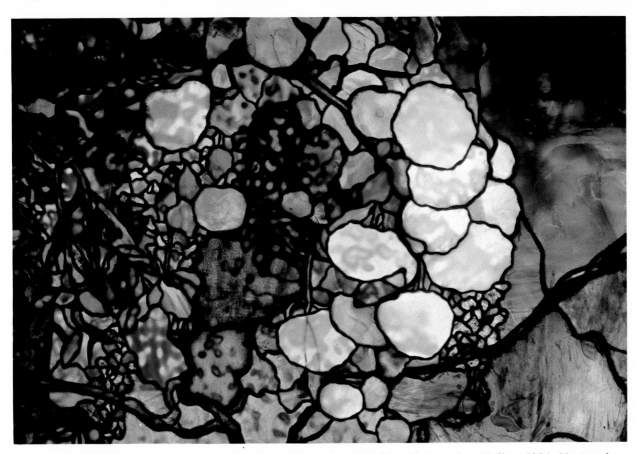

FIGURE 68 *"Snowball." Leaded transom. Designed by Louis C. Tiffany for Laurelton Hall, c. 1904. Unsigned. Height 27".*

FIGURE 69 *"Young Woman at a Fountain." Leaded window. Tiffany Glass and Decorating Company, c. 1894. Unsigned. From "Aurora," an oil painting by Will Low. Height 58".*

FIGURES 70, 71 *Details, "Young Woman at a Fountain."*

FIGURE 72   *"Butterfly" window. Designed by Louis C. Tiffany for the Tiffany mansion at Seventy-second Street and Madison Avenue, New York, N.Y. c. 1885. Unsigned. Transmitted light. Height 65".*

painter's interest in light reflected from images, not in the images themselves.

The "Four Seasons" is Impressionism. He is thinking as a painter. But whereas the impressionist painters used pigment to simulate their light, Tiffany is painting with light itself. The nonpictorial part of the "Four Seasons" was a glittering screen of lumps and chunks, symbols, and words that called attention to the beauty of glass. There was no conflict here—but, of course, it contained no human figures!

Tiffany was awarded a Gold Medal for his exhibit in the Exposition and the French government made him a Chevalier of the Legion of Honour. The "Four Seasons" was discussed and published,[6] but his exhibit was not the sensation his chapel had been in 1893. The world had seen his glass before.

Tiffany's workshops, of course, made thousands of windows. A rare few were from his own designs. Most were from designs by artists on his staff. "Young Woman at a Fountain"[7] (Figure 69) is after a painting in oils made in 1894 by Will Low, a well-known American. Here a young lady in a diaphanous robe stands beside a fountain on the edge of a forest. (The face varies markedly from that in the painting.) The figure, with the exception of the drapery, is executed in enamel. The outline of the body, which shows through the robe, is suggested by heavy lead cames in the next layer. The rest is untreated glass. The jet of water is a streak of clear glass worked into a sheet of dark glass while both were molten.

The middle-class gentility of the young woman, and the stocky plainness in all the forms, are suggestive of Tiffany's personal designs. The figure, however, has a sensuous, relaxed self-assurance that Tiffany's figures never achieved. She makes it very clear that Will Low knew more about painting classical nudes than Tiffany.

Among those windows Tiffany designed himself, sometimes for clients, often for exhibition purposes or for his own use, are the "Butterfly" (Figure 72), "Magnolia" (Figure 83), "Snowball" (Figure 68), "Rose" (Figure 87), "Wisteria" (Figures 1–7), "Heckscher" (Figure 77), "Pumpkin and Beets" (Figure 81), "The Scholar" (Figure 66), and the "Lily" window (Figure 64). All are made of untreated pot metal in the mosaic tradition. Those made before 1900 contain the "jewels," which gave them the third-dimensional quality of Celtic and Byzantine

jewelry (Figures 33, 35, 39, 40, 41). After 1900 the surface levels out, the brilliant chunks and lumps are gone, the style is more lyrical, more pictorial and often more Art Nouveau.

All reflect his belief that the coming new style would and should derive from a study of nature rather than historic art. They are a glassy search for art with less past and more future in it.

The "Butterfly" (Figures 72 and 73), originally made for the Seventy-second Street house, possibly as early as 1885, raises and solves a problem unique to leaded windows, which tend to "die" at night because the opaque whites shine while the rest turns a dull brown or gray. Much of its glass is backed with gold leaf thin enough to transmit light. It is crystal and yellow in daylight. In reflected light, it is a shimmering screen of gold. The circles are true mosaic of delicately interlocked sectiliae set in plaster. The wings of the large butterfly at the top are abalone shell. One butterfly in the lower mid-section flies on wings resembling goldstone. The marbleized circle in the center top is ancient Roman glass. In spite of its thousands of intricate cuts and hundreds of almost minute pieces, the window is leaded with cames. The result is dazzling in any light.

The double image is always a surprise. The images at first suggest a beehive in a tree. Then a butterfly appears, then another, and another, until all one sees is a cloud of yellow butterflies fluttering around a Japanese lantern. This window, made by Tiffany for his own home, represents no conflict. The flat pattern with its various kinds of magic could not be executed in anything except glass. Because of its history the window has remained almost totally unknown.

The "Heckscher" window (Figure 77), in reality four glass doors, gave the Heckscher family a view of their garden framed with a rhythmic design of grape vines, tomatoes, pumpkins, and eggplants. The window served several purposes. It shielded the Heckschers from the weather; it made the out-of-doors an integral part of the interior; in all seasons, it provided pleasure for the eye by relating a variety of colored shapes to each other. In a sensitive way, it also called attention to the wonder of the glass, not only to colored glass, but to glass that has no color at all. It made art an inescapable part of the Heckschers' daily life.

The window, but on grander scale, states once again the message of the "Kemp" window. It

6686684.

FIGURE 73 *"Butterfly" window. Reflected light.*

FIGURES 74, 75, 76   *Details, "Butterfly" window.*

FIGURE 77   *Leaded door panels, made for the Heckscher residence. Tiffany Studios, c. 1905. Unsigned. Height 122".*

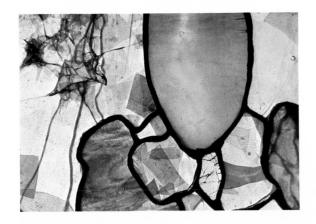

FIGURES 78, 79, 80   *Details, Heckscher leaded door panels.*

FIGURE 81 *"Pumpkin and Beets." Leaded window. Designed by Louis C. Tiffany, 1900–5. Unsigned. Height 47".*

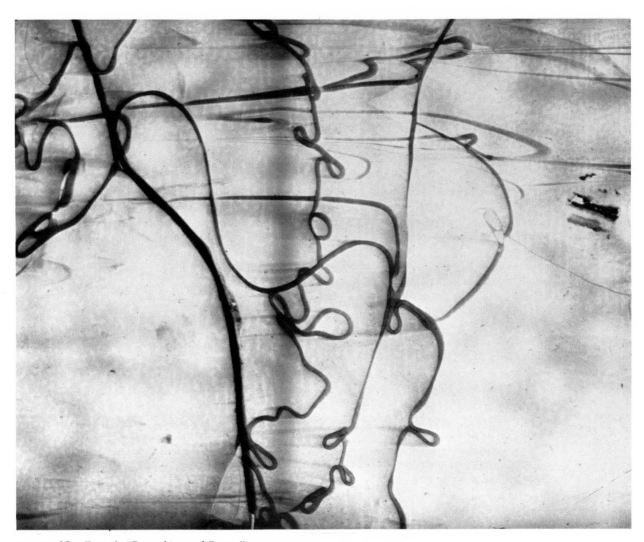

FIGURE 82 *Detail, "Pumpkin and Beets."*

FIGURE 83 *"Magnolia" window. Designed by Louis C. Tiffany for the Tiffany mansion at Seventy-second Street and Madison Avenue, New York, N.Y., c. 1885. Unsigned. Transmitted light. Height 45".*

FIGURE 84 *"Magnolia" window. Intermediate light.*

FIGURE 85 *"Magnolia" window. Reflected light.*

FIGURE 86 *Detail, "Magnolia" window.*

FIGURE 87 *"Rose" window. Designed by Louis C. Tiffany, for exhibition purposes, c. 1906. Unsigned. Height 57".*

FIGURE 88   "The Bathers." Leaded window. Designed by Louis C. Tiffany, c. 1912.

Photograph courtesy of the Corning Museum of Glass

calls attention to beauty we often overlook—the beauty of tomatoes, gourds, grapes, and eggplants. It also shows how effective panes of colored glass can be when cut in sensitive patterns and set in clear glass. That the window was made after 1900 is indicated by the fact that while the main leads are cames, the floral parts are coppered (copper foil). No documentary evidence indicates that it was, in fact, designed by Tiffany, but it has the characteristics of his personal work.

"Pumpkin and Beets" (Figure 81) has neither the Art Nouveau rhythm of the "Heckscher" window nor the intricacy of the "Butterfly" window. It is closer to the paintings "Duane Street" and "Sow with Piglets." "Pumpkin and Beets" is a glassy intimate view of a healthy earthy part of America. Nothing has been picked, scrubbed, and arranged to look nice. There is none of the elegance of the "Heckscher" window, none of the

glitter of "Christ, Ruler of the Universe," none of the drama of the "Entombment," none of the glassiness of the "Butterfly" windows—only the unselfconscious beauty of a vegetable garden.

The sheets of glass are rather large. Most are streaked with several shades. Some have dribbles of darker glass thrown and splashed with the inspired abandon of a Jackson Pollock. Plating adds to the depth of color, and in the pumpkin, the leads in the undermost sheet suggest its indentations.

"Pumpkin and Beets" does not have the heavenly turmoil of a Van Gogh landscape, but it is not unlike that master's work in some respects. It is a statement about life and art, not a window made to light a room. It comments that colors need not harmonize to be handsome, that they can express a set of ideas as well as describe a thing. It implies that beauty is never far away

FIGURE 89   *"View of Oyster Bay." Leaded window. Designed by Louis C. Tiffany for the William Skinner residence on Fifth Avenue, New York, N.Y., c. 1905. Unsigned. Height 72¾". The Metropolitan Museum of Art, New York.*

from those who dig, plant, and harvest. The "Pumpkin and Beets" window leaves pompous works of art with their emptiness showing.

The "Magnolia," a bay window in three sections (Figure 83), was also made for the Seventy-second Street house. That the one illustrated here came from the ruins of Laurelton Hall could mean that a copy of the original was used somewhere in the big place. It is more than probable, however, that the "Butterfly" and "Magnolia" windows were taken to Laurelton Hall by Tiffany after he decided to put his finest work in the collection of his Foundation.

The "Magnolia" was not only a strong, watertight shield against the rains and wind, it let light in and allowed one to see out. It also served in other ways. The heavy leading suggests, in a sculptured way, the angular grace of a magnolia tree. The drapery glass blossoms are a delight to the eye. Fragments of yellow and silver-gray tell of the tender beauty of leaf buds ready to open. In daylight, the "Magnolia" both pleased the eye and let one see the countryside. After dark it was a graceful silhouette against the night.

The "Rose" window (Figure 87) is not a fragment of nature. It provides no view of the out-of-doors; tells no story. It has the spirit of a greeting card and the look of an intricate piece of jewelry. The thousands of pieces of pastel colors say in a glassy way "all is well." Tiffany made the window as an exhibition piece early in this century and thought so well of it he included it in *The Art Work of Louis C. Tiffany.*

A glass wall was the only barrier between the Laurelton Hall dining room and the daffodil columns and wisteria vines beyond. In the fall, Tiffany probably missed the lavenders and blues of the wisteria blossoms. Either for that or for some other reason, he replaced the clear transoms with panels of wisteria blossoms (Figures 1–7). The designs are sensitive, and they gave that special room a rare beauty.

"View of Oyster Bay" (Figure 89) not only suggests Tiffany's personal involvement, but also how the design originated. It was made for the Skinner mansion on New York's Fifth Avenue and served as a divider between two rooms. The wisteria blossoms, which made a quiet pattern against a sky tinted with a rare rosy hue, and the view of a bay with hills beyond, suggest that it is a happy result of Tiffany's sitting on the terrace of Laurelton Hall looking out over Cold Spring Harbor and Oyster Bay.

All of these windows in one way or another helped solve some of the many challenges of leaded glass, but the nudes of Renaissance painting still haunted him. He longed to match their beauty in untreated glass.

In 1912,[8] Tiffany made what he considered a breakthrough in "The Bathers" (Figure 88). The central figure was a blond beauty gently brushing her waist-length hair. In the style of the Renaissance, her head turned to her left, her hips turned more toward the picture plane, her left knee bent slightly forward. She was a relaxed, naked naïve triumph, set in arcadian surroundings along with seven other beauties, gnarled trees, a waterfall, water lilies, and one stately peacock.

It was not the draughtsmanship in the figures that made Tiffany feel good about it, however. It was the fact that the flesh tones were in the pot metal, not enamels applied to the surface of the glass. The window satisfied the painter in him because it showed how ladies and peacocks look under romantic circumstances. It also satisfied his arts-and-crafts conscience because, in his opinion at least, the window was a triumph of pot metal over the brush.

In an address to the Rembrandt Club of Brooklyn,[9] he proclaimed:

"By the aid of studies in chemistry and through the years of experiments I have found means to avoid the use of surface-painting of glass, so that now it is possible to produce figures in glass of which even the flesh tones are not superficially treated!

"In Christ Church in your Borough you should examine the big window to see the proof of my statement; the heads therein are built up of what I call 'genuine' glass, genuine because there are no tricks of the glassmaker needed to express the flesh.

"Many of you who have not given any particular attention to the secrets of glassmaking may be surprised at the emphasis I give to this point; but those who have had the time to look into such matters, will understand the importance of the step taken. At Laurelton Hall near Oyster Bay I have a nude figure in glass which has no surface paint or etched parts to express the flesh, while the garments of other figures in the same composition are rendered by the artful adjustment of

FIGURE 90 *Detail, the "Peacock" window. Cutting glass away from a section is not too difficult. Cutting a "u" into a piece of glass is difficult because glass tends to break in a straight line. Tiffany's windows abound in difficult cuts such as these amber crescents necessary to suggest the eye of a peacock feather.*

FIGURE 91 *Detail, "Autumn." The hundreds of chipped jewels (glass given irregular facets by blows of a hammer) in the "Four Seasons" give it a twinkling effect with even the slightest movement of the observer. The borders gave Tiffany an excuse to use the abstract shapes and jewel-like colors he enjoyed.*

FIGURE 92 *Detail, "The Scholar." Because of the way the glass was made and cut, every piece in a Tiffany window has a quality of its own. Here, the large piece was cut from a sheet of light blue to white glass which had been sprinkled with darker chips before it cooled. This technique was one of many Tiffany introduced to call attention to the beauty of glass as a medium.*

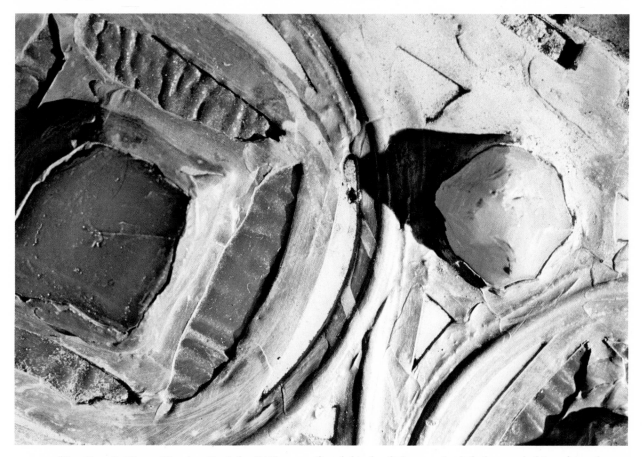

FIGURE 93 *Detail, "Jesus Blessing St. John." The use of such kinds of glass as rippled glass and chipped jewels gave parts of Tiffany's early windows a rich surface texture which must be seen at close range to be fully enjoyed.*

FIGURE 95 *Detail, the jeweled Gothic window. With a close look at Tiffany's finest windows, their inventiveness and quality become increasingly apparent. Traditional cames would not fit these chunks of glass. Tiffany therefore set them like jewels in masses of lead.*

glass in different thicknesses. Some day I hope to have the pleasure of welcoming this worshipful company at Laurelton—it is only about twenty-five miles from here—when you can satisfy yourselves that I am not indulging in exaggeration. This is one of the most important advances in modern colored windows."

Just how much importance the Rembrandt Club attached to Tiffany's great "advance" would be difficult to say. If they did journey the twenty-five miles to see the window, no record of the event exists. Tiffany did offer to exhibit it in the San Francisco Exposition of 1915, but the

fair authorities did not care enough about it to provide the artificial light needed to show it at night, and he withdrew the offer. The world simply did not share his excitement at capturing flesh tones in glass. His family, however, loved the window, which they called "Saturday Night."

"The Bathers" was built into the living room at Laurelton Hall along with the four cartouches from the "Four Seasons" and "Feeding the Flamingoes." When Laurelton Hall was burning in 1957, the firefighters, for reasons more clear to them than to others, chopped through the window.

"The Tree of Life," Tiffany's last window, made in 1930, with the help of his faithful chauffeur Jimmy Ryan, may explain the "secret" of "The Bathers." The first layer is a sheet of clear glass on which the features are suggested by manganese applied with a brush. The shadows are left heavily coated. In the lighter parts the coating has been thinned with a dry brush. In the highlights the glass has been wiped clean. In other words, the modeling was done in paint (brown enamel) on a layer of glass that was superimposed over a layer of pink-flesh-colored pot metal.

It is unlikely that Tiffany, having found a way to represent a naturalistic human figure with no brush work at all, would have abandoned the method later. It is also significant that in his remarks to the Rembrandt Club, although he said the flesh tones were in the glass, he did not say the window had not been touched with a brush.

"The Tree of Life" with its six panels, "Entombment," "Creation," "Science," "Religion," "Geology," and "Astronomy," reveal Tiffany's continued fascination with the problem of representing the human figure in untreated glass.

This time there is an interesting reverse twist. Having solved, to his own satisfaction, at least, the challenge of representing naturalistic figures in untreated pot metal, he now moves in a more decorative direction. Adam and Eve in "Creation" have a suggestion of the angular style of the figures in the thirteenth-century windows at Chartres and, curiously, a touch of the levitational qualities of the slender nudes that often float across the canvases of the American Arthur

FIGURE 94 *Detail, the "Lily" window. The rhythmic flow in all the carefully designed thousands of pieces of glass which make up the "Lily" window gives it a quality many observers enjoy for reasons they might not understand. The varying widths in the leading show it to be the copper foil technique.*

B. Davies. Even so, the window has a murky quality not found in the brilliant ones made of untreated glass in the mosaic tradition.

Some will always contend Tiffany was wrong in using paint and enamels, and that he should not have made "Feeding the Flamingoes," the "Entombment," and the "Botticelli" windows. Others will admire his skillful enameling and wonder what all the fuss is about. Many will always admire his leaded windows as some of the finest ever made. Others will think he should have made no windows at all.

But the windows will, at least, continue to speak about the integrity of materials, the goodness of life, the beauty of nature, the importance of quality and of going one's own way in art, and of working in good taste—and this will do no harm at all.

NOTES

[1] This description is made from a reproduction of the window in *The Art Work of Louis C. Tiffany* by Charles deKay.
[2] "American Stained Glass," *The American Art Review* (first article), Vol. 2, 1881, p. 234.
[3] "American Stained Glass," *The American Art Review* (third and concluding article), Vol. 3, 1881, p. 64.
[4] Townsend, Horace, *American and French Applied Art at the Grafton Galleries*, Vol. XVII, 1899, pp. 39–44.
[5] The date 1892 given in *The Art Work of Louis C. Tiffany*, by Charles deKay must be in error.
[6] *Deutsch Kunst and Dekoration*, Vol. VII, October 1900–March 1901, p. 86.
[7] On loan to the Metropolitan Museum of Art by the Charles Hosmer Morse Foundation.
[8] The list of illustrations in *The Art Work of Louis C. Tiffany* indicates that the window was "designed for Capt. J. R. Delamar in 1912."
[9] Tiffany, Louis C., "Color and Its Kinship to Sound," *The Art World*, Vol. II, No. 2, May 1917, pp. 142–43.

Chapter 7

WE ARE GOING AFTER
THE MONEY
THERE IS IN ART

Colman and de Forest and I are going to make a combination for interior decoration of all sorts. I shall work out some ideas I have in glass. De Forest is going to India to look up carved woods, and Colman will look after color and textiles. You had better join us. It is the real thing, you know; a business, not a philanthropy or any amateur educational scheme. We are going after the money there is in art, but the art is there, all the same.

LOUIS C. TIFFANY (quoted by Candace Wheeler)

In 1879, the thirty-one-year-old Tiffany with characteristic self-confidence announced that he and three recently acquired associates were ready to undertake all kinds of interior decoration. The associates were Samuel Colman, painter, friend, and former teacher; Candace Wheeler, an accomplished artist in embroidery and crewelwork, who suggested the name Associated Artists; and Lockwood de Forest, the collector of Far Eastern carvings.[1] The fact that none of them had been trained in the field did not seem to bother anyone. The Arts and Crafts Movement, led by William Morris, had encouraged the world to think in the spirit of the medieval art guilds. In those days the artist made what the patron wanted, whether it was a painting, a set of furniture, or a battering ram, and made it well. Many late Victorian painters were jumping the art traces.

The cocky American, James McNeill Whistler, for example, gladly undertook the job of redecorating the dining room of the fashionable London house of wealthy shipping magnate Frederick R. Leyland. The two up to that time had been friends. But after Whistler, carried away with enthusiasm, had painted peacocks not only where Leyland wanted peacocks but all over some costly leather hangings where he had *not* wanted peacocks, the feisty Englishman hit the ceiling and paid Whistler in pounds instead of guineas. (Tradesmen were paid in pounds; gentlemen were paid in guineas.) Whistler, who had spent three years at West Point Military Academy and did not take such things lightly, gave one of the birds an unmistakable resemblance to Leyland. The affair triggered merry laughs on both sides of the Atlantic, and called attention to the new mobility in the arts.

Tiffany turned to interior decoration for good reasons. It offered an opportunity to put art where the people are—pictures can be ignored easier than interiors. The engineer in him liked to solve mechanical problems. It also offered tempting financial rewards.

For the record, he was not totally without experience in the field. In 1878 he had made the top floor of the Bella, an apartment house at 48 East Twenty-sixth Street in New York City, into a stylish studio-home, which had attracted a lot of welcome attention.

By using bright red walls and hand-hewn beams studded with bits of glass and brass nail-heads, he had achieved a kind of medieval ruggedness in the lobby. At night it all glowed in the flickering (and flattering) light from a gas torch of his own design, a metal cone pierced with small holes and supported on a standard about shoulder high. The flame was controlled by an adjustable hood suspended from the ceiling. In daytime, light filtered in through colored leaded windows.

Tiffany's love of the arts of North Africa and of the Far East was much in evidence as well. According to George W. Sheldon, "A variety of styles present themselves, but not one of them is a copy. In this drawing-room, for instance, the Moorish feeling has received a dash of East Indian, and the wall-papers and ceiling-papers are Japanese, but there is a unity that binds everything into an *ensemble*, and the spirit of that unity is delicacy."[2] The wallpaper to which Sheldon refers was pink, and the ceiling paper was buff color highlighted with mica, an effect the Americans at the time attempted unsuccessfully to copy. "Old Japanese stuffs" hanging on brass rods supported by slender Moorish columns separated the drawing room from the hall. The upper part of the opening in the fireplace was covered by a screen of mica worked into the spiderweb pattern destined to become a Tiffany favorite. The fireplace was surrounded and enriched with his new iridescent glass tiles.

The main entrance to the drawing room could be closed off by a door hung on wheels running along an exposed metal track, a simple device used in many American barns. A heavy sash window in the hallway was raised or lowered easily because of a decorative counterbalance suspended on a chain which ran over an exposed wheel.

A painting of yellow pumpkins, field corn partly husked, and a turkey cock spreading his tail was secured to the mantel by narrow strips of plain brown wood.

The Bella apartment derived from sources other than renaissance palaces and medieval cathedrals. The candor in the solution of mechanical problems was disarming. Charm and surprise were everywhere. It was a "walk-in" work of practical art, designed to add aesthetic adventure to living. The Bella apartment demonstrated a new and attractive approach to the problem of designing a dwelling.

Several factors contributed to the success of the Associated Artists. In 1879 Tiffany was a well-known painter, and his father was on his way to becoming jeweler to the world. The Tiffany name was identified in the public mind with quality and taste. The Tiffanys moved in the same social circles as many potential clients. The law of supply and demand also worked to his advantage. Today, "interior designers" with dubious credentials can be found in almost every block. In 1879 relatively few were working in the field.

Another plus for the young firm was Tiffany himself. He was intense. He bristled with opinions. But his intelligent blue eyes, handsome head, cultured voice, generous supply of old-fashioned horse sense, and total commitment to his work, made him attractive to his clients, and he was talented and resourceful as well. He had everything anyone could ask for in an interior designer, except professional qualifications.

The firm's first commission was a drop curtain for Steele MacKaye's Madison Square Theater. This may not sound like interior decoration to some, but it did to the Associated Artists. They chose a riverbank in Florida as a theme, and introduced such tropical plants as oleanders, night-blooming cereus, Spanish bayonets, and wisteria. Fireflies and butterflies added color accents. It was executed in velvets, plushes, and other fabrics stitched to a background of yellow satin. The distance was suggested by powdery-blue silks.

The press greeted the curtain with hurrahs. Appleton's *Journal* declared it "a sort of poem in color, the subtle charm of which is wholly captivating," and continued, "An era in which a poet like William Morris devotes himself to paper hanging; an artist like LaFarge gives his time to designs for walls or windows; when a wealthy

Londoner decorates his dining room with designs by Whistler; and artists bring their mature knowledge and artistic science to the draperies and colors of a theater must have revived the ancient art spirit to a marked degree."[3]

Candace Wheeler has left an account of how the Associated Artists worked together. "Our very first order was the making of an embroidered drop-curtain for the new Madison Square Theater, and this enlisted us all—Mr. Tiffany for design and all sorts of ingenious expedients as to method; Mr. Colman casting the deciding vote upon the question of color; Mr. de Forest looking up materials, and I, directing the actual execution. . . . Mr. Tiffany was certainly a very inspiring and suggestive associate in art, and he had the recklessness of genius when it came to ways and means."[4]

The George Kemps were early clients. Kemp, a wealthy dealer in pharmaceuticals, commissioned the Associated Artists to decorate his mansion at 720 Fifth Avenue. The general effect, according to George W. Sheldon, was "Arabic with an inclination to the Persian." The drawing-room ceiling was covered with iridescent silver, the tones of which, according to Sheldon, would "glow and play in the embrace of the caressing light, inviting the attention of the spectator afresh with each change of his position."[5] Slender columns, made of wood from the holly tree, flanked a bay window. A piano, the door casings, and the chairs and tables were all made of the same wood, in a matching Arabic style.

Instead of the usual sliding door between the salon and the dining room, Tiffany, drawing on his experience in the Bella apartment, hung a decorative door on wheels running along an exposed iron track. A frieze in the dining room, painted by Tiffany on gilded burlap, featured pumpkins, half-shucked corn, branches laden with apples and golden pears, vines laden with peppers, and "heavy lustrous bunches of grapes."[6] A cove in the library was ornamented with iridescent seashells and sparsely placed iridescent fleur-de-lis. Leaded-glass panels over the doors included the "Eggplant" and "Squash" windows.

The Kemp house revealed a Japanese influence, but no place was beautiful solely because it contained nothing. The Associated Artists had not absorbed all there was to be learned from Japanese art. The rooms would look cluttered to us.

We are trained to prefer a minimum of ornament, and when we go back in time we take our prejudices along. If, however, the Kemp interiors are compared with those of other mansions of the period, the relative simplicity is evident.

What really counted was the happy fact that the Kemps liked their new house and so did their friends, and Louis C. Tiffany was on his way to success in another field and to fees that make the eyes of the greedy bulge even today.

By 1881 Mark Twain had written A Connecticut Yankee in King Arthur's Court and Tom Sawyer. He was on the crest of a wave of popularity, wealthy enough to own a somber mansion in Hartford, Connecticut, and sophisticated enough to ask Tiffany and his Associated Artists to brighten it up. Tiffany stenciled the woodwork in the hall with a silver pattern, which in certain lights looked like mother-of-pearl. The walls in the drawing room were painted salmon-pink and ecru, and stenciled (in silver paint) with grapes, bell flowers, and a paisley design. Candace Wheeler draped the windows with sheer Indian muslin and soft blue velvet. The walls in the library, where a knight's helmet and shield graced the mantel, were painted a rich peacock blue and stenciled with a gold pattern. A leaded window was placed between the upraised arms of a U-shaped flue to satisfy Mark Twain's desire for a leaded window over his fireplace. He wanted to sit in front of his fire and enjoy the falling snow at the same time. When Tiffany had finished, the house was alive with new colors and reflected lights that played here and there as the observer moved around. Mark Twain, his family, and their friends were delighted.[7]

An aura of prestige and success, an asset to any business, is an essential for any interior decorating firm that wants to get anywhere. And when, in 1880, Tiffany and his Associated Artists were asked to do the Veterans' Room and the Library of the Seventh Regiment Armory, Tiffany recognized the commission as the opportunity it was. The huge building, designed by Charles W. Clinton to serve as clubhouse, storehouse, and drill shed, was the first of its kind. It was to be opened on December 15, 1880, with a grand ball. The Associated Artists, providing they came up with something special, and completed it on time, had an important chance for exposure.

FIGURE 96 *Drawing room of the Mark Twain residence, Hartford, Connecticut. Interior by Louis C. Tiffany and the Associated Artists, c. 1882.*

FIGURE 97 *Dining room of the Twain residence, showing fireplace designed for a leaded-glass window.*

What they did *was* special, and it was ready on time. The Veterans' Room (40′×45′ with a very high ceiling) was heroic in spirit to begin with. When Tiffany had finished it had enough symbols of fury and conflict to suit the toughest old veteran. It also had elements intended to appeal to any veteran who might like to reflect on something else.

The room is a symphony of leather, oak, and iron and, as one contemporary writer sensitive to symbolism pointed out, oak is the "hardest, toughest, and most durable of woods" and "Sacred to Jupiter" as well, and iron is "the principle instrument of war."[8]

The mantel, the floor, the armchairs, and the ponderous center table are oak. An oak wainscoting, higher than the doors, encircles the entire room. The ceiling is supported by enormous oak beams which, as did those in the Bella apartment, show traces of the blows of the workman's ax. Iron, which had become the darling of the architects in addition to its popularity with the military, was used with equal enthusiasm. A wrought-iron crane supported a large copper kettle in the fireplace, and iron chandeliers, designed by Tiffany and made under his personal supervision, hung from the ceiling. A frieze, executed in "plaster and clinkers,"[9] depicting an unlikely battle between an eagle and a sea dragon, is secured to the chimney breast by an iron frame. Iron chains bound around the bulky columns to a height above a man's head not only make the columns impregnable to daily wear and tear, they suggest any number of things, all masculine.

Should all this not assuage the veteran's appetite for reminders of war, he can muse on: A

FIGURE 98 *The library of the Twain residence.*

frieze painted by Tiffany's associates, Messrs. Frank Millet and George Yewell, depicting, as described by one contemporary observer, the history of arms as used by the "Greeks and barbarians, heathens and Christians, from the earliest ages to the present day: Indians of North America, Mexicans, Egyptians, Assyrians, East Indians, Chinamen, Japanese, Persians, Greeks, Romans, Moors, Turks, Russians, Frenchmen, Englishmen, Germans, and men of the Seventh Regiment. . . ."[10]

Leaded-glass panels with decorative patterns in yellows and golden browns hung in front of the windows. Four generous and highly polished brass spittoons, now retired, were stationed strategically at the corners of the large Oriental rug and thus within reasonable range of the massive oak chairs and settees. The spaces between the crossbeams on the ceiling were livened with me-

tallic lusters. The green paper above the wainscoting was stenciled in gold and bronze. Candace Wheeler's influence was evident in the original plush draperies (two of which were Damascus red and two an antique blue) and also in the portieres of Japanese brocade bordered with plush in a leopard-skin pattern.

One feature, the small staircase leading to a narrow gallery along the Park Avenue side did cause some grumbling. Its spindles and bosses are in the Islamic tradition. This, in itself, was all right. But they also happened to be copies of those in the screened windows of the women's quarters of an Oriental palace. This did not sit well with the unimaginative.[11]

Why, they asked, introduce harem windows in the Veterans' Room of the Seventh Regiment Armory? *Harper's Weekly* came to Tiffany's defense by meeting the malcontents head on: "It has been said that this pretty piece of orientalism is foreign to the severe character of the decoration as a whole, and does not belong there. . . . But the veteran sitting there, thinking and dreaming of war, has only to turn his eyes to the left to be reminded of the 'rewards of peace.'"[12] The logic is unassailable.

The library was equally successful though less spectacular. The guests at the grand ball were greatly impressed with all of Tiffany's work. The Associated Artists were paid $20,000, and *Harper's Weekly*'s general assessment is as true today as it was then: "It's like is not to be seen elsewhere in this country or in any other country."[13]

In the same year, 1881, Louis Tiffany and his Associated Artists were asked to decorate two imposing mansions on New York's Fifth Avenue. One, belonging to the Ogden Goelets, stood in the northeast corner of Fifty-ninth Street. The other was Cornelius Vanderbilt II's residence, which graced the corner of Fifty-eighth and Fifth.

The Goelets got what must have been an overwhelming array of hangings and lacquered panels from the Orient; a great deal of carved woodwork, a fireplace, and window lattices from India; and, according to one newspaper account, a bill for $50,000 for the hall and parlor alone. The *Tribune* described the reception room as "occidental" [*sic*] to a bewildering degree, a combination of Japanese and Chinese, with lacquered panels and rich silk hangings on the walls." The same reporter referred to "carvings from old East Indian Temples" in the hall and to a fireplace from the "Transition Period"—"Gothic to Renaissance." The Goelets are said not to have been too pleased with it all.

Cornelius Vanderbilt II, in a move that reflected his total grasp of the finer points of the free enterprise system, commissioned Louis Tiffany to decorate the drawing room, John La-Farge the library, and the Herter brothers to do the upstairs bedrooms. All, understandably, gave the project careful attention. Tiffany's drawing room, according to a contemporary newspaper account, was "elaborate and rich to the last degree." As might be expected, a North African flavor was evident, but some touches were decidedly not North African. The maple wainscoting, for example, was inlaid with metal and glass in "Classic" designs. The ceiling was resplendent

with a nine-foot-square panel featuring a design "in the Moorish taste" surrounded by a "circle of cherubs." When all was finished, if the descriptions in the press even approached accuracy, the various rooms must have resembled exhibits at a world's fair, but Mr. Vanderbilt was reported as being highly pleased. One would hope so. His house cost a mere $300,000. The bill for his decorations (exclusive of furnishings), according to a contemporary newspaper,[14] approached $500,000.

In 1882 President and Mrs. Garfield lived in a noticeably run-down White House until a madman shot the President and Chester A. Arthur succeeded him. Arthur, a widower, but a sensitive man who knew what he did not want, settled into a cottage at the Soldier's Home (twenty minutes by fast horse from downtown Washington) and vowed he would stay there until the executive mansion was spruced up, adding that if the Congress would not come up with the funds he would pay for the work himself. Some imaginative bureaucrat decided that $15,000 was about what the United States Government should spend on the project, and the President asked Louis Tiffany if he would undertake it for that fee. Tiffany, realizing that no dollar figure could be put on the real rewards of such a prestigious commission, accepted readily. In characteristic orderly fashion he assembled a crew willing to work night and day because the January 1 deadline was only seven weeks away, and the time was unrealistically short for anyone except Tiffany. He closed the East Room, the Red Room, the Blue Room, the corridor, and the State Dining Room, to all visitors (except the President who followed the work with great interest). The secrecy added a touch of mystery to it all, and when Mr. H. M. Lawrence and Mr. E. N. Griswold, Tiffany's supervisors, held a press preview on December 19, 1882, an air of general excitement prevailed.

The reporters' reactions were understandably mixed. Tiffany, a romantic, had added whimsy, sparkle and surprise to a stately classic building. The Blue Room, traditional scene of the President's state receptions, had been "suffered to remain blue" according to one correspondent, but it now had an "antique blue rug with a wave-like pattern in gold yellow." The walls were a strange shade of green carefully selected to look the desired robin's-egg blue in gaslight. The dignified white marble pilasters of the mantel were still there, but the space between them was resplendent with opalescent glass jewels and tiles. The light-gray-and-silver ceiling led one correspondent to compare the plan with the out-of-doors where the colors "progress from the darker tones of the earth to the blues and grays of the sky."

Features like four rosette-shaped wall sconces in the Blue Room led some reviewers to explore the frontiers of their vocabulary. The sconces, three feet in diameter, supported seven gas jets of twisted brass. Five iridescent amber-colored glass balls dangled from each jet. Six hundred pieces of Tiffany's new opalescent glass "cut in fantastic shapes," were worked into every sconce, and bits of mirrors were set among them to add brilliance. The glass was described quite accurately by one as "wrinkled in order to catch light from the many angles." Another was fascinated with the "rough jewels of hammered glass placed at such angles as to flash back the light with charming effect."[15]

The "Old Turkey red carpet with the immense figures" in the East Room had been replaced by a pale yellow Axminster rug. The Green Room, recently redecorated by Mrs. Garfield, was left untouched. A glass screen containing a lot of "dull blue" and "dull smoky brownish-gray" glass, and highlighted with conventionalized eagles, flags, and other national emblems done in brilliant colors, now separated the long corridor from the square vestibule. Its predecessor had been made of ground glass.

The Red Room's walls were "tinted a dull Pompeian red," the wainscoting a deeper shade. Squares of "Japanese leather" as one reporter saw it, or of "brown Japanese paper which looks like wood" as another described it, had added a romantic reminder of the "exotic" and the "far away" to the mantel. The ceiling twinkled with a "complicated" pattern of metallic stars described by some as being of dull silver and by others as made of bronze and copper. All agreed the border was stripes "similar to those on the national emblem!" An upright piano was referred to by one reporter with a kindly, "for its presence I believe the decorators are not responsible."

Some hailed Tiffany's work as a triumph. One reporter lyricized, "No longer is the White House simply the home of a Republican President. Lo, it is the temple of high art." Another was so moved at the stained-glass screen in the corridor that he or she wrote: "It is so much bet-

ter than any glass which can be produced in Europe today that the typical American should point to it as one of our surest titles to respect when enumerating them for the benefit of the typical foreigner in Washington."

A special correspondent for *The World*, less enthusiastic, wrote of the effects: "They are not ideally good by any means, not 'monumental,' not 'high art' at all. In spite of all the abuse that has been heaped upon it, the White House is a fine old mansion, extremely well-planned for its purpose—except as to staircases—and being capable of being made into a beautiful building. It ought to be decorated someday from end-to-end in a truly good style with the best products of the chisel and the brush."[16]

George W. Sheldon's observation in *Artistic Houses* rings with sense: "The beauty and artistic value of the Messr. Tiffany's decorations are best appeciated by those guests who know how the White House used to look."

The President moved in without a moment's hesitation, held the traditional reception on New Year's Day, listened happily to all the enthusiastic comments about the modernization of the White House, and proceeded to live contentedly with his classic mantels ashimmer with iridescent glass, opalescent glass wall sconces brightened up with mirrors, wainscoting painted a deep red, and ceiling spangled with metallic stars. The publicity delighted Tiffany, who saved all clippings, complimentary or not.

By 1885 Tiffany was deeply involved in planning and building a massive residence that, for understandable reasons, would differ from everything he had done before. For one thing, there were no associates to make suggestions. (The Associated Artists had disassociated themselves amicably.) For another, the client, a descendent of one of America's "oldest families" was one Tiffany wanted especially to please. He was a civic leader. In addition he had taste. He wanted a residence that would house several families in style and comfort. He wanted it planned more to please those on the inside than to dazzle those walking by. Nor were there any particular limits on the cost because in addition to being one of the country's wealthiest men, he was Louis' father.

The site for the residence, the northwest corner of Madison Avenue and Seventy-second Street, was pretty far uptown. An open space lay

FIGURE 99 *Tiffany mansion, Seventy-second Street and Madison Avenue, New York, N.Y. Planning and interior by Louis C. Tiffany. Working drawings by Stanford White, c. 1885.*

FIGURE 100 *Main entrance, Tiffany mansion.*

to the south, but people did live in the area and many objected to the plan's unusual features. It was to be 100′×152′; 113′ from the sidewalk to the highest pinnacle, and constructed on a skeleton of iron. Of especial concern were the "jutting windows, incidental gables and other casual architectural eccentricities."[17] The Bureau of Buildings, after due consideration and greatly to their credit, granted permission for its construction.

The basic plans were by Tiffany. Stanford White was engaged to make the working drawings, all of which Tiffany approved in writing.

The style, which one reporter extolled as a good example of Dutch Renaissance, was, in fact, rugged, handsome, Richardsonian Romanesque with a good dash of Tiffany. The first two stories, built of rough-hewn blue stone, were pierced only by small windows placed high above the street. This gave it the austere character of the city palaces erected in fifteenth- and sixteenth-century Italy by wealthy families hoping for a little security during street riots. From there on up, it was Roman brick.

The two-floor apartment on the top, which Tiffany designed for himself, was of especial significance because of the way it anticipated architectural developments, which would emerge in Europe several years later. An elevator took guests to the lower floor of the apartment made up of a drawing room, dining hall, breakfast room, and an assortment of lesser rooms. Broad stairs led to the studio and bedrooms above. Entrance to the studio was through a vestibule described by Charles deKay as ". . . like a bit from the palace of an Indian Rajah. Beams and trim are carved wood from Hindustan and the wall supports a trophy of curious Indian weapons."[18] The rounded fountain, resembling a plumbing fixture, pictured in the window "Feeding the Flamingoes," stood on the left as one entered. Suspended over it was the goldfish bowl represented in the same window. A towering fireplace with four hearths, one facing in each of the cardinal directions, rose majestically from the center. Tiffany, demonstrating once again his Yankee ingenuity as well as his aesthetic sensibility, had combined its flues with those coming up from the floors below and enclosed them all in a molded shell of brick and plaster painted a dark blue. The handsome mass soared into the shadows above with a sweep that anticipated continental Art Nouveau by several years.

Much of what Tiffany was thinking when he designed his fireplace can be read from it. No cornices, columns, moldings, capitals, or anything else would be copied from the past. Neither did he want the verticals and horizontals that dominate most architecture. This fireplace would not be the progeny of a straightedge and a T-square. It would have the rhythm and freedom of growing things. It would provide the observer with a new visual experience and demonstrate the rewards of thinking for one's self. Tiffany was looking for a new style. He was thinking the thoughts that underlie all Art Nouveau.

In daytime, light came into the studio presumably through a north light (although none is mentioned by contemporary writers), and also through soft, yellow-green stained-glass windows which are frequently mentioned, but tantalizingly never described. Several other windows, apparently of the standard size, were glazed with single sheets of yellow-green opalescent glass.

The furnishings included potted palms, wicker chairs, oriental rugs, and ancient armor from India. Flowers and tropical plants were everywhere. Blown-glass globes and various other kinds of lights, some of them leaded glass butterflies in what the family describes as "black boxes," were hung at random heights in the shadows of the high gables. The supporting chains had links in the form of peacocks, gods, and elephants. The strange place, fascinating in daylight, was enchanting at night when the red, yellow, and cream lights seemed to float in the blackness above. Reflections of the driftwood fires would dance now in the blue of an iridescent vase, now in the brass of a Persian lamp, now in the gold of an Indian god, now in a jet of water in the fountain, and then be gone. And when the music of Wagner, Beethoven, or Brahms played on the pipe organ added another wonderful dimension, it all seemed bewitching—and it was. There was magic in the way Tiffany could relate light, forms, and colors.

Other parts of the apartment also reflected his creative spirit: The "Butterfly" window was like nothing anyone had even dreamed of before. The library contained "Magnolia" windows with blossoms of drapery glass set in clear glass. Here Tiffany *did* make effective use of empty space—one window held a single branch with only few blossoms. The apartment also reflected Tiffany's interest in mechanical devices. The fire-

FIGURE 101 *Entrance hall, Henry Villard apartment in the Tiffany mansion. Designed by Louis C. Tiffany,*
c. 1885.

place in the library, for example, was covered
with an adjustable hood counter-balanced by two
exposed iron balls.

Tiffany, realizing that his studio would have to
reach more than his family if it was to help
America become more conscious of beauty, frequently invited friends to view new paintings and
to hear the organ which could be played either
manually or by rolls. Events such as the Paasch-
Feest held early in April of 1888 brought others
who were not necessarily personal friends. According to the New York *Times,* a Paasch-Feest,
as "every New York Dutchman knows, is the

Dutch for Easter festival."[19] This event was
"under the management of Mr. and Mrs.
Tiffany, Mrs. Villard, Mrs. D. M. Stimson, Mrs.
Thomas Hicks, Mrs. Haydock, Mrs. John T.
Willetts, and Miss De Forest." The studio was,
according to the reporter, "a perfect fairyland,
with its East India vestibule and decorations, soft
lights and lofty arched ceilings." Young socialites "attired in the quaint costumes of the
Dutch peasantry, tended the booths and sold
Dutch cake, tulips, potted plants and Easter eggs
from the egg tree." The event was so brilliant, according to the *Times,* it "would have made the

FIGURE 102 *Music room, the Henry Villard apartment.*

old Dutchmen themselves open their eyes and forget to watch their dikes." Organized to raise funds for the New York Infirmary for Women and Children, of which Mrs. Tiffany was a founder, it raised over $2,500, an impressive sum at a time when $500 would build a modest house. Among those present were Tiffany's parents, Bishop Potter (the Episcopal Bishop of New York), and Mrs. John Taylor Johnston (wife of the president of the Metropolitan Museum of Art).

Louisine and Henry Osborne Havemeyer proved to be two of Tiffany's most satisfactory cli-ents from every point of view. She was bright and loved art. Henry played the violin, collected old masters, and made fortune after fortune. In 1890 they asked Tiffany to decorate their mansion at 848 Fifth Avenue, and he was delighted.

The color scheme was mellow and the fabrics were rich; one from Japan was shot through with gold threads. The furniture was simple and showed a Celtic influence in its carving.

One feature, however, was a standout—a metal staircase that hung from the ceiling and was supported by a spine of iron. It was painted gold and led to a balcony of the same con-

FIGURE 103   *View of drawing room of the Havemeyer mansion, New York, N.Y. Designed by Louis C. Tiffany, c. 1890.*

FIGURE 104   *View of balcony and section of hanging staircase, Havemeyer mansion.*

struction. The effect must have been light, airy, and somewhat dazzling, with its crystal balls held in the metal in a manner similar to that used in the slender bronze candlesticks to come a decade later. The staircase was lighted by an electrolier of the same construction, and it is no wonder that the great house, which would have been talked about anyway because of its Rembrandts, its musicals with its owner playing his Stradivarius, and the brilliant woman who presided over it with such charm, was a sensation in a city that was throbbing with them.

Tiffany's father died in 1902, long before estate or income taxes had begun to cast their everlengthening shadow over America. Tiffany's share of his estate was at least $3 million, the equal of at least $20 million today. (In those carefree days $75 would buy a player piano, $480 a lot in New York City, and $2.95 would bring four full quarts of Queen City rye or Bourbon whiskey to one's door in a plain wrapper, express prepaid.) In the same year, possibly not by coincidence, Tiffany bought Laurelton Hall, an old and once-fashionable hotel located on approximately 580 acres of rolling land on Cold Spring Harbor in the town of Oyster Bay, Long Island. He tore the old buildings down and began planning a new summer place for himself, which he would call by the same name, Laurelton Hall.

He approached the matter with characteristic thoroughness. First, he studied the configuration of the land, then the distribution of its tulip, cedar, oak, locust, and dogwood trees, and its thousands of azaleas and laurels. The next step was a model of the entire project in clay and wax: the house, gardens, stables, tennis courts, ponds, streams, masses of trees and shrubs, yacht basin, and driving and service roads. Then came a careful study of how the contours, the views, the prevailing winds, the existing gardens, and the wooded areas related to each other. In glass he liked the chance effect, the happy mistake, the planned accident. It was different with Laurelton Hall.

The drawings were made by Robert L. Pryor, a twenty-four-year-old architect employed by the Tiffany Studios who was sympathetic to Tiffany's plans and thinking.

When completed two years later Laurelton Hall extended 280 feet from porte cochere to stables, covering a space nearly as long as a football field. It was built on several levels, and all under one roof in the New England tradition. The complex included ten or so bedrooms, a pipe organ, hanging gardens, terraces, a bowling alley, a squash court, a large conservatory, and an assortment of other subdivisions that defy classification. A cork-lined tunnel provided electric-lighted access to the swimming beach. Estimates of Laurelton Hall's cost varied from $200,000 to $16 million. (In 1904, the taxes on the property came to $157,000.) Tiffany never disclosed the actual cost—Laurelton Hall was not built to call attention to his wealth—but a statement dated January 16, 1906, from Charles T. Wills, builder, 156 Fifth Avenue, to L. C. Tiffany, Esquire, gives the total cost of the erection of a residence at Cold Spring Harbor, Long Island, as $212,365.20. The statement adds $1,714.44, bringing the total to date to $214,079.64. On December 20, 1906, Tiffany added a greenhouse to his residence, which cost $8,791.00.

The big place gave an appearance of resting possessively on its hill overlooking Cold Spring Harbor. The site played a key role in determining its form—it could not have been built anywhere else. The progression was logical: from porte cochere to the Fountain Court, to the dining room, to the kitchen, to servants' quarters, to a conservatory, to a series of greenhouses, to a bowling alley, to a coach house, to stables (built around a paved court). Hanging gardens complete with tropical plants, fountains, and waterfalls extended out from the terrace on the harbor side. The hill on the land side was covered with terraces and gardens, one of which made picturesque use of stone masonry left from the old hotel. The main masses of Laurelton Hall had the molded look of a Pullman car. The greens in the copper cornice, the cream of the stucco, the wine-reds and butter-yellows in the flowers on the capitals, and the blues and golds of the mosaics suggested the freedom with which North Africans use color in their villages and cities.

It is always classified as "Art Nouveau," and with good reason, but Laurelton Hall had none of the restlessness of European Art Nouveau architecture. It was Art Nouveau becalmed by Tiffany's ingrained inclination to quiet art forms. It had character and a style of its own.

Guests approached Laurelton Hall over a mile or so of blue gravel drive through wooded areas filled with rhododendrons and laurel, past a totem pole, a waterfall, and a solid field of

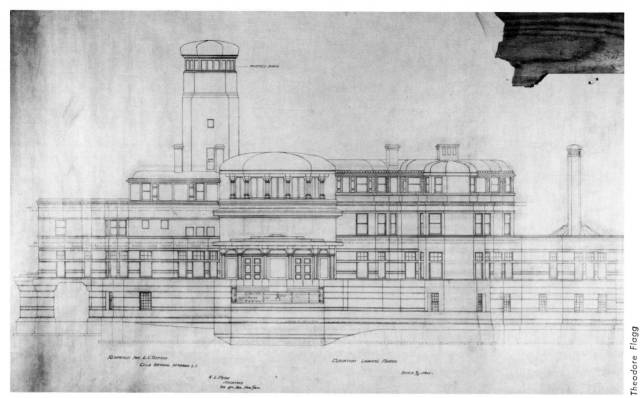

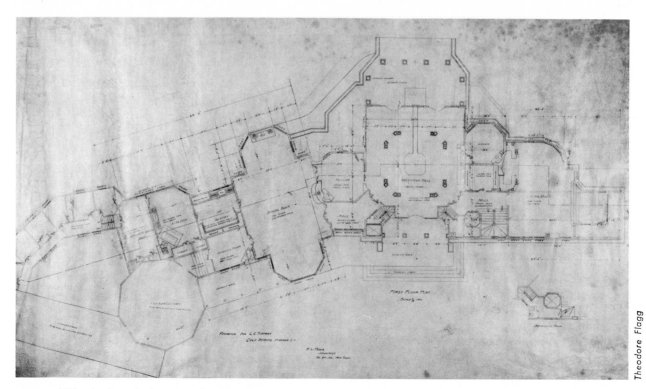

FIGURE 105   *Architect's drawings for Laurelton Hall by Robert L. Pryor, Tiffany Studios, 1903.*

daffodils, under a hundred-yard-long arch of espaliered apple trees, and around pools and streams lined with day lillies, joe-pye weed, Japanese iris, marshmallow, boneset, wild rice, forget-me-nots, goldenrod, and other wild flowers, to a porte cochere containing a marble table. From there, a stairway led to the Fountain Court. The main entrance, however, was from a garden on the land side where two brilliant turquoise-colored late seventeenth-century Kang-hsi Chinese dogs stood guard on a colorful loggia with columns that would have made a pharaoh glad. The limestone shafts rested on granite bases and supported cement capitals abloom with wine-red ceramic oriental poppies. The buds on the left progressed to wilted blossoms on the right. As is the case with their Egyptian prototypes, the cord binding their Favrile glass stems is indicated in the design (Figure 108). The entablature above was faced with iridescent blue, white, and gold Favrile glass mosaic bronze lanterns (Figure 109), hung between the columns. They were sixteen feet from the ground and weighed forty pounds. Their leaded-glass panels, which could be seen only with the sharpest eye, contained some pieces of glass no larger than a grain of corn.

The loggia led into a three-storied court topped with a translucent blue Favrile glass dome. Suspended from the top of the dome was a spherical leaded-glass lamp, which at night resembled a large moonstone. Under the lamp was one of the most serene shapes ever to come from Tiffany's restless mind, a pear-shaped vase (Figure 110) of colorless glass. It stood in the center of an octagonal basin and changed color slowly from violet to blue to green. It was lighted from underneath. The water had made its way through two pools, dropped over a waterfall, and come into the house through an underground conduit. It entered the vase from the bottom and flowed almost imperceptibly down its sides into the octagonal basin and from there through a marble trough across the room and out to the fountain on the terrace. Two clear-glass vessels, about the shape and size of maple sugar kettles, flanked the end of the trough. They, too, were fountains; the water flowed quietly over their sides into short, marble troughs which emptied into that from the central fountain. The water continued down over falls in the terraces, splashed into a fountain from a dragon's mouth, and eventually wound up in ponds far below.

The divans around the central fountain were covered with Tiffany velvets stenciled in powder-blues and golds. The basic colors in the court were green, purple, rose, lilac, and black. The flowers (definitely *not* to be picked by grandchildren), which were always banked around the fountain and troughs, came from the estate's greenhouses and gardens. The marble floors were inlaid in geometric patterns, and the walls were covered with heavy canvas stenciled with a cypress tree design taken from a tiled wall in the Seraglio of the Topkapi Palace in Istanbul, Turkey (Figures 113 and 114). Glass doors on the bay side afforded a panoramic view of the hanging gardens, the fountains, the valley, and Cold Spring Harbor.

The living room and library opened onto a short hall which led off the court. Windows that Tiffany considered milestones in his career were built into the walls of the upper level of the living room. Among these were "Feeding the Flamingoes," the cartouches from "Four Seasons," and "Flowers, Fish and Fruit." "The Bathers" was installed across the back of the raised section in 1914.

Three steps led to the lower level and an inglenook with hospitable curving seats and fur-covered hassocks where the entire family could gather around a fire on a cold night. One feature typical of Tiffany the engineer was a decorative iron yoke suspended from the ceiling over the living room table (Figures 115 and 116). Five green turtle-back lamps hung from the yoke; three attached directly to it; two from wheels that used it as a track. The result was an adjustable light on the table underneath.

The table's legs had the postlike simplicity of an elephant's, and consequently the sturdy look found in much of Tiffany's work. The table itself was always happily cluttered with orchids, books, magazines, vases, a tall and ungainly radio, and a model of the hand of Queen Elena of Italy, cast in bronze. A small circular iron staircase led from this room to the floor above. On this same side of the house was a small library furnished in a style suggestive of that which Frank Lloyd Wright was to introduce later.

The dining room held a large rectangular table (for formal dining) and two octagonal and progressively smaller ones (Figure 119). All were simple and oriental in spirit, as were the thirty-foot mazarin-blue rugs with large medallions in the same warm gray of the furniture. An inverted

Tiffany Studios, photograph courtesy of Robert A. Koch

FIGURE 106   *The hanging gardens of Laurelton Hall as seen from second floor, c. 1908.*

FIGURE 107   *Daffodil Terrace of Laurelton Hall, c. 1910.*

Tiffany Studios, photograph courtesy of Robert A. Koch

FIGURE 108   *Poppy capital from the loggia of
Laurelton Hall. Designed by Louis C. Tiffany,
1902–4. Cement, ceramic poppies with glass stems.
Height 41¾". The Metropolitan Museum of Art,
New York.*

FIGURE 109   *Lantern from loggia, Laurelton Hall.
Designed by Louis C. Tiffany, 1902–4.
Bronze with leaded-glass panels. Height 35½".
The Metropolitan Museum of Art, New York.*

FIGURE 110   *Vase from Fountain Court, Laurelton Hall. Designed by Louis C. Tiffany, 1902–4. The vase cracked
from time to time and was replaced by a duplicate. The colorless glass appears red in color due to minerals deposited
on the interior by the flowing water. Height 49".*

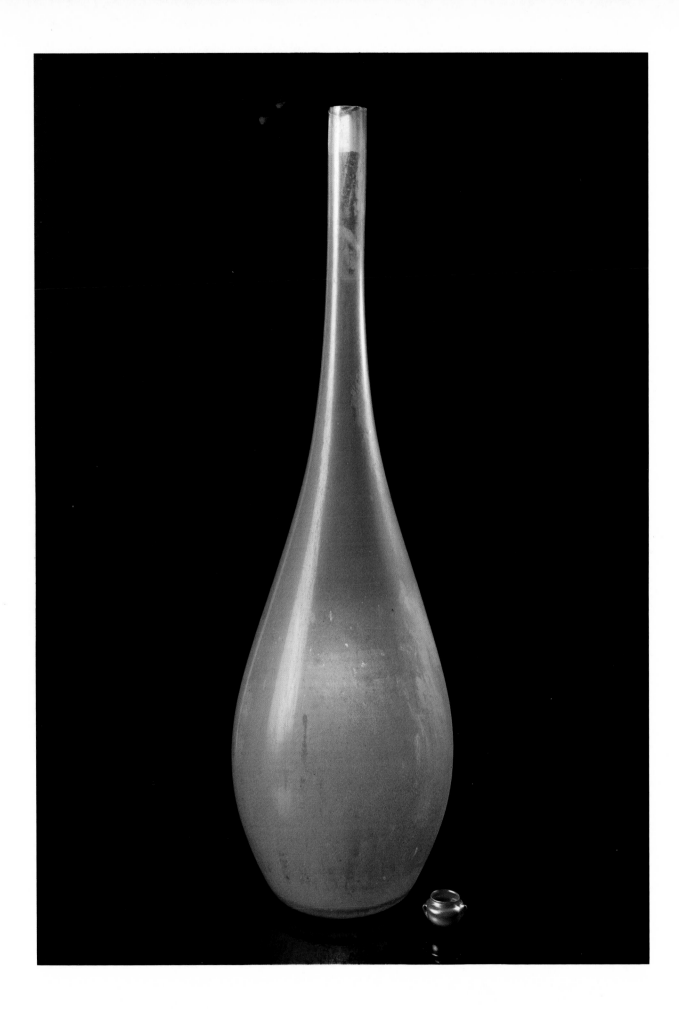

FIGURE 111   *Fountain Court, Laurelton Hall. Designed by Louis C. Tiffany, 1902–4.*

FIGURE 112 *Fountain Court, Laurelton Hall, showing portrait of Louis C. Tiffany (and his dog "Funny"),
by Joaquin Sorolla.*

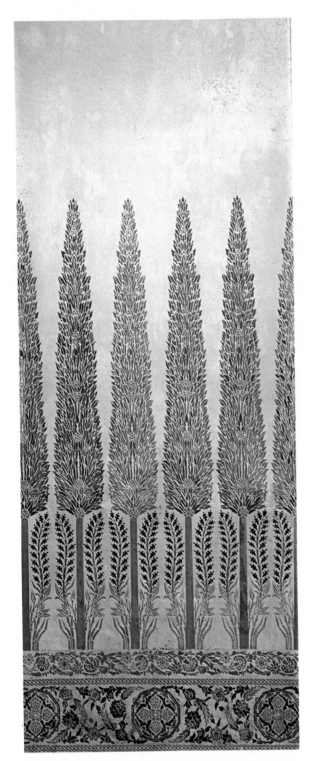

FIGURE 113 *Section of wall covering from*
Fountain Court, Laurelton Hall, c. 1904. Stencil
design adapted by Louis C. Tiffany from tile mural,
Topkapi Palace, Istanbul, Turkey. Oil on canvas.
Height 136½".

FIGURE 114 *Section of tiled wall in corridor*
leading to Harem, Topkapi Palace, Istanbul,
Turkey. From photograph in research files of Tiffany
Studios.

dome made of thousands of pieces of Favrile
glass, mostly a soft blue with bits of green, yellow, orange, and gold, hung over the central table
close to the ceiling (Figure 117). Its design of
small units on a theme of flowers and birds repeated that of the central medallion in the rugs
(Figure 118). Leaded green lamp shades hung
over the octagonal tables. The mantelpiece,
essentially a floor-to-ceiling sheet of light-colored
marble, held two candelabra on its narrow shelf.
Its three instrument faces set with blue mosaic
recorded not only the hour but also the day and
month.

The dining room extended the full 38-foot
width of the house. A bay at each end repeated
the octagonal shape of the table it held. Their
glass walls had the effect of making the gardens
and the Daffodil Terrace on one side and the harbor on the other extensions of the room. The

subtleties of its muted colors and the simplicity and sense of endless space gave the dining room at Laurelton Hall a timeless quality which will make its design forever contemporary.

The smoking room led off the far side of the dining room. From it one could enter the Daffodil Terrace where marble columns, topped with cement capitals set with glass daffodils, all from the Tiffany Studios, supported a wooden ceiling from Algiers. Originally, the daffodils sparkled with a high sheen. In time the weather gave all, except those few protected from the winds and rain, a soft matte finish (Figure 121). An opening in the roof, left to spare an old pear tree, was transformed into a special feature by a lining of iridescent blue glass made of 5½" squares and so designed that when assembled they created a pattern of branches, complete with leaves and fruit, from a pear tree (Figure 120). Wisteria vines growing around the terrace undoubtedly led Tiffany to place the leaded transoms on a wisteria theme over the glass doors.

The smoking room also opened into the series of glassed-in gardens which led down the hill to the bowling alley, the carriage house, and the stables.

Many of the extensive (4,000+) collection of Japanese sword guards which Tiffany had assembled as a young man were embedded in its walls and fireplace. They were also incorporated into its lamps and stored in cabinets that doubled as end tables. These alone would have given the little room a fascinating character. In addition, it held "The Opium Fiend's Dream," a painting of a man in trouble. A dark beauty obviously unencumbered either by garments or principles lay beside him, but his habit had involved him in a nightmare, and the opportunity was going to waste. Tiffany himself scumbled paint over the picture's more lurid passages.

A Chinese room on the second floor, also octagonal in shape, which might have been taken from the stage setting for one of the musical plays on an Oriental theme so popular at that time, was an Occidental's version of a Chinese room—an unauthentic assembly of carved and colored panels from the East—but it added to the quality of surprise and unreality of Laurelton Hall.

The second floor also contained four full-sized bedchambers (each with its bath or bath-boudoir), a sewing room, and ten servants'

rooms. A gallery filled with display cases packed with both ancient glass and Tiffany's own collection of Favrile glass ran around the open Fountain Court.

What was Tiffany thinking when he built Laurelton Hall? It was, of course, an expression of himself. The farmer in him, his love for growing things, for the earth and all it means, was everywhere, in the greenhouses, gardens, and in the fact that Laurelton was also a model farm complete with dairy cattle and vegetable gardens. The glass walls, which made the showers, the storms, the sunlight, and the harbor all a part of it, told of his joy in the environment and the earth's natural beauty. His fascination with mechanics was reflected in the lighting and in the fountains fed by storage tanks holding forty thousand gallons, and in their complicated lighting systems. (Three sets of synchronized colored lights played on the crystals in the terrace fountain from underneath.) His love of collecting, and possibly a desire to escape reality, could have led to the cases, cabinets, and shelves on the balconies of the court that were loaded with ancient Roman glass, American Indian artifacts, and Chinese and Japanese ceramics and metalwork. His urge to find new ways in the arts led to a use of stucco applied to both sides of a wire mesh with an air space between for insulation. The freedom in its design and the fact that it was so different, reflects the maverick in him. The Chinese room, the painting of the opium fiend, the ceiling from Algiers in the Daffodil Terrace, and all the references to the long ago and the far away were romanticism. The Westminster chimes in the clock tower were a musical statement of the importance those in the Puritan tradition attach to work, promptness, and order. The tower itself with its milk-bottle shape may have been a father symbol. His commitment to quality led to such things as the delicacy of the loggia lanterns hung so high their details could not be seen from the ground. Whatever else it was, Laurelton Hall was an introduction to a fascinating and complex mind.

But Laurelton Hall also revealed that even orderly, creative, careful, Louis Tiffany did not think of everything. With its glass walls, many windows, and three-storied court, it was impossible to heat. When the need for a power plant became apparent, so did the fact that the only possible site for it was on the shore of Cold Spring

FIGURE 115   *Living room, Laurelton Hall. Designed by Louis C. Tiffany, 1902–4.*

FIGURE 116 *Hanging lamp from living room, Laurelton Hall. Designed by Louis C. Tiffany, 1902–4. Green glass turtlebacks set in bronze. Diameter 18½".*

Harbor, which meant a smokestack marring the view that was one of the reasons for the house in the first place. The result was a resplendent Tiffany-type smokestack with all the grace of a handsome minaret! (The wooden model used to study its proportions is pictured in Figure 123.)

He also may have overlooked another matter—the feelings of his family. They loved "The Briars," the first summer home he had designed and built in Oyster Bay. It had sweeping verandahs high enough to let one see over the trees, a commanding clock tower, large and gracious rooms, and it was furnished in an elegant, warm, and comfortable style. The Briars was in many ways "home," and they did not want to leave it.

In the summer of 1904, as the final bright touches were being added to Laurelton, Louise Tiffany, a gentle woman whom all loved dearly, died. When the saddened fifty-six-year-old widower moved his three teenaged daughters to Laurelton Hall, the event was not the happy one it might have been. His family admired Laurelton Hall, and it was to become the setting for many happy house parties and social gatherings, but they had no feeling for it.

It is tempting to assume that Laurelton Hall was an intentional manifesto on domestic architecture, that it was built to show Americans how creative a dwelling can be. Possibly that had occurred to Tiffany, but under no circumstances could Laurelton Hall ever have taken this message to very many. The place was built to be lived in, not to be visited. Seeing it once would not have sufficed. Laurelton Hall said one thing in the sunlight; another in the evening. It was one place in the spring and another in the fall when the winds were stripping the leaves from its trees. Laurelton Hall took time.

That Tiffany planned it from the start as a retreat for creative young people is unlikely, and yet his comments, as recorded in the Minutes of his Foundation, especially those in which he declares the Foundation's sole purpose is to provide young artists an opportunity to work in the atmosphere of Laurelton Hall, sound as though this might be the case. Under one set of circumstances, and perhaps only then, Laurelton Hall seemed to explain itself. At night when the lights in the court hung like Japanese lanterns in a garden, and the slender fountain was changing color slowly, and the globe over it glowed with a soft yellow light, and the organ was playing, and palm trees and flowers were everywhere, and with Louis Tiffany sitting benign and content on a divan among young people whose lives he wanted so much to touch with beauty, Laurelton Hall made a great deal of lovely sense. Then it seemed to state its purpose in clear terms.

In his address to the Rembrandt Club, he observed, "Today we are beginning to realize that these light vibrations have a subjective power and affect the mind and soul producing feelings and ideas of their own in the recipient brain."[20]

By October 21, 1902, with the exception of the glasshouse at Corona, which he renamed the Tiffany Furnaces, his enterprises had been brought together as the Tiffany Studios. The name was not new. It had appeared on his publications as early as 1896. In the fall of 1905 the Tiffany Studios moved to new headquarters, the former Manhattan Athletic Club located on the southwest corner of Madison Avenue and Forty-fifth Street. Everything was now under one roof, the decorating establishment and the show rooms

FIGURE 117   *Hanging inverted dome lamp from dining room, Laurelton Hall. Designed by Louis C. Tiffany, after 1904. Favrile glass set in silvered copper foil. Diameter 66".*

FIGURE 118 *Medallion from dining room rug, Laurelton Hall. Designed by Louis C. Tiffany, after 1908. Wool. Length of rug 25'7"; width 8'8".*

FIGURE 119 *Small table and four chairs from dining room of Laurelton Hall as shown in The Morse Gallery of Art. Diameter of table 54".*

FIGURE 120 *A "Pear Tree" panel from opening in Daffodil Terrace, Laurelton Hall. Designed by Louis C. Tiffany after 1904. Sections of four-inch squares of decorated iridescent Favrile glass mounted on wood. Height 25¼".*

FIGURE 121   *Capital from Daffodil Terrace, Laurelton Hall. Designed by Louis C. Tiffany after 1904. Cement set with Favrile glass daffodil blossoms and stems. Height 22¼".*

Theodore Flagg

Michael M. Fairchild

FIGURE 122 *Smokestack on Laurelton Hall powerhouse. Designed by Louis C. Tiffany after 1904. Stucco, Favrile glass. Height 60′.*

FIGURE 123 *Model for Laurelton Hall powerhouse smokestack. Designed by Louis C. Tiffany. Wood and modeling clay. Height 60″.*

which carried Oriental rugs, antiques, Rookwood and Grueby pottery, as well as all the things Tiffany made: windows, mosaics, lamps, furniture (contemporary and traditional), pottery, blown glass, enamels, and metalwork. Clients selecting furniture for an entire room could see it all assembled on a trial basis in one of the studios provided for that purpose. In addition, there were large displays of rugs, textiles, and hangings of every description from designs by Tiffany and by members of his staff made in such places as Belgium, Bohemia, Ireland, China, and Japan.

Tiffany seems by this time to have left much of the interior design work to his staff. This may have been due to a lack of clients interested in his personal style with its emphasis on fabrics and wood carvings from North Africa, the Middle East, India, China, and Japan. The Tiffany Studios advertisements made it clear that they carried "reproductions of English, French, and Italian models of all periods," and that they did "distinctive work" at "reasonable prices."[21]

There was no diminishing interest on Tiffany's part in architecture, however. If anything, it increased. He built houses for each daughter as she married, and one for Miss Hanley complete with dining-room furniture similar to that in Laurelton Hall.

The Tiffany Studios continued to be a prestigious name, and when in 1915 the President of Cuba decided to have a Presidential Palace befitting his station in life, he commissioned Tiffany to decorate it. The plans called for a lot of furniture including twenty-three rugs and fifteen lamps. The original bill, totalling $1,167,392 was followed by a subsequent invoice for $199,123 to cover "incidentals."

After that the studios did less and less decorating. After the 1920 reorganization Tiffany continued as president and art director, but change was in the air. The world was being encouraged by the Bauhaus to think of architecture in terms of unadorned rectangular masses. After 1925 Art Deco, a geometric descendent of Art Nouveau, came into fashion. Grandparents and great aunts still loved Tiffany's floral elegance, but it looked dated to many. Before long, there were cruel giggles. The Tiffany Studios, bankrupt in 1932, were liquidated in 1938. For many years if critics mentioned Tiffany's Favrile beauty, it was with a sigh of relief that the world had not succumbed to the threat of its iridescent decadence.

FIGURE 124   *Tiffany Furnaces at Corona, Long Island (from a damaged glass plate).*

What happened to Tiffany's major architectural projects reads as much like fiction as the story of his successes. The New York mansions, including the Seventy-second Street house, were cleared away in the name of progress. The glass screen in the White House was "removed and broken into bits" on the express orders of President Theodore Roosevelt.

Laurelton Hall and four acres of land were sold in 1948 for $10,000. The sale was referred to in the January 1950, issue of *Cosmopolitan*, as "the rarest of all white elephant transactions." In 1957 it burned in a three-day fire which curiously spared many of its finest parts, the Daffodil Terrace, the glorious columns in the loggia, the vase in the Fountain Court, many of the leaded windows, and the furniture and fireplace in the dining room.

A few examples of his "decoration" have survived intact. Mark Twain's house in Hartford, Connecticut has been carefully and lovingly restored to the look Tiffany and Candace Wheeler gave it in 1881. The Ponce de León Hotel in St. Augustine, Florida, which is now a college, still has its windows. The Regiment has wisely preserved the Veterans' Room and the Library in the Seventh Regiment armory. But that is about all.

FIGURE 125   A showroom of the Tiffany Studios, c. 1926.

FIGURE 126   *A showroom of the Tiffany Studios.*

Tiffany Studios

NOTES

1 First he incorporated himself as Louis C. Tiffany &
   Co., with headquarters at 333 Fourth Avenue,
   New York. The Associates, with an embroidery department at 115 East Twenty-third Street, were a
   subsidiary, as was another short-lived association,
   Tiffany and de Forest.
2 Sheldon, George W., *Artistic Houses—Interior
   Views of Homes in the United States*, 1883. Re-
   issued by Benjamin Blom, Inc., Publishers, New
   York, 1971, Vol. I, Part I, p. 1.
3 From a clipping in Tiffany's scrapbook (no date).
4 Wheeler, Candace, *Yesterdays in a Busy Life*,
   Harper & Brothers, New York, 1918, pp. 233–34.
5 Sheldon, Ibid., pp. 53–56.
6 Taken from an unidentified clipping in Tiffany's
   scrapbook, p. 31.
7 In 1955 the Mark Twain Memorial Board of Trustees voted to restore the house and return in to its
   original state.

8–10 In an undated clipping from *Harper's Weekly*, in
      Tiffany's scrapbook.
11   The staircase and balcony were introduced at the
     suggestion of Stanford White, whom Tiffany had
     engaged as a consultant. White collaborated with
     Tiffany on other projects until a bullet fired by a
     wealthy Pittsburgher ended his career.
12–13 From an undated clipping in *Harper's Weekly*, in
       Tiffany's scrapbook.
14   The unidentified clipping is preserved in Tiffany's
     scrapbook.
15   *Washington Post*, December 20, 1882.
16   January 1, 1883.
17   Taken from a clipping from an unidentified news-
     paper preserved carefully in Louis Tiffany's scrap-
     book.
18   DeKay, op. cit., p. 58.
19   The New York *Times*, Sunday, April 8, 1888.
20   As reported in *The Art World*, May 1917.
21   They also called attention to the "Chicago office in
     the Orchestra Building," and to the "Boston office
     in the Tremont Building."

Chapter 8

TIFFANY MOSAICS

Glass mosaic is appropriately applied to the enrichment of walls and ceilings and to mantel facings.

From an advertisement used in March 1902
by the Tiffany Studios

The term "Tiffany mosaic" raises a familiar question. Does it mean designed by Louis Tiffany? The answer is "not necessarily." Tiffany did design some, his staff designed many more. Who designed which? We know about some, at least.

Mosaics are pictures made of bits of colored materials (usually glass, pottery, and/or stone) set in fresh cement or mud and applied to a floor, a wall, or to some other support. By nature they are a group project. One early example is a palm log encrusted with bits of black, white, and red limestone and mother-of-pearl set in mud. It was made for a gentleman who lived in El-Ubaid, Iraq, more than four thousand years ago (as in the case with so many world treasures it subsequently found its way to the British Museum). It was probably designed and made by the carpenters who built the house.

The ancient Greeks liked floors made of colored pebbles. The Romans used cut stones—marble was a favorite. In the sixth century the Emperor Justinian adorned the halls of his Basil-ica of San Vitale in Ravenna, Italy, with stately mosaic portraits of himself, his newsworthy Empress, and all his court. By this time, the favorite material was pieces of glass about one-half-inch square and one-quarter-inch thick. (When geometric the bits are called tesserae; when cut in free forms they are sectiliae.) Glass, lighter than stone and easier to cut, comes in a wider range of colors. The bits of glass in the early mosaics were set by hand and intentionally tilted at different angles so at least some would catch light from every source. The glass gave mosaics brilliance, and this refinement of method was also used to draw attention to important parts of the design.

By the latter part of the nineteenth century most mosaics were copies of oil paintings. There was little interest in the medium itself. Dr. Antonio Salviati, the bald and bearded Venetian who did the mosaics in the Albert Memorial in Kensington Gardens, had won endless honors by developing a type of do-it-yourself mosaic in which bits of glass, all of a uniform thickness,

FIGURE 127 *Planter, c. 1900. Bronze set with Favrile glass mosaic. Planter signed, "Tiffany Studios/New York/29117 B" (stamped) "S/C 305/S/C 5407" (incised). Insert signed, "Tiffany Studios/New York/29117" (stamped) "S/C 305/S/C 5407" (incised). Both pieces stamped with Tiffany Glass and Decorating Company monogram. Height 4."*

were pasted face down on sheets of heavy paper just as they were to appear in the finished work on the wall. The "ready-to-install" results were easily shipped. All the recipient had to do was push them into the wet plaster, let the plaster set, and remove the paper! In 1889 three young Germans named Wagner established a glasshouse in Berlin that produced 15,000 shades of glass. They too made mosaics using the "indirect" pasted-on-paper method. The series of Indian chiefs in the Cincinnati Union Terminal was from their studios. The method was ingenious, quick, and much less expensive than that employed by the mosaicist who draws his design on the wall, plasters over as much of the drawing as he can cover at one time, and sets the glass, piece by piece. It was also one more compromise with quality made by a society with a ravenous appetite for culture and a taste for bargains.

Louis Tiffany began to think this over. Here was another art form involving glass that had fallen into the hands of the unimaginative. It was absurd to limit mosaics to copying paintings.

They can liven up a fireplace and serve as a foil for a wall sconce. They can be used in other ways. And they are an art for any light—day, candle, gas, or electric. He used them first in his Bella apartment, then in nearly all his decorating projects including the Seventh Regiment Armory, the Union League Club, the Havemeyer house, and his Seventy-second Street home. He also used them on his metal lamps, planters, and trays.

The Columbian Exposition Chapel was his first major statement in mosaics. The altar front is covered with one-fourth-inch squares of pearly-gray glass; some a little lighter than most, some a little darker. The variation gives it a cloudlike softness. Set in this quiet background are five circular devices. The central one contains the Alpha and Omega symbol of the Savior; those on either side the symbols of the four evangelists. All are executed in mother-of-pearl and glass sectiliae set in a background of pearly-white pebbles. The emphasis is on form. The materials are played against each other to underscore the beauty of each. St. Matthew's angel, Saint Mark's lion,

St. Luke's bull, and St. John's eagle are abstract designs, sophisticated enough to suit the intellectuals and understandable enough to suit the rest of us.

The retable glows with a quotation from the scriptures done in tesserae in which gold leaf is sandwiched between a layer of opaque glass and a layer of clear. The door to the tabernacle has the exuberant ruggedness of Byzantine jewelry. The niche above the altar is a mass of sectiliae cut from wrinkled, fractured, folded, lumpy, iridescent glass. It has the freedom and rhythm of the glass in leaded windows. The design is two peacocks (an ancient symbol of immortality and a favorite Tiffany motif) facing each other and surrounded by a vine (to symbolize the Eucharist). Above them a crown floats in a halo of beads made, obviously, for another purpose but serving in this case to stand above the surface of the mosaic so their faceted surfaces can create a cloud of light. Under the crown seven large simulated amethysts have replaced the original garnets stolen by some turn-of-the-century blackguard. A string of gilded beads embedded in the plaster beneath and glass hemispheres about the size of a golf ball set here and there throughout the design give an element of surprise and glassy wonder to it all.

The design is sensitive, and logically related to the medium. It is consistent, with one exception which only the close observer would discover. The peacocks study the viewer with the fixed stare of a stuffed bird. The eyes are not Tiffany glass. They are from a taxidermist.

Above the niche is a mass of opalescent and iridescent glass mosaic set in concentric arches. The uppermost arch is mainly painted plaster brightened with glass jewels.

The dome-shaped cover of the baptismal font is made of hundreds of sectiliae cut in the rhythmic patterns of glass in leaded windows. They are set in cames, but backed with metal paint so the whole will function as mosaic. (Without the metal backing it would make a magnificent leaded lampshade.)

The entire chapel was, in effect, a first viewing of the kind of beauty with which Tiffany was soon to infiltrate thousands of American offices, drawing rooms, dining rooms, libraries, and boudoirs. While he did not and could not have made the mosaics and all the furnishings in the literal sense that one "makes" a painting, it was all from

FIGURE 128   *Door to Columbian Exposition Chapel, Laurelton Hall. Designed by Louis C. Tiffany, c. 1916. Oak and wrought iron. Height 77."*

his designs, a fact he made clear in his pamphlets and personal letters. He might have resisted the urge to set some of the tesserae and sectiliae himself, but that would be unlikely.

More than a million interested visitors gazed at the chapel's windows, furnishings, mosaics, vestments, and other ecclesiastical accoutrements (Figures 129–137). Some were properly awed. Others, under the spell of the stately classicism of "The White City," thought the treatment and color "too rich." Many discerning critics, especially those from other countries, recognized it (along with Louis Sullivan's door in the Transportation Building) as an island of creativity in a sea of colorless conformity. Tiffany was awarded fifty-four medals for his exhibits, and the Columbian Exposition exhibit won him a position of

FIGURE 129   *Furnishings from the Columbian Exposition Chapel. Designed by Louis C. Tiffany, 1892. Height of altar 39".*

artistic leadership in America and launched him as a major influence in Europe. Regardless of who thought what, it was a personal triumph.

The chapel was his favorite among all his works, not least because it was a trial run, a proving ground for nearly everything he made later. All his innovations in the decorative arts derive in one way or another from something he tried in it. When the fair closed, however, he faced the problem of what to do with a treasure for which there is no place.

He took the mosaics and windows to his showrooms in New York, where during April 8–15, 1894, he exhibited them to raise funds for the Bethlehem Day Nursery (admission—$.25), and he continued to exhibit them for several years after that. This, of course, was not a permanent solution, but one soon appeared in the

person of Mrs. Celia Whipple Wallace, Chicago's "Diamond Queen," who paid Tiffany $40,000 for the mosaics and windows (in those days men worked ten hours a day for a dollar, and the country had several good five-cent cigars) and gave them to the Cathedral of St. John the Divine, then under construction in the high rolling country on the upper west side of New York's Manhattan Island. The reassembled chapel was to serve as a memorial to her son.

The Cathedral was, in fact, little more than a Romanesque hole in the ground, since only the crypt and part of the apse had been completed. The round arches and bulky piers were suggestive of the style of America's Henry Hobson Richardson, and the chapel fitted in beautifully. The warm friendship between Presbyterian Tiffany and Episcopalian Bishop Potter made the ar-

FIGURE 130 *Central medallion, altar, Columbian Exposition Chapel. Mother-of-pearl, glass jewels, copper beads. Diameter 21".*

FIGURE 132 *Medallion. Symbol of St. Luke, from the altar. Mother-of-pearl, quartz pebbles, Favrile glass. Diameter 10½".*

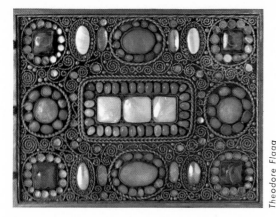

FIGURE 131 *Tabernacle door from the altar. Gilded grill set with jade, amber, quartz pebbles, mussel, and abalone shell. Height 11¾".*

FIGURE 133 *Medallion. Symbol of St. Matthew, from the altar. Mother-of-pearl, abalone shell, Favrile glass. Diameter 10½".*

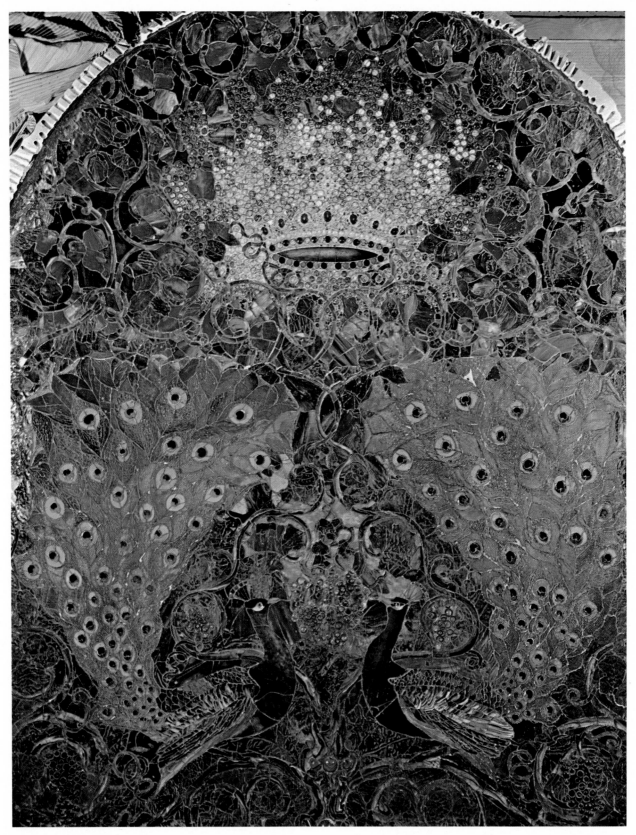

FIGURE 134 *Peacock niche from the reredos. Mosaic of Favrile glass, glass buttons, abalone shell, and found objects. Height 90".*

Theodore Flagg

FIGURE 135 *Detail of the cover of baptismal font. Leaded glass. Reverse backed with silver paint. Diameter 42".*

FIGURE 136 *Section of the electrolier from Columbian Exposition Chapel. Height of section 22½".*

rangement especially satisfying to both of them. The Cathedral was destined to become one of America's great monuments, and Tiffany drew pleasure from the fact that down through the years the chapel would come alive regularly with the prayers and chants of an ancient service.

But stories do not always end where they should—even those about chapels—and what became of Tiffany's beloved little masterpiece is sad to tell. Services were held in it for about ten years. Then Bishop Potter died and Ralph Adams Cram, a testy little man, blinded by the glory of Europe's Gothic style and set in his aesthetic ways, was appointed architect for the Cathedral. Cram did not care for Byzantine art and he did not like Tiffany at all. One reason was a window in a very Gothic and beautiful church

Mrs. Russell Sage had commissioned Cram to design for Far Rockaway, Long Island. While Cram was in Europe, Mrs. Sage bought a Tiffany landscape window to fill the openings for which Cram had planned Gothic windows. Tiffany's window featuring an ancient tree on a bluff was so wrong and the effect so beautiful that it made Cram's Gothic blood boil. His revenge came when he changed the style of the Cathedral from Romanesque to Gothic, and soon Tiffany's chapel was boarded up and forgotten.

What happened after that is a flawless model of stupidity. The chapel became a soggy pocket of neglect. Its condition is described in the following letter (addressed to Tiffany's manager) from one of the caretakers, the quality of whose English did not match his eloquence:

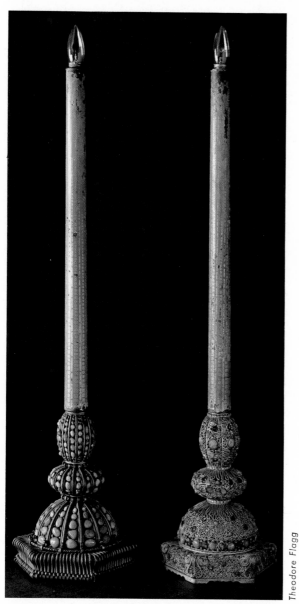

Theodore Flagg

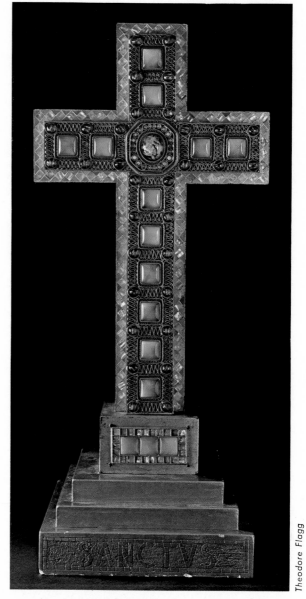

Theodore Flagg

FIGURE 137 *Altar candlesticks from Columbian Exposition Chapel. Gilded metal filigree, quartz pebbles, Favrile glass jewels. Height 36".*

FIGURE 138 *Cross from Columbian Exposition Chapel as installed at Laurelton Hall. Designed by Louis C. Tiffany as a replacement for the original, c. 1916. Brass, Favrile glass, mother-of-pearl. Height 24".*

FIGURE 139 *Fire curtain, National Theater, Palace of Fine Arts, Mexico City. Made by the Tiffany Studios from a design by Harry Stoner, 1911. Two hundred mosaic panels, each 36" square. Height 36'.*

Tiffany's or Harry Stoner's or that of the twenty or thirty artisans who selected the correct colors and cut and set the pieces of glass?

The answer is not the same as it would be for the chapel. Those who enjoy it for the mountains are drawn partly by Harry Stoner's ability to record what he saw in the mountains. Those who also appreciate the skill needed to select the right color and cut and set the pieces of glass are drawn by the skill of the workmen as well. Those who know enough to understand the skill necessary to produce the glass are enjoying one of Tiffany's achievements.

President Porfirio Diaz should not be overlooked either. True he had scurried into history before the screen was installed, but it was his idea. The drawing power of the curtain, therefore, is its own personality, which is the creation of many thoughtful people.

In 1914 the Tiffany Studios covered 300,000 square feet of the interior of the Roman Catholic Cathedral of St. Louis with mosaics designed by the Italian Aristide Leonori. The style is, of course, Leonori's. The brilliance of the material is Tiffany's.

The "Dream Garden" in the Curtis Publishing Company Building in Philadelphia was Tiffany's last great mosaic. In 1915 Edward Bok, the immigrant who had made a fortune publishing the *Ladies' Home Journal*, was planning a new building for his publishing company. Because he loved the meticulous phantasies created by the American painter-illustrator, he wanted Maxfield Parrish's pictures in the foyer of the handsome new building.

By fortunate happenstance Parrish was planning to build an actual "Dream Garden" at his home in New England. Bok who had seen and become entranced with the fire screen in Mexico, persuaded him to make a picture of it instead, and approached Tiffany about translating the result into Favrile glass mosaic. After several conferences Parrish and Tiffany agreed to cooperate on the plan. The mosaic was executed in New York by thirty artisans who were aided by a series of bromide photographs enlarged to a size never before attempted. Each artisan had a "palette" of pieces of rainbow-tinted glass, a wheel with diamond points, and a design showing the exact shape and size of each tessera and sectilia. As the pieces of glass were cut to exact size, they were glued in place on a color sketch. As each section was completed it was covered with waxed paper and turned face down on a bench. Then the glued sketch was removed, the whole covered with cement, reinforcing bars put in place, and more cement added. When these unwieldy sections were assembled, the result was a mosaic fifteen feet high and forty-nine feet long.

The fire curtain, the niche in the reredos of the chapel, and the "Dream Garden" are all different. The fire curtain is like an immense window opening on a view of snow-capped mountains. It calls attention to some of the beauty of Mexico.

The niche with its peacocks is not a "place." The peacocks are flat patterns, ideas recorded in glass. It calls attention to the beauty of form in art, to the dynamic relationships that can be established between lines, shapes, color, texture, and space.

The "Dream Garden" invites the observer into a lovely world, something like the real one but with a difference. Three-dimensional shapes take the light, cast shadows, and occupy space. Gnarled and gentle trees grow happily—free from any threat from "progress." Flowers bloom in peace. Water tumbles happily. Time, troubles, worry, and tension do not exist. The "Dream Garden" is a private "this is the way I wish it were" world, the creation of a man who was raised a Quaker and who wanted to share his daydreams with others.

Tiffany's attitude toward this mosaic is a matter of interest and also of record. In a brochure published by the Curtis Publishing Company, speaking of the difficulty of translating a painting into mosaic, he said: "I have been studying the effects of different glasses to accomplish perspective, and effects of color of different textures, of opaque and transparent, of lustrous and nonlustrous, of absorbing and reflection glasses.

"The mosaics of the past, although of the greatest beauty, were all made to copy pictures of flat decorations, and these modes of mosaics would not have answered this purpose.

"When Mr. Maxfield Parrish's painting was shown to me, with all of its beauty of suggestion, I saw the opportunity of translating it into a mosaic which would bring, to those who could see and understand, an appreciation of the real significance of this picture.

George Gelernt

FIGURE 140 *"Dream Garden" mosaic. Made by the Tiffany Studios after a design by Maxfield Parrish. 1915. Height 15'. The Curtis Publishing Company Building, Philadelphia.*

"In translating this painting so that its poetical and luminous idealism should find its way even to the comparatively uneducated eye, the medium used is of supreme importance, and it seemed impossible to secure the effect desired on canvas and with paint. In glass, however, selecting the lustrous, the transparent, the opaque and the opalescent, and each with its own. texture, a result is secured which does illustrate the mystery, and it tells the story, giving play to imagination, which is the message it seeks to convey.[1]

"As a matter of fact, it is practically a new art. Never before had it been possible to give the perspective in mosaics as it is shown in this picture, and the most remarkable and beautiful effect is secured when different lights play upon this completed mosaic.

"It will be found that the mountains recede, the trees and foliage stand out distinctly, and as the light changes, the purple shadows will creep slowly from the base of the mountain to its top: That the canyons and the waterfalls, the thickets and the flowers, all tell their story and interpret Mr. Parrish's dream.

"I trust it may stand in the years to come for a development in glass-making and its application to art which will give to students a feeling that in this year of nineteen hundred and fifteen something worthy has been produced for the benefit of mankind, and that it may serve as an incentive to others to carry even farther the true mission of the mosaic."

There was no trace in Tiffany's thinking that using natural forms is tantamount to pandering to public ignorance. Tiffany believed that to create an illusion of reality not only requires skill but that it can be done creatively. He admired Parrish's picture *because* of its depth and other illusory qualities, not in spite of them. He was pleased to capture these qualities in his mosaic.

It is equally clear that he still thought as a painter, that he looked on tesserae as something like brush strokes, and that in some ways he considered his glass superior to pigments. He was proud that small bits of Favrile glass could simulate the images in the Parrish painting. He was pleased with the smooth surface. He was proud, too, that with changing lights, the mosaics had qualities not found in the painting.

Then what about the "Dream Garden" is Tiffany?

The images are the inner world of Maxfield Parrish. The Favrile glass, which put them on a wall where they can be seen by hundreds of viewers, and the planning that enabled artisans to reproduce them in pieces of glass were Louis Tiffany at work.

The answer, then, to the question, what does

the term "a Tiffany mosaic" mean, is not a simple one. The fire curtain in Mexico's National Theater is from a design by Harry Stoner; the "Dream Garden" is from a design by Maxfield Parrish; those in the Roman Catholic Cathedral in St. Louis are from designs by Aristide Leonori; the panel of "The Church Fathers" shown in the chapel in the Chicago Exposition, the mosaics in the Wade Memorial Chapel in Cleveland, Ohio, and those in the Huntington Mortuary Chapel in Columbus, Ohio, are from designs by Frederic Wilson. (The mosaics in the Columbian Exposition Chapel, however, are Tiffany all the way.) But we must not forget that every Tiffany mosaic glows with a special beauty, and that regardless of who made the design, Tiffany made the glass.

NOTES

[1] Happily, even though the *Ladies' Home Journal* has moved its headquarters, the building is still one of the many joys of Philadelphia and is likely to remain so.

Chapter 9

BLOWN GLASS

Among the artists who have led the way in this change there is none who has affected the taste of the public more profoundly than Louis Comfort Tiffany. And the reason is not far to seek. With a tenacity rarely seen among those who, when young, have been subjected to the high sounding claims of academical painters, he has refused to limit his curiosity as an artist to one or two paths in art. He has followed first one road, then another, without heeding the formulas of his fellows, who seem always singularly enraged if one of the fraternity deviates from the unwritten rules of the guild.

CHARLES DEKAY

The Art Work of Louis C. Tiffany, written but not signed by Charles deKay, art editor of the New York *Evening Post,* was published at Tiffany's behest and expense. The Foreword begins: "This volume is not written for the public, but for the children of Louis Comfort Tiffany and at their request." That 502 copies were printed, and that he had only five living children indicate that he might have published it for other reasons as well, one being to set the record straight on his views on art, and on what he thought was his proper place in the history of American art. This would have been in character. Tiffany took other steps to achieve the same end. He gave interviews to the press and to authors preparing magazine articles about him. He wrote articles, and published pamphlets and booklets about himself and his work. From his eighteenth year until his death at the age of eighty-five, he

intentionally lived a public life. The press was encouraged to cover his new ventures, his exhibitions at world's fairs, his honors, and his dazzling fetes and social events. Even so, the record is full of gaps and contradictions, and the historical Tiffany has become something like the yeti in that it is easier to see the footprints than it is to see the man. When did he begin to work in a new medium? What part did he play in it himself, and what did he delegate to others? Which is his personal work, and which is the work of his staff? These questions are not easily answered.

If he had limited his activities to painting and interior decorating, it would have been different. The puzzles begin with the windows, increase with his blown glass, and multiply with each venture in a new medium.

Why he made blown glass is no mystery. Many Americans were wealthy, but the number who wanted a leaded window or a complete interior in the "modern" taste was limited. Vases were something else! The Belle Époque's appetite for ornament was ravenous, and for vases it was insatiable. Through vases you could get art's nose under a lot of tents.

Ancient Roman glass was another reason Tiffany turned to blown glass. The way its flaky surface turns daylight into bits of rainbows fascinated him. He collected it. He used fragments of ancient Roman and medieval glass in leaded glass and in mantelpieces. He longed to make vases with that same kind of beauty.

Then, too, the sheets of glass (tons of it were piling up in his storeroom bins) set the businessman in him to thinking. The number of windows he could make and sell was limited. If his glasshouse were to make readily salable wares of another kind, it might make a lot of budgetary sense.

The Art Work of Louis C. Tiffany covers these matters this way: "Yet the fact that things of daily use like lamps, flower-vases, and toilet articles reach a wider public than do paintings and sculpture make the 'decorative' arts more important to a nation than the 'fine' arts. Hence the value to a community of artists who devote their talent to making things of use beautiful. They are educators of the people in the truest sense, not as school masters laying down the law, but as masters of art appealing to the emotions and sense and rousing enthusiasm for beauty in one's environment.[1]

"Much pot-metal of very glorious color could never find a place in windows. Stores of it had accumulated; it was evident that an industry pushed so far ought to strive to lower the annual deficit by the utilization of by-products, just like any other. This was one but by no means the only reason for the attention he turned to small glass and the production of a very popular, very varied and beautiful glass of novel quality which received the title FAVRILE as a name easily spoken and readily recalled, the root being 'faber.' "[2]

But if the reasons for his making blown glass are clear, when he began to make it and what his role was in its production are not. Furthermore, his own attempts to clarify the matter are of questionable help. In 1896, for example, a pamphlet called *Tiffany Favrile Glass* containing "A Brief Chronology of the Art of Glass Making"

was published by the Tiffany Glass and Decorating Company. The entry for 1893 is: "Tiffany Favrile Glass first given to the public." It is not specific whether the reference is to blown glass or to the glass in his windows. The year 1893 is when he began using the trade name "Favrile." It applied to all his glass—window and blown. But he was making the kind of window glass he later called Favrile long before 1893. (The Musée des Arts Décoratifs in The Louvre provided one firm date in the chronology of his blown glass by buying a bowl through S. Bing in 1894. The Smithsonian Institution helped by buying a number of vases in 1896, as did the Cincinnati Museum Association by buying a number of vases in 1897—one at half price, $3.50, because it was cracked.)

In the fall of 1895 Tiffany invited the public to his workshops to inspect a selection of blown Favrile glassware. On October 17, 1895, the New York *Times* described the exhibit in enthusiastic terms: "Astonishing results have recently been accomplished by Louis C. Tiffany in experiments with glass. The results of his investigations may now be seen at the rooms of the Tiffany Glass and Decorating Company, on Fourth Avenue near Twenty-sixth Street, where there are on view numerous vases, jugs, and different attractive and artistic forms of glassware, curious and entirely novel both in color and texture. Effective combinations have been obtained in the blowing of the material, the placing of color over color, the union of metal with glass, the embedding of lines and threads of one colored glass in those of another while in a molten state, and, finally, the cutting of the glass into attractive designs. A remarkable lustre is apparent in some of the work, while others show delicate, iridescent colors, similar to those on glass recently exhumed from Greek, Roman, and Phoenician tombs. These pieces of Favrile glass now shown have cost great study, almost innumerable experiments, and are absolutely unique of their kind. This much accomplished, the possibilities seem practically unlimited and ramify out in almost every direction that decoration can suggest, but more particularly in mosaics and colored windows. They will remain on exhibition for some time to come."

From the foregoing, one might conclude that Tiffany made his first vases in 1893, but that may not be the case. Some art glass, with all the characteristics of Tiffany's, is marked with a large

FIGURE 141   *Two vases, Favrile glass. Left: C. 1896. Signed, "LCT/E150" (engraved), "1710" (canceled) "2222" (incised). Height 17½". Right: C. 1914. Signed, "L.C. Tiffany-Favrile 1564J" (engraved). Height 6½".*

FIGURE 142   *Three vases. Favrile glass. Left: Possibly before 1892. Signed, Tiffany Glass Company monogram (acid etched). Height 2¾". Center: C. 1910. Signed, "L. C. Tiffany-Favrile 1578E" (engraved script). Top has been ground down. Height 8¾". Right: 1892–1900. Signed, "Louis C. Tiffany-Favrile" (engraved script). Height 4½".*

"T" flanked by a small "g" and a small "c" (Figures 142, left; 144, left and center; 145). (See Appendix B: The marks for photographs of this and other, subsequently mentioned, Tiffany signatures.) The letters could stand for the Tiffany Glass Company which was reorganized as the Tiffany Glass and Decorating Company in February 1892. It would be out of character for him to use the initials of a company no longer in existence. To compound the matter further the vases so marked are perhaps more sophisticated than those generally considered his earliest pieces. That he stopped signing his windows "Tiffany Glass Company" and began using "Tiffany Glass

and Decorating Company" as soon as the reorganization was completed lends credence to this supposition.

The iridescent glass turtlebacks Tiffany was making (in a press) before 1893 (the year he established his famous glasshouse at Corona)[3] might also point to the early date. They appear in the electrolier made for the Columbian Exposition Chapel, which would date them as early as 1892. Turtlebacks are iridescent ovals about six inches long and shaped like the shell of a small turtle. But they also look something like a small dish. It is unlikely that he would have come that close to making vases and bowls without actually having done so.

FIGURE 143   *Vase. C. 1893. Favrile glass.
Unsigned. Height 4½".*

What part Tiffany himself played in making the blown glass will always be something of a pleasant mystery. A look at what went on inside the Tiffany furnaces might illuminate the matter. The workers were organized into teams, called "shops," that worked together to make a given piece of blown glass.

The gaffer was the master craftsman. The others—a blower, a decorator, a gatherer, a dip boy, and a taking-in boy—served under him. Each shop had its own tools, glory hole (for reheating an unfinished glass vessel), and benches. They worked from drawings supplied by management.

The gatherer started the process by heating the end of his blowpipe so molten glass would adhere to it. He then turned it in the molten glass to gather a ball of pot metal the exact size needed for whatever the project was. The process might take fifteen or twenty minutes. The next step was blowing the gather into a small bubble. What came after that varied from bubble to bubble. If it was to be decorated, the decorator might, for example, add prunts, or threads of molten glass of different colors. Bubbles thus embellished were sometimes rolled on a "marver" (a sheet of iron) to embed colored glass fragments or powdered glass into their surface. They could be dipped in pots of other colors to give them a layered effect, and they could be ringed with bands of a different color which were then pulled into patterns with metal hooks, not unlike a crochet needle.

After the bubble was blown to its final size but still attached to the blowpipe, a solid metal rod called a "pontil" or "punty," with a dab of molten glass on its tip, was attached to the far end, and the blowpipe detached (this could be done with a sharp tap on the blowpipe), leaving the unfinished vessel affixed to the pontil rod. The finishing was done by the gaffer who, rolling the pontil rod continually back and forth on the arms of his chair (to prevent sagging), shaped the soft glass with "jacks" (charred sticks of fruitwood). Glass that cooled to the point where it would not yield to pressure was reheated at the glory hole.

The completed vase was then detached from the pontil rod. Since thinner parts cool more quickly than the rest, thereby setting up internal stresses, the vase was placed in an annealing oven, reheated almost to its softening point, and cooled slowly, sometimes for several days. This process relieves the stresses. The scar left by the pontil rod was often polished to form a smooth disc. In some Tiffany vases the blob on the pontil rod appears as a waferlike pad with the pontil mark in the center of it.

Blown glass was made by sweating teams working in intense heat. Tiffany's furnaces made literally thousands of pieces of Tiffany glass. Since they were only one part of a large art-making complex, all of which made demands on Tiffany's time, it is obvious that neither Tiffany nor any other single individual was solely responsible for a finished piece of blown glass.

Nevertheless, all Tiffany vases are his in one sense. He knew how to make glass and how to

FIGURE 144 *Three vases. Favrile glass. Left: Possibly before 1892. Signed with the Tiffany Glass Company monogram (acid etched). Height 4″. Center: Possibly before 1892. Signed with the Tiffany Glass Company monogram (acid etched). Height 10″. Right: 1900–10. Signed, "L.C.T. o5112" (engraved). Height 2″.*

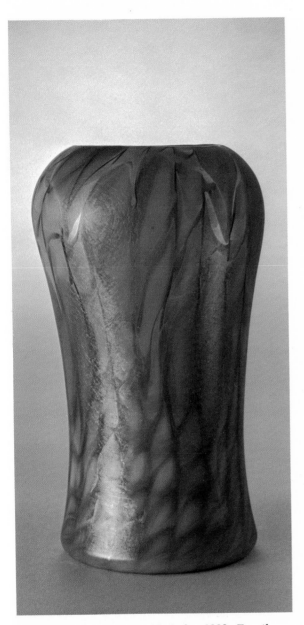

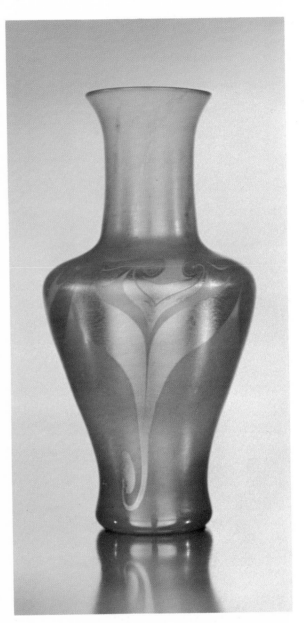

FIGURE 145   *Vase. Possibly before 1892. Favrile*
glass. Signed with the Tiffany Glass Company
monogram (acid etched). Height 7½".

FIGURE 146   *Vase. C. 1897. Favrile glass. Signed*
"L.C.T. H 1252" (engraved). Height 9¼".

FIGURE 147   *Three vases. 1897–1900. Favrile glass. Left: Signed, "L.C.T. N 1441" (engraved). Height 3". Center: Signed, "L.C.T. H 1750" (engraved). Height 6". Right: Signed, "L.C.T. H 1433" (engraved). Height 5".*

FIGURE 148 *Two "Cypriot" vases. 1899–1900. Favrile glass. Left: Signed, "LCT K241. Favrile-Exhibition Piece"*
(engraved). Height 5⅞". Right: Signed, "o3167" (engraved). Also has two original paper labels: the Tiffany Glass
and Decorating Company monogram and "L'Art Nouveau, Paris." Height 3".

FIGURE 149 *Vase. C. 1896. Favrile glass. Signed,*
"L. C. Tiffany-Favrile, 1938" (engraved script).
Height 5½".

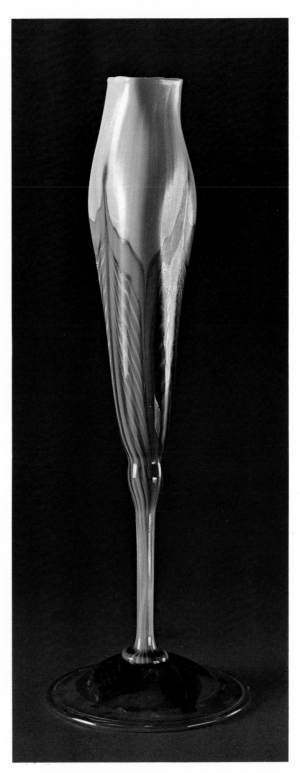

blow it.[4] He could show his workers what he had
in mind with quick skillful sketches. He "talked
the language" of glass with his men. His ability
to organize and to lead was such that his employees wanted to carry out his wishes. He knew
what he wanted. He visited his glasshouse at
Corona regularly, even in winter, when it meant
the long drive by carriage from Seventy-second
Street and crossing the East River by ferry boat.
He loved the place. According to his employees,
"he always seemed to be around." He liked the
suspense of experiment and the excitement of
success. His ability to foresee what a white-hot
ball of glass dabbed with bits of glass of other
colors would look like when blown, decorated,

FIGURE 150 *Floriform vase. C. 1905. Favrile glass.*
Signed, "L.C.T. Y6535" (engraved). Also original
black and white "LCT" monogram paper label.
Height 13".

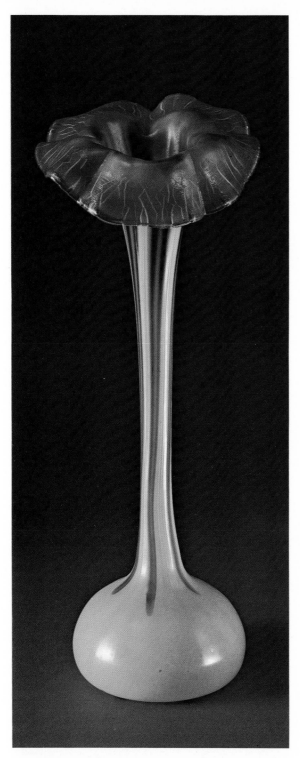

FIGURE 151 *Floriform vase. C. 1900. Favrile glass. Signed, "L.C.T. M 2068" (engraved). Also original Tiffany Glass and Decorating Company monogram paper label. Height 13".*

FIGURE 152 *Floriform vase. 1896–1900. Favrile glass. Signed, "L.C.T./o7731" (engraved). Height 9¼".*

FIGURE 153 *"Jack-in-the-Pulpit" vase. C. 1912. Favrile glass. Signed, "3918G L.C. Tiffany-Favrile" (engraved). Height 18½".*

FIGURE 154 *Vase. C. 1902. Favrile glass. Signed, "Louis C. Tiffany" (engraved script) "R4017" (engraved). Height 11".*

FIGURE 155   *Aquamarine vase. Shown at the Turin Exposition 1902. Favrile glass. Signed, "Louis C. Tiffany" (engraved script)/"R2401" (engraved). Height 8⅛".*

FIGURE 156 *Aquamarine vase. C. 1915. Favrile glass. Signed "L.C. Tiffany, Inc. Favrile, 5399 M, Panama-Pacific Ex^N" (engraved). Height 12".*

and cooled was uncanny. He was quick to spot the potential in a "mistake" by one of his workmen. Tiffany vases are Tiffany's vases, all of them.

His personal involvement is also indicated in the way the changes of style in his blown glass parallel those in his windows. Early vases and bowls tend to be abstract shapes, sometimes of lustered or iridescent glass, assuming, of course, that the T.G.C. mark does stand for Tiffany Glass Company. One, a deep blue "free form" miniature vase with a velvety sheen, ornamented with trailings of silver-colored glass applied at random and left to stand well up off its surface, suggests the techniques later called "lava glass" (Figure 142, left). The baluster-shaped vase ornamented with bands of cream, green, and gold which were worked with a hook into a wavy pattern (Figure 144, left) is further evidence of his interest in the glass itself, and in ways of treating it with metallic salts to give it the iridescence of peacock feathers, butterfly wings, and ancient Roman glass. His vases, as is the case with his early windows, are to be enjoyed for the interplay among the shapes, colors, and textures.

By 1896 many different kinds of vases were flowing from Tiffany's furnaces at Corona. Some were crumpled into surprisingly modern-looking freeforms (Figure 147, left). One popular series inspired by sixteenth-century Persian water sprinklers reflects Tiffany's interest in the art of the Middle East. Some early gold iridescent bowls and smaller items, such as salt and nut dishes, might be termed commercial since they were made in sets, but they were simple, handsome shapes determined largely by the nature of the material itself. The vase in Figure 148, right, bears an Art Nouveau Bing label, which would place it among the early ones.

It was not long, however, before Tiffany's conviction that nature points the way to new art forms was to be reflected in his blown glass. Vases shaped like single flowers, and sensibly turned up to make them useful containers (Figure 149), were the first. Others suggest single blossoms on long slender stems (Figures 150, 151, 152). This development is paralleled in the early windows such as the "Magnolia." The glass is now being asked to describe a natural image. The observer is to be attracted to it partly because of the beauty of the material, and partly because the material suggests the beauty of a flower.

FIGURE 157 *Aquamarine vase with dogwood motif. C. 1915. Favrile glass. Signed. "1335N Louis C. Tiffany. Favrile-Special Exhibit" (engraved script). Height 7½".*

FIGURE 158 *Aquamarine vase. Interior view of Figure 159. Diameter 4¼".*

FIGURE 159 *Aquamarine vase. C. 1912. Favrile glass. Signed, "5197G L.C. Tiffany-Favrile" (engraved script). Height 7".*

After 1900 vases appear with flowers embedded in the glass (Figure 154). Others were made by adding slices of glass canes (colored rods melted together and drawn into sections often not much bigger in diameter than a lead pencil) to the surface of the original bubble, rolling the whole on a marver to smooth it out, blowing it to the desired size, and dipping the whole in a pot of clear glass to give it a crystal coating. One of this type was exhibited at the International Exposition in

Turin, Italy, in 1902 (Figure 155). Its several layers of white flowers and slender stems float in a gray-green mist. The vase is, in effect, a circular bit of atmosphere with flowers in it.

The aquamarine series, introduced around 1913 and featuring flowers or butterflies embedded in heavy masses of clear crystal, came later. (These are often called paperweight glass, a term not used by Tiffany.) One aquamarine vase (Figures 158 and 159) suggests a miniature lily pond. The stems make a handsome pattern when viewed from the side. The blossoms and leaves make an equally attractive pattern on the "surface" of the "pond." This is still another approach. The flower is *growing* there. The vase is more than a fragment of atmosphere, it is a complete miniature environment.

A "Morning Glory" vase (Figure 166), made for the Paris Exposition of 1914, reveals still another development. The edges of the flowers are blurred, the images are less precise. One does not see the flowers as much as one sees the light reflected from the flowers. It is Impressionism in glass made after Tiffany had been influenced by the paintings of the great impressionist master, Monet. The same effect can be seen in late Tiffany windows and paintings. Tiffany was not at the worker's side when each vase was made, but his ability to organize and to lead was such that as he became an impressionist, so did his gaffers.

Tiffany also made "commercial art glass," commercial in that it came in patterns; art in that each piece was blown individually. Sets include decanters, wine, sherbet, and water glasses, salt and nut dishes, berry bowls, finger bowls, and dinner plates. They bore such names as Dominion, Earl, Ascot, Royal, Victoria, Queen, Prince, Princess, Manhattan, Savoy, York, Flemish, and Colonial. The pieces match, but each has those individual characteristics (commercial glassmakers would call them flaws) that give handmade things the rhythm of music. In a row of iridescent gold wine glasses, one will lean a little to the left, another to the right, one will be taller and another a trifle short. The inside of most will be iridescent gold. A few may give the illusion of brimming with blue mist.

The diversity of Tiffany's blown art glass, a result of his intense curiosity about the medium itself, is a typical, albeit confusing, characteristic.

FIGURE 160 *Goblet, "Princess" pattern. 1900–20. Favrile glass. Signed, "L.C.T." (engraved). Height 8¾".*

FIGURE 161   *Tulip-shaped drinking goblet. 1915–25. Signed, "L.C.T. Favrile" (engraved script) "Ex. Ex." (engraved). Height 6½".*

FIGURE 162   *Wine glass. 1900–25. Favrile glass. Signed, "L. C. Tiffany-Favrile" (engraved script). Height 6½".*

FIGURE 163 *Two vases. Favrile glass. Left: C. 1896. Signed. "L. C. Tiffany-Favrile" (engraved script) "5576E" (engraved). Height 5¼". Right: C. 1914. Signed, "L. C. Tiffany, Inc. Favrile" (engraved script) "3990N" (engraved). Height 6½".*

He seems literally to have tried everything one can do with glass, no matter how difficult or how costly. Vases will have three or more layers, some with "windows" cut in the outer layers to reveal the color beneath (Figure 170, center). Cypriot vases (Figure 172, left and center) were rolled on a marver covered with crumbled glass to give them a rich and unpredictable surface. In lava glass (Figure 171), one color was poured over another and let cool in the imaginative patterns of drips. The entire surface of some agate glass was cut away to reveal patterns buried in the material (Figure 168). Bubbles were blown inside some to give them a special lining. Ivy vines were engraved on some. Parts of heavy bowls were cut in the "brilliant" tradition but with large red flowers embedded in the parts not cut (Figure 173). The iridescence may be in the surface, on a layer covered with clear crystal, or on the inside. Threads of one color were applied to a ground of another and worked into waves with metal hooks. Sometimes an entire vase was twisted sufficiently to give an applied pattern a swirled effect. Some vases have surface textures deceptively similar to that of metals—iron or bronze, for example (Figure 175). Vases range in size from two inches to a height of two feet or more.

The glass bud vases in enameled bases (Figure 176) came after 1920.

The markings are, no doubt, an effort to keep the record straight, but they have been less than successful.

Signatures include: L.C.T.; LCT Favrile; Louis C. Tiffany, Favrile; Louis C. Tiffany, A-Coll. (A-Coll. indicates artist's collection); Louis C. Tiffany Exhibition Piece; Louis C. Tiffany Favrile Exhibition Piece. Some are block letters; others script. Most are on the bottom, but they can be on the side. Many pieces were not only signed but given numbers, or numbers and letters, and special pieces were identified with codes. A small "o" as a prefix indicated a special order. An "x" meant experimental. Some, including many in the collection of the Smithsonian Institution (acquired in 1896) and the Metropolitan Museum of Art (acquired in 1896) are not signed.[5]

Robert Koch, in *Louis C. Tiffany's Glass-Bronzes-Lamps*, suggests that those with no prefix were made before 1894, those with prefixes from A to L were produced from 1894 to 1900; those with a prefix from M to Y from 1901 to 1905; those with a suffix from A to G from 1906 to

FIGURE 164 *Three plates with added rims. C. 1915. Favrile glass. Top: Signed, "L. C. Tiffany-Favrile" (engraved script) "X87" (engraved). Diameter 9." Middle: Signed, "X87 3965 (engraved) "M.L.C. Tiffany Inc. Favrile (engraved script). Diameter 8⅞." Bottom: Signed, "L. C. Tiffany-Favrile" (engraved script) "X87" (engraved). Diameter 9⅜."*

FIGURE 165 *Carved rock-crystal vase. After 1902. Signed, "115 L.C. Tiffany" (wheel-cut block letters). Height 7".*

FIGURE 166 *"Morning Glory" vase. 1914. Favrile glass. Signed, "L. C. Tiffany-Favrile 8566H/Paris Salon 1914" (engraved script). Height 5".*

FIGURE 167 *Turquoise vase with orange inclusions.*
C. 1912. Favrile glass. Signed, "L.C.
Tiffany-Favrile 3087J" (engraved script). Metal
base unsigned. Height 9½".

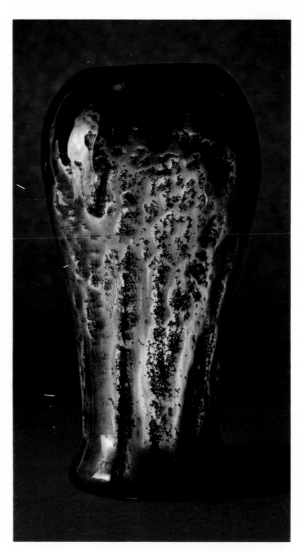

FIGURE 169 *Vase. Made for the 1914 Paris Salon.*
Favrile glass. Signed, "L. C. Tiffany-Favrile
8568H/Paris Salon 1914" (engraved script).
Height 7¾".

FIGURE 168 *Three vases. Favrile Glass. Left: Leaf*
pattern. After 1902. Bears the original black and
white "LCT" monogram on paper label. Height
2⅞." Center: Decorated green. C. 1900. Signed,
"L.C.T. K2973" (engraved). Height 8½." Right:
Faceted agate Favrile glass. 1900–10.
Signed, "L.C. Tiffany-Favrile" (engraved script)
"104A-Coll." (engraved). Height 3¼."

FIGURE 170   *Three vases. Favrile glass. Left: C. 1897. Signed, "L.C.T.H1374" (engraved). Height 3¼". Center.*
C. 1918. Signed, "3301P L. C. Tiffany-Favrile" (engraved script). Bears green and gold "LCT" monogram paper
label. Height 9¼". Right: C. 1895. Signed, "L.C.T.o9965" (engraved script). Bears "TGDCo" monogram paper
label. Height 2½".

FIGURE 171   *Two lava vases. Favrile glass. Left: C. 1908. Signed, "L. C. Tiffany-Favrile 2328C" (engraved).*
Height 5". Right: C. 1913. Signed, "L. C. Tiffany-Favrile" (engraved script) "9771K" (engraved). Height 7½".

FIGURE 172 *Three vases. Favrile glass. Left:*
"Cypriot" vase. C. 1896. Signed, "L.C.T."
(engraved) "Louis C. Tiffany" (engraved script)
"E 1771" (engraved). Bears original "TGDCo"
monogram paper label. Height 7¾". Center:
"Cypriot" vase. C. 1899. Signed, "L.C.T. K1462"
(engraved) "2461" (incised). Height 8½". Right:
Vase. 1895–1910. Signed, "L.C.T." (engraved).
Height 2¼".

FIGURE 174 *Vase. C. 1910. Favrile glass. Signed,*
"L. C. Tiffany-Favrile" (engraved script) "7008D"
(engraved). Height 7½."

FIGURE 173 *Marquetry bowl. 1892–1901. Favrile*
glass. Signed, "Louis C. Tiffany" (engraved script)
"o3440" (engraved). Bears original "TGDCo"
monogram paper label. Height 7."

FIGURE 175 *Vase, acid-etched and scratch-*
engraved. C. 1895. Favrile glass. Signed, "L. C.
Tiffany-Favrile" (engraved script) "E752"
(engraved) "E752" (wheel cut). Height 8¼".

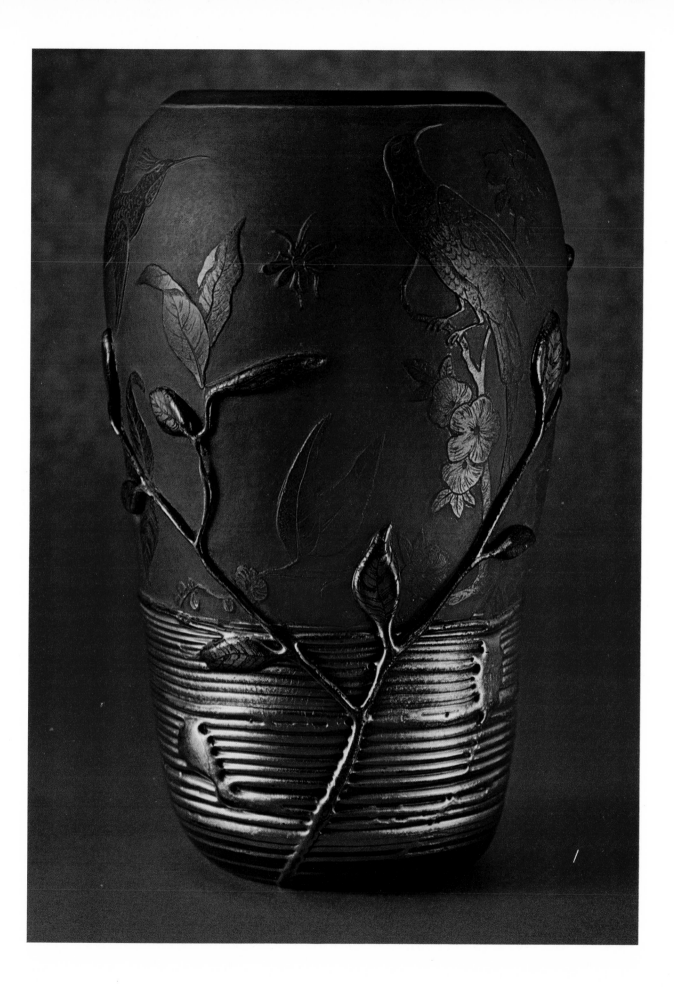

FIGURE 177　*Two vases. Favrile glass. Left: C. 1894. Signed, "L. C. T." (engraved script) "1460" (engraved). Bears two paper labels: "Tiffany Favrile Glass" and "1460." Height 4½". Right: C. 1921. Signed, "3917 P L.C.T." (engraved) "Favrile" (engraved script). Bears green and gold "LCT" monogram paper label. Height 2¼".*

1912, and those with a suffix from H to W from 1913 through 1928.

One early vase (Figure 177, left) numbered 1460 bears a paper label with the same number. By 1892, a paper label with a large T flanked by the letters G D Co. (standing for Glass and Decorating Company) came into use. In 1902, this was superseded by a new label bearing an Art Nouveau version of Tiffany's initials. The design is circular, a small ribbon-shaped L is encircled by a C which develops into a floriate T. This design is similar to but distinct from the curvilinear "TS" design which stands for Tiffany Studios and which was used in their brochures and advertisements.

Smaller numbers incised or scratched, also on the bottoms, have attracted very little attention. These may be related to the distribution methods. Ordinarily, Tiffany sold no art glass to dealers. Everything was consigned for a stated period. Glass that did not sell was returned to be tried somewhere else or destroyed. It was entrusted (with the exception of New York where it was carried by Tiffany & Company and Tiffany

FIGURE 176　*Vase. Enameled copper and Favrile glass. 1921–28. Signed, Glass—"LCT/Favrile" (engraved); Base—"LCT" monogram "Louis C. Tiffany Furnaces Inc./Favrile/151" (stamped) "6103" (incised). Height 13¾".*

Studios) only to such stores as Neiman Marcus in Dallas and Marshall Field in Chicago. In 1910 the Shreve Company of San Francisco issued a catalogue of their Favrile glass; hence one would assume they had a special arrangement with the Tiffany Studios.

A letter from The Louis C. Tiffany Furnaces, Incorporated, to *Antiques* magazine which appeared in 1926, under "Questions and Answers,"[6] reads as follows,

> The Louis C. Tiffany Furnaces, Incorporated, inventors and sale (*sic*) manufacturers of Favrile glass have furnished the following notes: "Favrile glass was invented in 1893, and was the result of Mr. Tiffany's desire to produce a glass which would serve as a medium for interpreting his ideas for ecclesiastical windows. It was originally made only for this purpose. Very shortly, however, Mr. Tiffany developed an interest in blown glassware, but he felt that in order to preserve the true characteristics of glass it should always be handmade— hence the name FAVRILE, a derivation from an old Saxon word meaning hand-wrought.
>
> Each article of Favrile glass is marked with the Tiffany name or initials, and all unusual pieces bear a number, the letters of the alphabet being used first as a prefix, later as a suffix to the numbers."

The letter was unsigned. Whether it was from Tiffany or from someone else is not known but it may give all the answer there is. There may be no planned relation between any number and any year. When an agreed upon limit had been reached, the next piece might have been numbered 1 plus the succeeding letter. In other words, if 10,000D came in July, the next number might have been 1E.

Sometime in the twenties, a handsome undated and unsigned brochure issued by the Tiffany Studios, 391 Madison Avenue at Forty-seventh Street, announced that production of Favrile glass vases had ceased and that the remaining stock would be marketed in the usual way. It also predicted that the glass would enhance in value in "the years to come." The voice was as grand in style, as anonymous, as prophetic, and as prone to ambiguity as those originating in fissures in the earth. The glass did increase in value, but when production ceased is unclear.

Favrile art glass seems to have been made until 1928.

In 1920 the Tiffany Furnaces were reorganized as Louis C. Tiffany Furnaces, Inc. Tiffany continued as president and art director. Arthur Nash continued as vice president and general manager. Nash's son, A. Douglas Nash, served as treasurer and assistant manager.[7] The glass changed somewhat in character. The colors were more pastel and there seems to have been more emphasis on matched sets. Jimmy Stewart's drawings for vases from these years are reproduced in *Louis C. Tiffany's Glass-Bronzes-Lamps* by Robert Koch.

In 1928, Tiffany sold the glass works to a corporation owned by the Nashes and headed by A. Douglas Nash. They made handsome glass, but the venture was not a financial success and the fires went out for the last time in 1931. Douglas Nash was employed by the Libbey Glass Manufacturing Company in Toledo, Ohio, for the next three years.

Tiffany art glass came into being because Louis Tiffany wanted to make the world more beautiful and because he could train skilled artisans such as Thomas Manderson, his first and perhaps finest gaffer, to make their hands serve as his own. Its shapes and colors mirror his thinking, express his taste, reveal his personality. Some of it has the rhythmic grace of Art Nouveau. Some pieces are exuberant, some flamboyant. Most, however, are becalmed to some extent by the Puritan reserve that ran in his blood. This quality becomes apparent when his pieces are compared with the European art glass of the time. Tiffany's blown glass may posture, flourish, swing, and turn, but it does not mince, flutter, prance, or skip. Cecilia Waern, the eminent English critic, put it very well when in 1898 after seeing his art glass she wrote: "The shapes are often capricious but with all the sweet waywardness of this exquisite material: they are almost invariably simpler, less slight, less tortured, and more classical in the deepest sense, than the blown glass of Europe."[8]

NOTES

1 DeKay, op. cit., pp. 27–28.
2 Op. cit., p. 25.

3 This is the year given in *The Art Work of Louis C. Tiffany*. Cecilia Waern in her article in the *International Studio*, Vol. XIV, No. 63, pp. 16–18, June 1898, states, "In 1892 he started the glassworks at Corona."

4 On one occasion he blew three glass toys, for his grandchildren. Each was a glass rod with a chicken on the end of it.

5 This matter is discussed fully in Appendix B.

6 December, No. 329, p. 478.

7 This is as the letterhead on their stationery lists them in 1921.

8 *The Studio*, Vol. XIV, No. 63, June 1898, "The Industrial Arts of America: II. The Tiffany or 'Favrile' Glass," pp. 15–21.

Chapter 10

ART GUARDED BY THE DEAD

THIS IS THE FIELD AND ACRE OF OUR GOD:
THIS IS THE PLACE WHERE HUMAN HARVESTS GROW.

Memorials in Glass and Stone,
TIFFANY STUDIOS, 1913.

As the last century approached its end, a change was taking place in the way Americans thought about their dead. Shrouds went out of fashion. The dead were dressed in party clothes and "laid away." Grave markers were no longer adorned with a skull or some equally grim reminder of the inevitable.[1] The era of the intimate burying ground such as that surrounding New York City's Trinity Church was over. High land prices had forced city churches to build up to the sidewalk. Churches in the towns occupied landscaped lots. The dead now slept in some of the finest land in the suburbs. Cemeteries bore comforting names such as Fairview, Forest Lawn, and Brookhaven.

The shift in American wealth had something to do with it. Many of the new elite, not content to sleep under modest grave markers, wanted at least a symbol of their status near them. This required space. Another factor was a change in the intellectual climate. The roaring religious revivals of the early part of the century had left the country drenched, if not in religion, certainly in sentiment, and a good bit of this was focused on "the departed."

As a result, cemeteries had evolved into a popular new community art form. Americans were enthusiastic about but inexperienced in funerary art. Some of their efforts were terrible; some ridiculous. A few monuments like the marble shaft in a midwestern cemetery which supports a marble replica of the deceased's rocking chair, are amusing. Many of the marble angels have a decided charm. Egyptian obelisks are always impressive in a way. Some of the Greek temples are attractive. A good many mausoleums from the period are impressive at least because of their size and cost.

Louis Tiffany, always keen to help out in situations offering an opportunity to demonstrate the power of good taste, and especially if they involved glass as well as an opportunity to make money, was attracted to the field of outdoor memorials as irresistibly as a honey bee is drawn to a marigold. He had been making memorial windows for years. The Columbian Exposition

Chapel had been one of his triumphs. Making memorials in stone did not involve a new way of thinking.

When he resolved to enter the field, he added a complete new division to the Tiffany Studios, the Ecclesiastical Department. It was organized, as one would expect, with meticulous care. It had its own engineers as well as artist-designers. By offering a wide variety of memorials and services, it revealed an awareness of a fact about Americans as true today as it was at the turn of the century; namely, the diversity of their views on what relationship, if any, exists between the body and the departed soul.

The influence of such attitudes is apparent when the art of India is compared with that of the ancient Egyptians. Hindus cremate their dead. Anything else might be inappropriate since the soul is already on its way to another body, human or animal, unless the gods have decided to spare it the pain of another go at life. The Parsees, latter-day Zoroastrians who do not defile the earth with dead bodies, expose them in "Towers of Silence" where vultures are always waiting. Needless to say, the cemetery is not an important art form in the sub-continent.

The ancient Egyptians, on the other hand, preserved the bodies of their loved ones in their dry desert air, confident that this would make the inevitable future life more like that in fair Egypt. Those who could afford it took gold, furniture, clothes, flowers, food, and slaves into the tomb for use in the next life. It is not by happenstance that pyramids are the most expensive and most permanent structures on earth. They are visual expressions of a determination to spend what is necessary to make things comfortable in the next life. Americans' attitudes toward death have never been as clearly delineated or as cohesive as those of the Indians or the Egyptians.

Turn-of-the-century Americans knew death more intimately than those living today, however. Nursing homes had not yet appeared on the American scene. People died younger and in their own beds. Funerals were held in the living room or in the parlor if there was one. Sentiment was respected. Grief was expressed openly. The deceased were viewed with a mixture of fear, awe, and respect. (Consequently, cadavers were difficult for medical schools to come by.) But as to what had happened to the liberated soul, it was every man for himself. Some considered the body a "temple of the Holy Spirit." Some believed the soul hovered around following earthly events with interest. Many held that souls were confined to heaven and denied the pain of knowing what was going on below. Many believed that soul and body would eventually be reunited. Mediums kept many Americans in touch with loved ones on a regular basis. A few believed in reincarnation. Some believed the soul could be baptized into a new faith. A rather silent group looked on death as a sleep that lasts forever.

That Americans should vary in their burial customs was inevitable. Most bodies were embalmed and buried in the ground. A small number were entrusted to mausoleums which were above ground, dry, and more costly. Some were cremated. Wealthy Americans of the Belle Époque spent less on their dead than the wealthy ancient Egyptians, but they were not niggardly. Cemeteries often became showplaces which drew crowds on Sundays and holidays.

At the peak of their activity, the Tiffany Studios were ready to meet the funerary needs of anyone, regardless of his or her views. Those preferring a simple marker could choose from traditional headstones. As a slightly more costly alternative, the client could have a ledger stone (a slab of marble or granite covering the entire grave, handsomely ornamented and marked). Table monuments (like a ledger stone but resting on four legs) and sarcophagi (a stone monument large enough to contain a casket, but serving only to mark the grave) were also available, as were obelisks and bench memorials. For those wanting to protect the body "from the elements," there were small tombs, complete with a door, a window, and niches for several coffins. On occasion, however, members of the "better families" wanted to rest in something truly fine, complete with portico, bronze doors, crystal chandeliers, marble catacombs, custom rugs, bronze sarcophagi, mosaic floors, and leaded windows. This was so much the better!

The destitute, of course, slept somewhere else —under a number.

A posh brochure published by Tiffany in 1913 entitled *Memorials in Glass and Stone* and intended for very special clients not only illustrated many kinds of Tiffany memorials, it offered help (on a high plane of course) in clarifying one's thinking in the delicate area of memorials to loved ones. To this end it quotes from an essay entitled "God's Acre" by James Burrell. The essay reasoned: "The custom of erecting memorials to the dead is as old as love and sorrow. The saddest thing in the world is an unmarked grave . . . The heart that ever truly loved cannot forget. And of all tributes paid by memory to affection there is none more natural or time-honored than the fit adornment of the resting places of our beloved. This is the least that sorrowing hearts can do."

On the crucial matter of displaying good taste in the selection of a memorial, the essay had this to say: "How much there is that is simply vulgar; how much that is grotesque and bizarre! And this in the sacred suburb of the heavenly city where all should be dignified and reverent." The brochure then examined the term mausoleum, disclosing that it derived from the tomb erected in 352 B.C. for Mausolus, the King of Caris, by his widow, Artemisia. It described the tomb (one of the seven wonders of the ancient world) as consisting of a podium (foundation), a pteron (a circle of columns), a pyramid, and a pedestal topped by a "marble chariot group of the King drawn by an attendant god." Relating such data to the present it continued: "To persons of considerable wealth, this form of memorial is commended, as affording a large field for the display of genius, originality and artistic skill as well as giving expression to a regard for the dead adequate in some measure to the unsparing devotion paid to them in their earthy home."

Lest the reader get the impression that the Tiffany Studios catered only to the well to do, the brochure made it clear that they stood ready to meet any exigency. Tiffany may not have known about Captain Samuel Jones of Washington, New Hampshire, who, while moving a house in the early days of the Republic, caught his leg between the building and a fence and later lost it to a surgeon (without benefit of anesthetic). The leg was interred in the Washington Cemetery under a marker reading: "Captain Samuel Jones's leg which was amputated July 7, 1804." The rest of the Captain sleeps in far away Rhode Island.

As might be expected, Tiffany's clients were given every consideration. When a proposed memorial was on the scale of a mausoleum, plans were first translated into renderings and then into an elaborate model executed in great detail.

In 1914, after an exhaustive search for the best,

FIGURE 178 *Celtic crosses. C. 1898. Tiffany Glass and Decorating Company photograph (from a damaged photographic glass plate).*

FIGURE 179 *Baptismal font. Before 1900. Tiffany Glass and Decorating Company photograph (from a damaged glass plate).*

Tiffany purchased an entire granite quarry in Cohasset, Massachusetts. Before making the purchase he had tests made on samples by two Boston scientists. The results of these tests were published in detail in the brochure. Professor H. W. Hayward of the Massachusetts Institute of Technology, found the "maximum compression load" of Tiffany Granite to be 110,400 pounds or "equal to 26,037 pounds per square inch," and that it "broke explosively at maximum load, chipping off very slightly before this load."

Professor Charles H. Warren of Boston, Massachusetts, found that Tiffany Granite contained: "Quartz, gray to smoky; potash feldspar, generally of a pale pink or flesh color; a soda-lime feldspar, in part white or cream colored, in part a pale yellowish-green; chlorite with epidote forming small black or dark green specks scattered rather plentifully among the other mineral grains, with the exception of the black mineral, which forms smaller grains. The other constituents have a rather equal development as to size . . ." He found the specimens "agreeably free from the deleterious constituent pyrite (di-sulphide of iron), that a small portion was in a soluable condition, that its density was 2.72 compared with water at 4° centigrade, or about 2.66 at room temperature, that the rock behaved well under the action of heat being 'free of explosive effects,' and that as a result one could assume that the granite 'should withstand the usual processes of weathering and corrosion.'" He added that "its structure density and low porosity" would insure "high strength," and concluded that since its "texture, or pattern, and the color scheme were both characteristic and pleasing to a higher degree" and since it had both "durability and strength" it could be "heartily recommended for churchyard memorials . . ."

Tiffany was unspecific about the extent of his personal involvement in designing the memorials. No doubt the pattern was the same as that followed in other departments of the Tiffany Studios. His guidelines were very likely so firm and so precise that all reflected his standards; many surely evolved from a quick sketch on his drawing pad, while some he must have designed in detail.

Being a good businessman, however, he assembled a staff of artists capable of designing memorials in any style. That this was the case is indicated by the fact that some have the characteristics of his personal style, and some do not. Those in the crisp impersonal Classic Revival tra-

Michael Melford

Michael Melford

FIGURES 180, 181   *David Belasco Mausoleum, Brooklyn, N.Y. Tiffany Studios, c. 1913. Tiffany rough-hewn granite.*

dition such as the H. McK. Twombly Memorial in New York's Woodlawn Cemetery would not be his. Others less conventional, more romantic in approach, such as the Mary E. Wright Mausoleum in Bridgeport, Connecticut, have the rugged, stony Romanesque look he gave to many things. The same is true of Bradford Cogwell's granite monument in Albany, New York.

The Wade Memorial Chapel in Cleveland's Lake View Cemetery was designed by a Cleveland firm, Hubbell and Benes, but the interior was by the Tiffany Studios. Facing the congregation (its handsome pews would seat approximately fifty) is a leaded window, the "River of Life," which Tiffany exhibited at the Paris Exposition Universelle in 1900. The lectern of white Carrara marble sparkles with Favrile glass mosaic, as do six marble candlesticks rising between the chancel and the nave. While the Favrile glass mosaics are known to have been designed by Frederick S. Church, the simplicity and low-keyed richness of the project as a whole suggests Tiffany. The candlesticks and the lectern are reminiscent of those in his Columbian Exposition Chapel, which preceded it by five years.

A design for a mausoleum commissioned by Chester W. Chapin in 1914 (but possibly not built since it is not in the Springfield Cemetery for which it was destined) called for building blocks of Tiffany granite. Entrance was through a Romanesque portico complete with round arches, stocky columns, and Favrile glass mosaics. Two marble benches flanked a specially designed Tiffany bronze door. Inside were twelve catacombs of richly veined white marble, a Favrile glass window, and a Favrile glass mosaic ceiling. The style had a dash of Richardson's Trinity Church in Boston, and of the Tiffany house on Seventy-second Street in New York. It also reflected Tiffany's fascination with Romanesque buildings of the eleventh and twelfth centuries.

The Currier Mausoleum published in the Tiffany Studios brochure on mausoleums in 1914 (the location is not given) is a simple and elegant building with Ionic columns, a decorative iron grill, a pair of elaborate bronze doors, and a Favrile glass window. With the possible exception of the doors and the window, the design does not suggest Tiffany's hand.

Charles Hamilton Paine's grave in Boston's Forest Hills Cemetery is marked by an elaborate baroque sarcophagus in white marble which bears little relation to Tiffany's personal work. But the reproduction of St. Columbkille's Cross, Kells, Ireland, which marks the Stickney family graves in New York's Woodlawn Cemetery, and the monolith in the Arlington National Cemetery, Virginia, ornamented with a Celtic Cross, which marks the grave of Thomas Mayhew Woodruff, are rooted in Tiffany's love of the simple and elegant carvings by the Irish stonemasons who worked a thousand years ago.

Somewhere a family of Pooles is at rest in a handsome Egyptian mausoleum. (It is pictured in the Tiffany brochure on mausoleums, but no location is given.) The catacombs are in white Italian marble and the interior is decorated with Favrile glass mosaics. The leaded window is "Egyptian in treatment and coloring." The slanting walls, the pattern in the mosaic, the grillwork on the door, and the columns of the portico all reflect that stately tradition.

Possibly the most Tiffany of all is a mausoleum built for David Belasco that sits on a hilltop in Brooklyn (Figures 180 and 181). Even the original landscaping was the work of the Tiffany Studios. The Tiffany granite used in its construction carries the marks of massive sledgehammers. The columns on the portico look like boulders left by glaciers. The interior is soft, more elegant. The twelve catacombs of Italian marble are nicely adjusted to the rotunda shape of the building. A circular marble seat in the center was originally covered with cushions made of Tiffany velvet. A circle of especially woven Tiffany rugs covered that part of the mosaic floor that would be under the feet of those sitting on the seat. A Tiffany bronze lantern massive enough to hold its own in such awe-inspiring surroundings hangs from the Favrile glass mosaic ceiling. Light enters through a field of leaded-glass peonies in full bloom. For many years a homey wicker chair awaited those planning to spend an hour or so amidst all the beauty near those they loved.

The ways this mausoleum calls attention to the granite and the glass and the elegance of its detail are typical of Tiffany, as is its determination to defy time. Tiffany designed this mausoleum to last until the day of judgment, and it will unless some fool tears it down.

Other good examples of Tiffany monuments

are the Celtic cross marking the grave of E. A. Cummings in Forest Home, Chicago, Illinois; the Celtic cross for Mary Watson Borup in Sing Sing (now Ossining), New York; and the granite cross decorated with bronze marking Julia J. McClure's grave, in Albany, New York.

Americans of the period did not bother to analyze their fascination with cemeteries, which was probably just as well. They saw their elaborate memorials only as symbols of love and respect. Even a hint that the extravaganzas could also have been status symbols might have shocked and hurt. Regardless of why they came into being, the cemeteries of the Belle Époque offered personal involvement in art and its inevitable satisfaction to many. They also kept the Tiffany Studios in the black during the later years.

But that, of course, is not the whole story. Richardson, Sullivan, White, and other American greats designed mausoleums. But Tiffany not only designed them—he built his. And his Celtic crosses, ledger stones, mausoleums, and other memorials, were often islands of good taste in a sea of the second rate, and some are gems of American art. In his brochure, *Mausoleums*,[2] he states: "In the United States the great development in cemetery memorials along artistic lines may be considered as having had its inception when the department of out-of-door memorials became a branch of the Tiffany Studios," and he was right. His memorials opened many eyes to beauty.

The Tiffany mausoleums may serve in another way. The Parthenon was shattered by gun powder, but we find undamaged art in Greek tombs. The Sphinx lost its nose to vandals, and the pyramids at Gizeh were "skinned" for the stone to build Cairo. What art we have from ancient Egypt was discovered in tombs. Man destroys far more art than time. Most of Tiffany's work will eventually go the way of the Bella apartment, the Madison Square Theater curtain, the Seventy-second Street house, the Columbian Exposition Chapel, the White House screen, and Laurelton Hall. And eventually all that is left may be that which has been guarded by the dead.

NOTES

[1] A favorite was "Remember me as you pass by, as you are now, so once was I, as I am now, so you must be; prepare for death and follow me."

[2] Tiffany Studios, 1914.

Chapter 11

LAMPS

Now he has turned toward stained glass, and again to mosaic, or to pottery, or to enamels, or else to tapestries and rugs, or at another time to jewelry. He has made special studies of decoration and lighting, and though for many years interested in floriculture, he has given much attention to landscape architecture and house building.

CHARLES DEKAY

Why *The Art Work of Louis C. Tiffany* refers to Tiffany's interest in lighting but does not mention his lamps is one secret he may have taken to the grave. There may be at least a partial explanation, however. When all things are considered, his lamps were an inevitable development in his career. He was fascinated with light and with all kinds of illumination. He loved color for itself. He loved glass for itself. Lamps were one art form that offered an opportunity to satisfy all three interests. He took them very seriously.

The blown-glass lampshades developed from the blown vases and bowls. The leaded shades very likely stemmed from the exhibit at the Columbian Exposition. The leaded windows glowed day and night, thanks to back lighting by Edison's incandescent bulbs. (A sheet of diffusing glass prevented hot spots.) The cover on the baptismal font was a dome made of a thousand or more pieces of colored Favrile glass leaded with cames, but was otherwise constructed in the manner later used in leaded shades. The electro-

lier was made of green turtlebacks lighted from behind with incandescent bulbs. A leaded shade is, in a way, a combination of all three.

Tiffany had made gas light fixtures for the White House in 1882, and for the Havemeyers and other clients in the decade that followed. He and Thomas Edison installed clustered globes in the Lyceum Theater in 1885. His blown-glass lamps were on the market shortly after the Columbian Exposition. He was quick to see the electric light bulb as an important new tool for the artist, and from the very start it became an integral part of his own plans.

Leaded shades appeared shortly before 1899. One of the earliest was the "Nautilus" (Figure 182) for which he filed patent claim No. 30,665, on May 2, 1899. It appeared in several forms; one had a genuine nautilus-shell shade, one a leaded-glass shade, and one a base designed by the sculptor, Louis A. Gudebrod. The "Dragonfly" after a design by Clara Driscoll, one of the most accomplished artists in Tiffany's employ, was awarded

FIGURE 182 *"Nautilus" lamp. 1899–1902. Bronze and Favrile glass. Base stamped, "Tiffany Studios/New York"/Tiffany Glass and Decorating Company monogram/"21345." Shade unsigned. Height 13½".*

FIGURE 183   *"Dragonfly" lamp. This example after 1902. Doré bronze and Favrile glass. Base stamped,* *"262/Tiffany Studios New York." Shade stamped, "Tiffany Studios New York 1495." Height 27". Diameter of* *shade 20".*

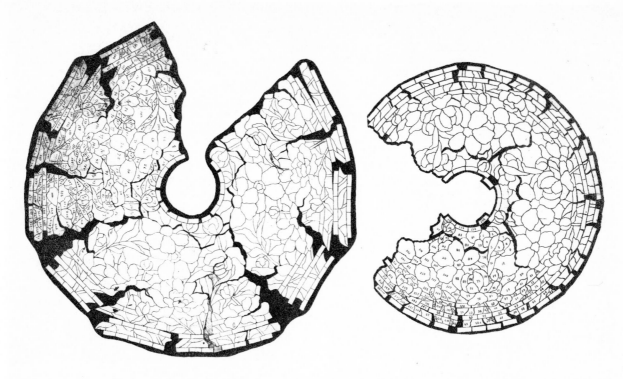

FIGURE 184 *Working design for a "Peony" leaded lamp.*

FIGURE 185 *"Peony" lamp. Given by Tiffany to his son Charles. After 1902. Bronze and Favrile glass. Base stamped, "Tiffany Studios/New York 6006." Shade stamped on plate, "Tiffany Studios/New York." Height 32". Diameter of shade 22".*

a prize at the Paris International Exposition in 1900.

The "Light Fountain," designed for the Buffalo Pan-American Exposition in 1901, in which water was simulated with colored lights, must have been a landmark in electric light bulb art. By 1915 the number of patterns of leaded shades ran into the hundreds. The *Tiffany Blue Book* (a catalogue of all things sold at Tiffany and Company) for that year mentions "Favrile glass candle lamps, globes for candle and electric fixtures; lamp screens, desk lamps and hanging shades."[1]

Obviously the shades were made on an assembly line basis, and obviously Tiffany viewed the matter with sensible satisfaction because a lot of

FIGURE 186   *Left: "Wisteria" lamp. C. 1902. Bronze and Favrile Glass. Base stamped, "Tiffany Studios/New York/27770"/monogram of Tiffany Glass and Decorating Company; and incised "2076." Shade stamped, "Tiffany Studios/New York." Height 27". Diameter of shade 18". Right: Miniature "Wisteria" lamp. 1902–18. Bronze and Favrile glass. Base stamped, "Tiffany Studios/New York/7805." Shade stamped, "Tiffany Studios/New York." Height 16¾". Diameter of shade 10½".*

FIGURE 187   *"Spider Web" lamp. C. 1900. Leaded Favrile glass shade. Bronze base with glass mosaic. Tiffany Studios. Unsigned. (Unlit.) Height 30". Diameter of shade 20½".*

FIGURE 188 *"Spider Web" lamp, lighted.*

green eyes and blue wings. "Wisteria" lamps vary from deep blue to pale to silvery blues. The leaded shades are, in reality, diminutive, useful, portable, relatively inexpensive, leaded windows, back-lighted to look lovely anytime and especially at night.

Some lamps are known to have been designed by Tiffany himself. A design in the Metropolitan Museum of Art indicates that Tiffany designed a special-order lamp for a Miss Perkins. The overwhelming electrolier in the Columbian Exposition Chapel, so unlike anything else before or since, has Tiffany's personality built into every unusual part of it (Figure 136). Tiffany made it clear that it was his design. (He also made it equally clear that the sanctuary fixture in the Columbian Chapel was designed by J. A. Holzer and that the "Dragonfly" lamp was designed by Clara Driscoll.) The living room lamps at Laurelton Hall (Figure 116) with their large turtlebacks which were iridescent in reflected light and emerald-green in transmitted light, are obviously derived from the Columbian Exposition electrolier. The inverted dome over the center dining table in Laurelton Hall (Figure 117) with its silvery color scheme, silvered copper-foil leading, and intricate design identical with that in the rug beneath surely has his look.

Some table lamps have the marks of Tiffany's personal style. His fascination with spider webs is reflected in the massive "Spider Web" lamp (Figures 187 and 188) and in the "Spider" lamp (Figure 189). (The famous "Wisteria" lamp is a special case and is discussed in some detail in Chapter 13.

As is the case with windows and blown glass, *all* Tiffany lamps reveal his guiding hand. In spite of their diversity, a certain common look runs through all. Compared to the unornamented functionalism of today, to many they seem overly rich. When, however, his lamps are compared with the decorative arts of their time, the relative quiet in their shapes and color harmonies is apparent. Tiffany extolled simplicity, and within the context of the prevailing taste of the Belle Epoque, he achieved it.

Then, too, both bases and shades suggest Tiffany's taste. Shades will often contain as many as a thousand pieces of glass, and yet each piece has a handsome, fluid character of its own. The lamps' designs are so sophisticated that while they can be copied, they are not easily imitated.

beauty was going into American homes and a lot of sales were being entered on his books.

Construction methods for leaded lampshades were similar to those for leaded windows. A cartoon in color was followed by a cut line which served as a pattern for the leads as well as to give the shape (template) for each piece of glass (Figure 184). The templates for the lamps, however, were cut from thin sheets of copper because they were to be used hundreds, perhaps thousands, of times.

The leading (the copper-foil technique to which Tiffany brochures refer as "coppering") was done by women who were free to select the general color scheme, with the fortunate result that many lamps have a character of their own. One "Dragonfly" lamp, for example, may have red eyes and iridescent wings. Another may have

FIGURE 189   *"Spider" lamp. After 1902. Doré bronze and Favrile glass. Base stamped, "Tiffany Studios/New York/337." Shade stamped, "Tiffany Studios, New York, 1424." Height 18". Diameter of shade 16".*

Theodore Flagg

FIGURE 190   *"Spider" lamp. Detail of shade and finial cap.*

Theodore Flagg

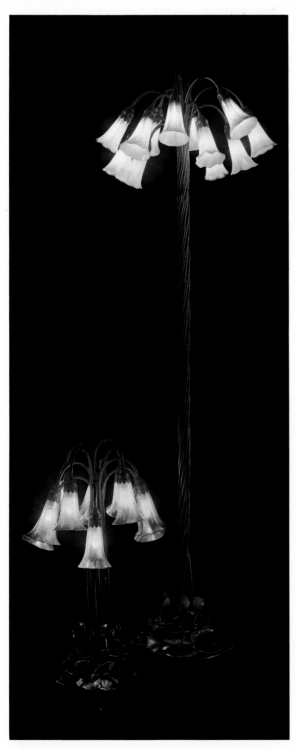

FIGURE 191   *Left: Ten branch "Lily" lamp. After
1902. Bronze and Favrile glass. Base stamped,
"Tiffany Studios/New York/381." Shades engraved,
"L.C.T." Height 21". Right: Twelve-branch "Lily"
floor lamp. After 1902. Bronze and Favrile glass.
Base stamped, "Tiffany Studios/New York/685."
Shades engraved, "L.C.T." Height 55".*

FIGURE 192   *Bamboo floor lamp. After 1902.
Bronze and Favrile glass. Base stamped, "Tiffany
Studios/New York/10923." Shade stamped,
"Tiffany Studios, New York." Height 63".*

FIGURE 193 *Student lamp. After 1902. Bronze and Favrile glass. Base stamped, "Tiffany Studios/ New York/416/S207." Shade engraved on fitter rim, "L.C.T." Height 15½". Diameter of shade 7".*

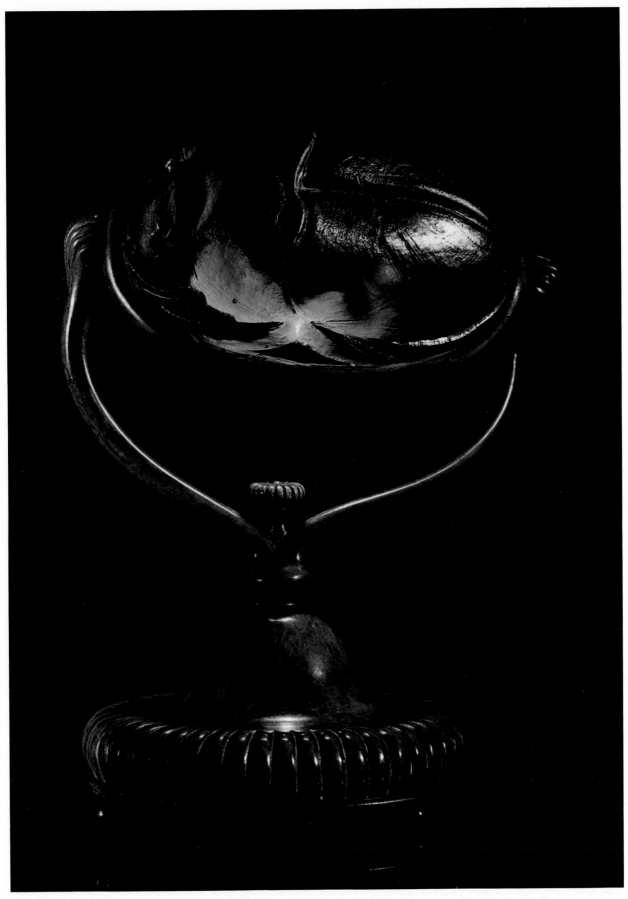

FIGURE 194 *"Scarab" lamp. 1900—2. Bronze and Favrile glass. Base stamped, "269/Tiffany Studios/ New York"/monogram of Tiffany Glass and Decorating Company. Shade unsigned. Height 8½".*

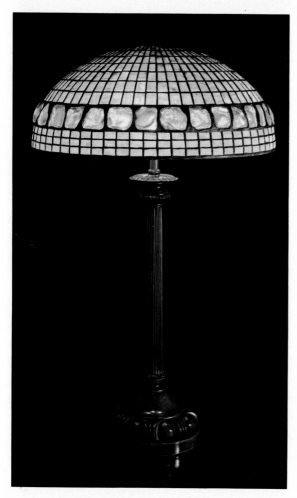

FIGURE 195 *Table lamp. Geometric design with band of turtlebacks. 1900–20. Base unsigned. Shade stamped, "Tiffany Studios/New York." Height 37½". Diameter of shade 20½".*

The use of dandelions, black-eyed susans, Queen Anne's lace, and bamboo as motifs is another factor. They are typical of Tiffany's love of calling attention to forms of beauty many consider commonplace. They also reflect the farmer in him, that side which loved the earth and was fascinated with what can be brought from it.

The way the lamps changed in style parallels a similar change in his paintings and windows. In the electrolier from the chapel and in the cover for the baptismal font, the interest is in the material, the glass itself. The electrolier was basically of emerald-green glass suspended in a framework of gilded pipes and lighted by incandescent bulbs. The cover to the baptismal font is a leaded-glass dome. The design of each is rooted in the material and in the technique involved. After these came shades patterned on individual objects and flowers such as the nautilus, the dragonfly, and the wisteria blossoms. The nautilus is presented as an object—not in the sea, not on a beach, not surrounded by atmosphere. The dragonflies are placed *on* the lamps as though they were mounted in an exhibit. They are not darting here and there on a summer day. The same is true of the "Wisteria" lamp. The base is the vine, the shade is the blossom. There are no implications of light and shade or atmosphere.

The last phase came with roses, Oriental poppies, and other flowers, treated not as isolated entities, but as growing in a garden, lighted by the sun, and reflecting colored rays back through the air. The hand of Tiffany the painter is obvious. The shades are, as were many later windows, impressionist pictures in glass.

So, even though Tiffany did not design all the lampshades himself, they reflect his thinking. Why, then, did he ignore them in *The Art Work?* The answer may lie in the fact that to a certain extent he always thought as a painter, but a painter who had never learned to step outside himself and look back. Painters rarely make copies of their pictures: versions, yes; replicas, no. Gilbert Stuart, with his copies of his famous portrait of George Washington, was one exception, but the exceptions are few. Tiffany's workers were free to vary the color schemes, but the lamps were still essentially replicas. Even though Tiffany disliked the term "fine art," and believed no art form was "finer" than any other, without realizing it, he may have had the painter's prejudice against copies, and this was not logical for an industrial designer.

Tiffany believed in using new business techniques to make beauty a more common experience in the day-to-day life of Americans. But when it came to deciding what aspect of his own art he wanted covered in his own book, he had to draw the line somewhere, and he drew it this side of the lamps.

FIGURE 196 *"Arabian" lamp. 1900–10. Favrile glass. Base engraved, "L. C. Tiffany-Favrile" (script). Shade engraved, "L.C.T. Favrile" (script). Height 14".*

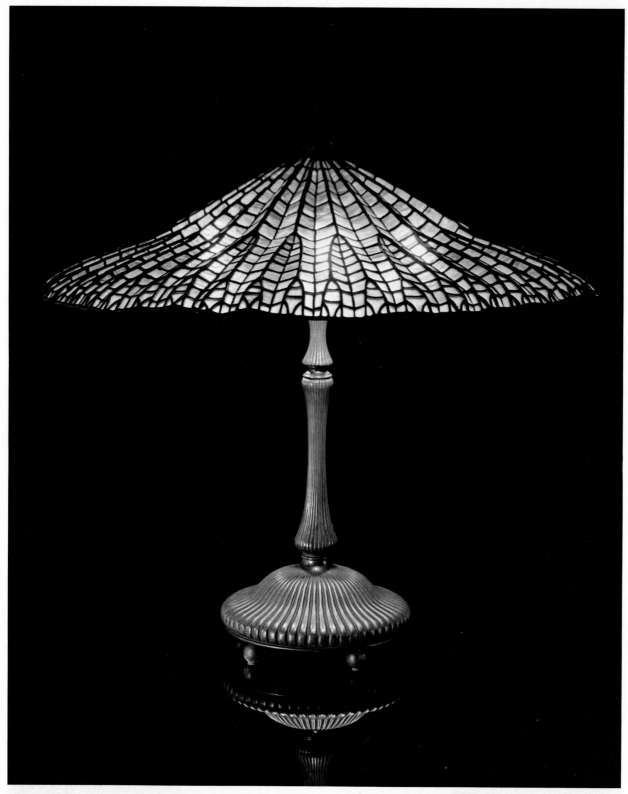

FIGURE 197   *"Lotus Leaf" lamp. Bronze and Favrile glass. 1898–1902. Base stamped, "Tiffany Studios/New York"/monogram of Tiffany Glass and Decorating Company "D795 25/66." Shade stamped, "Tiffany Studios/New York." Height 24½". Diameter of shade 16".*

FIGURE 198   *"Laburnum" lamp. After 1902. Bronze and Favrile glass. Base stamped, "Tiffany Studios/New York/ 529." Shade stamped, "Tiffany Studios, N.Y. 1539." Height 32". Diameter of shade 20½".*

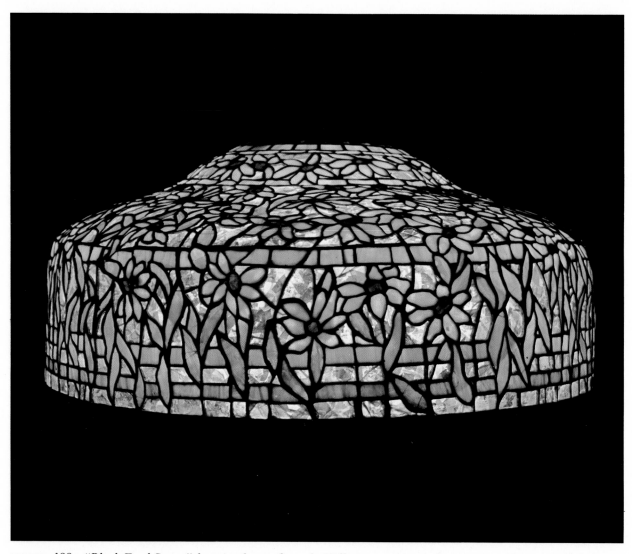

FIGURE 199   *"Black-Eyed Susan" hanging lamp, from the Tiffany mansion on Seventy-second Street. 1902–20.*
Favrile glass. Stamped, "Tiffany Studios, New York." Diameter 25".

FIGURE 200 *"Dogwood" hanging lamp. After 1902. Bronze and Favrile glass. Stamped, "Tiffany Studios, New York." Diameter 28".*

was not offered for sale until a year later. But a vase lent to the Metropolitan Museum by the Tiffany Foundation in 1925 was assigned to the year "1898" in a letter of transmittal from Tiffany himself. Another date may be even more significant: In 1879, Tiffany taught (for a brief time) a class in unglazed pottery at the New York Society of Decorative Arts. This would raise the probability of work decades before any one has ever suggested. What were the early pieces like? Where are they?

If there is uncertainty about the timing and the nature of the early pieces, there is little about the later ones. Nearly all are "high fired" china, meaning white and cream colored clay brought to "maturity" (hardened in a kiln heated to a temperature close to 2,366° F.). They include no porcelain, which required about 2,453° F., and very little stoneware (heated to about 2,291° F.). Neither is there any reason to believe Tiffany made any earthenware (heated to somewhere between 1,733° F., and 2,120° F.), but it is risky to rule out anything where he is concerned.

Earthenware is made from clay as it comes out of the ground, is red-brown in color (terra cotta) and is not vitreous (glassy) enough to hold liquids. China, including Tiffany's, is made of a carefully prepared mixture of clays such as kaolin (the finest white clay), ball clay (a good white clay), feldspar (a mineral found in igneous rock), flint (beach pebbles heated and then reduced to a fine white powder), and ground glass (added to lower the maturing point).

Glazes are an important part of pottery since they may be a determining factor in color and in some cases, in the surface texture. Glazes can be of many kinds from a thin coat of salt to a thin coat of glass melted directly on the surface. They serve not only to make a pot attractive, but in the case of earthenware, they make it watertight. Glazes begin as a mixture of such ingredients as clay, alumina (to give sufficient viscosity to keep it from running off the ware), metallic oxides (the same as those used to color glass), and flux such as soda, lead oxide, potash, and feldspar. They can be applied to green (unfired) ware or to bisque (fired). The pot can be dipped in the glaze, the glaze can be poured over the pot, or it can be applied with a brush. The pot is then heated in a kiln to a temperature sufficient to turn the mixed ingredients into glass (a glaze). Glazes must contain sufficient flux to make cer-

FIGURE 201 "Calla Lily" vase. C. 1906. Pottery. Signed, "LCT" monogram (incised). Height 11¼".

FIGURE 202   *"Fern Tendril" vase. C. 1906. Pottery. Signed, "LCT" monogram (incised). Height 10½".*

Theodore Flagg

FIGURE 203 *Vase. C. 1910. Pottery. Signed, "LCT" monogram (incised). Height 15".*

FIGURE 204 *Vase. C. 1910. Pottery. Signed, "127 A-Coll. L. C. Tiffany-Favrile Pottery" (engraved script). Height 4".*

Theodore Flagg

tain they vitrify at a temperature lower than that of the melting point of the pot. In too much heat, the pot itself will turn into glass.

The color of a piece of pottery depends not only on the metallic oxides in the glaze, but on such other things as the color of the clay, how the glaze is applied, the temperature of the kiln, the rate of firing, and the amount of oxygen in the atmosphere of the kiln. Under certain conditions, copper oxide turns a glaze black. The same oxide in a lead glaze produces an apple- or grass-green. In an alkaline glaze, fired at a low temperature, it will produce turquoise-blue. If the glaze is highly alkaline and contains boric and tin oxides, and if the kiln atmosphere is low in oxygen, and if the body of the clay is relatively free of iron, copper oxide will produce a rich red.

Iron oxide gives various effects depending on many factors. In a lead glaze, it produces a dark red. In large amounts, it can make a goldstone or "aventurine" (shot through with gold flecks). When the oxygen in the atmosphere of the kiln is limited, the iron oxide will give up its oxygen and the result is a green or a blue-gray celadon.

Much Tiffany pottery was left in the bisque state, i.e., fired but not glazed. The bisque pots have a light matte finish easily soiled by handling. The plan may have been to glaze the pieces to order. The interior of most bisque pieces was glazed a blue-green or a brown. Many glazes are an ivory, which runs occasionally into tans and in places a dark brown. Pale greens, ivory-whites and matte greens and blues are fairly common. A limited number have bubbly rough textured surfaces (Figure 203) glazed in two or three shades of blues, greens, creams, browns, or tans. Some were finished with a gold glaze (Figure 206). These were covered first with an opaque glaze fused at a high temperature then removed to a muffle and cooled to 1,103° F. Pure gold in powdered form mixed with a clear glaze was then introduced to the muffle. The hot pot picked the gold from the air and fused it to its surface.

Which colors came first is one of the questions for which the answers vary. Clara Ruge in *The International Studio* for March 1906, in an article "American Ceramics," states, "The color was at first almost exclusively a deep ivory, sometimes shading into brownish effects. Of late, greenish tints have been effectively employed."

FIGURE 205 *Four vases. 1900–10. Left: Favrile bronze pottery. Signed, "LCT" monogram (incised) "BP346/L.C. Tiffany-Favrile Bronze Pottery" (engraved script). Height 16½″. Center left: Favrile pottery. Signed, "LCT" monogram and either an "L" or "7" (incised) "P825" (engraved). Height 5¼″. Center right: Favrile bronze pottery. Signed, "LCT" monogram "6262" and either an "L" or "7" (incised) "L. C. Tiffany-Favrile Bronze Pottery" (engraved script) "BP279" (engraved). Height 13″. Right: Favrile pottery. Signed, "LCT" monogram and either an "L" or "7" (incised). Height 12½″.*

Theodore Flagg

FIGURE 206 *Vase, mushroom motif. C. 1910. Favrile pottery, gold plated. Signed, "L. C. Tiffany-Favrile/Bronze Pottery" (engraved script) "BP511" (engraved) "LCT" monogram (incised). Height 2".*

Tiffany's is what is called "art pottery," i.e., vessels good to look at whether they are useful or not. Much art pottery of the time was decorated with pictures painted by hand. This was not the case with Tiffany's. Favrile pottery was never covered with pictures. Its beauty was due to the colors in its glazes and to its shape.

Tiffany pottery progressed through the same changes of style as those of his windows and art glass. The shapes of some evolved from the fact that hands can do certain things with soft clay. The shapes of others were suggested by fern tendrils, leaves, or flowers (Figure 202). Some have strange beasts (the kind used centuries ago in the Middle East) marching around them (Figure 210). Later pieces are modeled into shapes that suggest a little bit of the world, perhaps a cluster of flowers growing in a garden, or weeds with all their tangled charm. In these the glazes and the forms are a little fuzzy around the edges so that the general effect is one of light rays coming through the air. One late bowl is encircled by fish swimming in a fast stream (Figure 211).

Most of Tiffany's pottery has the sturdy simplicity found in his personal work in all fields

(Figure 204). His love of the modest and at the same time the lovely forms in nature is shown in his use of weeds, cattails, pussy-willows, and grasses (Figure 214).

Tiffany's indifference to rules and to boundaries in the arts also turns up in the pottery, as one might expect. After 1910 he began to cover pieces with a sleeve of metal (Figure 205) and to electroplate others in bronze, gold, or silver.

Many pieces were from a mold. Pots can be "thrown" on a potter's wheel or built by hand. In throwing a pot, the clay is placed on a disc that spins. The centrifugal force throws the clay outward, the potter's hands force the clay inward to give it shape. Ornament, if desired, is then added by hand and perhaps finished with tools. A plaster cast can be made of the finished original, and duplicates made from this cast. Tiffany's were then carefully finished off by hand.

Those built by hand are made from coils of clay in a way similar to that used by sculptors. These, too, were reproduced by using casts. If this sounds like mass production, it was. Tiffany never wavered from his dream of placing more good art in the American home, and unlike William Morris, the English prophet of the arts and crafts movement, Tiffany believed in using modern business techniques. His pots, priced from $5.00 up, were less expensive than his vases. It should be remembered, however, that the original was handmade; that each cast from a mold was carefully and meticulously carved, trimmed, and finished by hand; that each could have its own glaze; that glazes are complicated and tricky; that many of the effects in Tiffany's glazes are as sophisticated as those in his Favrile glass; and that each finished piece is therefore unique.

Most Favrile pottery was signed with the initials "LCT" incised in the green ware in a conjoined monogram. Some pieces were signed in script "L. C. Tiffany Pottery." The latter was often engraved on the pot after it had been fired. Some bear initials as well, apparently the glazier's. Occasionally, there is a 4-digit Arabic number, and sometimes a "7" which might also be an "L." Bronze pottery was signed in several ways, one being "L. C. Tiffany-Favrile. Bronze Pottery." One example has "B. P. 270" on a lower line.

Two pieces of iridescent pottery may be of special interest. One, a free-form vase with an iridescent blue glaze (Figure 216), was sold as glass, and for only $40, in 1958. The second (Figure

FIGURE 207 *Two vases. 1900-10. Favrile pottery. Left: Lustered "artichoke" vase. Signed, "LCT" monogram and either "7" or "L" (incised). Height 5". Right: Signed, "LCT" monogram (incised). Height 3¾".*

217), a pitcher with a rich iridescent blue glaze, hollow handle, and hollow fruit ornament, was sold in 1955 for only $110. Both were difficult to make. The iridescent glaze on the latter has deep blue tones with rich magenta highlights. Its quality is not often seen in glazes.

The marks on these pieces are suspect, however. The vase is signed with three acid etched initials, "LCT" and the Arabic numerals "2927," followed by the Roman numeral VII, incised before firing. The pitcher has three initials (in script), which suggest, at least, LCT incised in the clay along with the Arabic numerals "7602" followed by "19."

If they were made seventy or eighty years ago by some rascal who forged Tiffany's initials, his ineptness in business matched his skill in pottery, because Tiffany's pottery was one venture that did not succeed. His workmen put pieces out of sight to spare him the realization of how few had sold. To have made these two pieces twenty years ago and sold them at such modest prices would have been equally unrewarding. The style is not similar to what is known as Tiffany's, but the question does arise—are they two of the early pieces in lusterware made before Tiffany had settled either on a style or a signature? Or are they

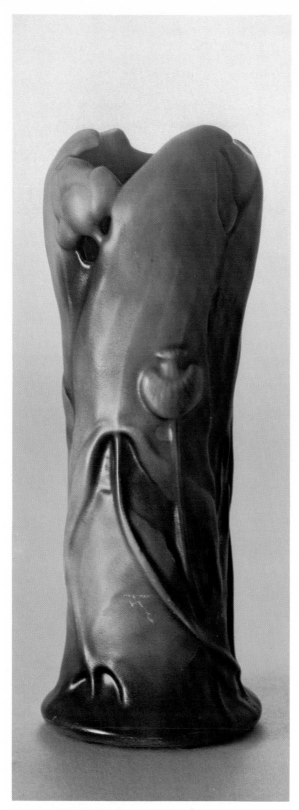

FIGURE 208 *"Water Lily" vase. 1900-10. Favrile pottery. Signed, "LCT" monogram (incised) "L.C. Tiffany-Favrile Pottery" (engraved). Height 8½".*

FIGURE 209 *"Peapod" vase. C. 1914. Favrile pottery. Signed, "LCT" monogram (incised). Height 9".*

Theodore Flagg

FIGURE 210 *Vase with lion motif. 1910-15. Favrile pottery. Signed, "LCT" monogram (incised). Height 6⅜".*

FIGURE 211 *Three bowls with swimming fish motif. C. 1910. Favrile pottery. Left: Bisque with glazed interior. Signed, "LCT" monogram and either "7" or "L" (incised). Height 4½". Center: Bronze pottery. Signed, "L.C. Tiffany-Favrile Bronze Pottery" (engraved script) "B.P.392" (engraved) "47" (incised). Height 4½". Right: Glazed. Signed, "LCT" monogram (incised). Height 4½".*

merely two interesting pieces with fake signatures?

A third piece is equally fascinating (Figure 213). It has two glazes. One, a dark blue-black, was permitted to run down over the other, a golden lemon-yellow. This vase is not only lustered, it is signed with the conjoined "LCT" monogram and with "A-COLL," which indicates it was part of Tiffany's personal collection. There is no question as to its authenticity, and it could be one of the hitherto unknown first pieces.

Tiffany did not blow all the glass himself. He did not design all the windows or all the mosaics or metalwares. But with the pottery, it might be different. To have made the original pots would have involved no intense heat, no crews, and no great amount of time. And since the number of pieces is limited, one person, working in a com-fortable studio, could have made them all. Then there is a significant statement in *The Art Work of Louis C. Tiffany:* "Glazes on pottery claimed much of his time during certain years."

Wilhelm Jenkins, for five years chief muffler (until 1910) in the Pottery Division of the Tiffany Furnaces, who is quoted at length in *Glass-Bronzes-Lamps* by Robert Koch, indicated that Tiffany was involved personally with his pots. According to Jenkins, Tiffany himself threw the first pieces on the wheel, made the master pots for those he reproduced from molds, and incised the conjoined monogram "LCT" on the bottoms. Jenkins is also quoted as describing Tiffany as "a nice man, but a hard man to work for . . . as one who had to have things exact," and, "a hard man to know." Jenkins sounds like a man who knew what he was talking about.

FIGURE 212 *Vase. 1900-10. Favrile pottery. Signed, "LCT" monogram (incised) "82A-Coll. L. C. Tiffany-Favrile Pottery" (engraved). Height 16".*

FIGURE 213   *Vase. C. 1906. Favrile pottery. Signed, "84 A-Coll. L. C. Tiffany Favrile/Pottery" (engraved) "LCT" monogram and "7" (incised). Height 14¾".*

Theodore Flagg

FIGURE 214 *"Milkweed" vase. C. 1906. Favrile pottery. Signed, "LCT" monogram (incised) "AG" with over-painting and "P" (incised). Height 10".*

FIGURE 215 *Goblet. 1900–10. Favrile pottery. Signed, "LCT" monogram (incised) "L. C. Tiffany-Favrile P1241 Pottery" (engraved script). Height 9¼".*

Theodore Flagg

FIGURE 216   *"Art Nouveau" vase. 1910-20.*
Iridescent pottery. Signed, uncharacteristic "LCT
2927" (acid etched) "VII" (incised before firing).
The style is European. Height 9".

FIGURE 217   *Pitcher with cherry motif. C. 1900.*
Iridescent pottery. Signed, three unclear initials
which suggest "LCT" (incised before firing) "7602"/
"19" (impressed). Height 7¾".

NOTES

1 *Keramic Studio*, Vol. III, No. 2, June 1901: "At
present there is a choice exhibition at the Tiffany Studios of artistic pottery from the famous French potters
Delaherche, Dalpayrat, Jeannency, Hoentschel, Chaplet
and Doat . . . but we urgently advise every one to see
this collection, for these potters have never exhibited
in this country before (excepting Delaherche) . . .
Every student should see the work at these studios . . .
not only to study form and glazes from the pottery,
but the wonderful color effects in the glass."

2 *Keramic Studio*, Vol. IV, No. 2, June 1902: "French
Pottery": "The lustres of different colors which Clem-
ent Massier has so cleverly used, and he has many
imitators, are, I think, obtained from gold, Massier's
lustres are at any rate. However, copper mixed with
the glaze as protoxide and heated in a sufficiently
reducing atmosphere, gives a great variety of colors
and iridescent effects of every shade. I sent a sample
of red lustre of copper to Mr. Volkmar last year, and
you mentioned it in *Keramic Studio* but took it for
red of copper (letter from Dr. Chaussegros to editor)."

FIGURE 218 *Vase. C. 1910. Favrile bronze pottery. Signed, "L. C. Tiffany-Favrile Bronze Pottery/B.P. 325/40A-Coll." (engraved) "LCT" monogram (incised). Height 7¼".*

Chapter 13

BUTTONS, BLOTTERS, ET CETERA, ET CETERA, WITH STYLE

For beauty in the home has little or nothing to do with the amount of money spent; extravagance does not produce beauty; and many of our richest people, like some of our poor people, have not yet come to see the value of good taste.

In fact, money is frequently an absolute bar to good taste, for it leads to show and over-elaboration.

LOUIS C. TIFFANY, 1910

Few artists who have made a success in the "fine arts," even those swayed by the arts and crafts, have deigned to make such things as blotters, pin trays, and ordinary buttons. But then Louis Tiffany was not the usual artist. Such things sold, of course, but cash flow alone would not account for his interest in them.

One reason for the wide variety of Tiffany productions was the steady stream of new ideas flowing through his mind. Another was his conviction that the world *needs* art. His desire to add beauty to the daily life of America was real. Like William Morris, Tiffany was looking for more than ways to parade his talents before an admiring audience. He wanted a better world; one with more people who knew what makes life worth

the trouble. He believed in good industrial design. He was convinced useful articles made with care and taste could help the world with its values and he may not have been entirely wrong.

Take, for one example, the human dynamo, the man on the make whose interest is money, who knows intuitively when to buy, when to sell, when to remain loyal, and when to double-cross. This kind of man might curse incompetents, fire fools, grind his teeth at scatterbrained secretaries, hate the world and himself for years, and then one day notice a blotter on his desk, one made with care, one that says some things are better than others, that quality does exist. The experience might make him a little curious about what life is for, or about what, if anything, has real

---

meaning. Should that lead to any objectivity in the way he sees himself, life might assume a new dimension, and eventually that string of factories along that river which is no longer full of fish might not look so good. In time, he might find his associates and even himself a little more tolerable.

Then there is the matron whose nerves are frazzled by chefs who cannot cook, or butlers who pinch maids, or other equally weighty problems. After years of wringing her hands in desperation, she might notice the Tiffany pin tray on her dresser, *really* notice it: how the lines have the freedom of vines and the order of art, how it repeats a handsome shape to call it to one's attention, the way its parts relate in terms of scale and shape and size, and how it contrasts a bit of sea shell with the rich yellow of gold, to make them both more lovely. She might even get the complete message it contains; the implication that life is, or can be good. She might even sense the artist's desire to make life better for someone. This might arouse her curiosity about what she is making of herself. After a while chefs bumbling in the kitchen and butlers capering in the pantry might seem less important—who knows?

And those bustling millions who probably never should go anywhere but who, because it makes them feel important, dash pointlessly all over the place, need not necessarily be left to their scrambled fate. A few, as they dash past, *might* notice a good ash stand in the hall, and how the bowl not only looks attractive but holds cigar butts properly. Some might even develop an interest in the connection between good workmanship and beauty, and in what makes useful things attractive. This might generate an interest in art in general and possibly a visit to a museum. At first, of course, they would have to dash in and right out again because of a "tight schedule," but eventually a few might sit down for a few minutes, and think about the reason for life and beauty, and why all the rush.

We cannot expect too much from blotters, pin trays, and ash stands, but civilizing this world is never going to be easy, and Tiffany was convinced every little bit of beauty helps.

In *The Art Work of Louis C. Tiffany*[1] deKay discussed Tiffany's thoughts on this matter:

"His taste in color has found expression in a thousand articles of applied art; these occupying

FIGURE 219 *Ornamental plaque. Designed by Louis C. Tiffany, possibly in the 1890s. Plaster painted, gilded, and set with Favrile glass. Height 32½".*

prominent places in households, have exercised a happy influence on the taste of citizens. It is obvious that such influences exist and make themselves felt; but that is seldom thought of. Yet the fact that things of daily use like lamps, flower-vases, and toilet articles reach a wider public than do paintings and sculpture makes the 'decorative' arts more important to a nation than the 'fine' arts. Hence the value to a community of artists who devote their talent to making things of use beautiful. These are the educators of the people in the truest sense, not as school masters laying down the law, but as masters of art appealing to the emotions and the senses and rousing enthusiasm for beauty in one's environment."

Those words are like the pieces of glass in Tiffany's leaded windows. They may have been put together by someone else, but they say what Tiffany thought. The "thousand articles of applied art" Tiffany made to "exert a happy influence on the taste of citizens" included (in addition to his glass) wallpaper, metalwork, fabrics, rugs, furniture, buttons, and books. Many were designed by artists on his staff, and some were designed by Tiffany himself.

A series of plaster plaques (Figure 219) that turned up in the ruins of Laurelton Hall are one more example of Tiffany's interest in combining mediums in new ways. Made apparently to be screwed to a wall and roughly 3′×2′ in size, they bear floral patterns in low relief which are painted, gilded, and livened up with inserts of Favrile glass, some of which is backed with foil. The hemispheres and chipped jewels used in the early windows also appear in the plaques.

One of Tiffany's ventures in designing books was *On the Road to Slumberland, or My Boy and I* by Mary D. Brine, published by Mr. George W. Harlan in New York in 1881. It is a fragile and lovely early example of Art Nouveau. This book, illustrated by drawings bearing a strong resemblance to early drawings by Tiffany, was praised in lavish terms by the Liverpool *Mail*:

"As an instance of the gratifying recognition our art productions are receiving in England, we submit the following from the Liverpool Mail:

"The interest manifested in England in American wood-engravings prompts us to give absolutely the first news given to anybody of what promised to be something notable in that department. Mr. Geo. W. Harlan, a young publisher in New York, has in preparation for the holidays a book, the text of which is a series of juvenile songs and poems by Mrs. Mary D. Brine. The piece is called, "On the Road to Slumberland"; but that is a matter of small moment. The important thing is that upon its art side the book is to be unique and notable.

"Louis Tiffany, the artist, whose attention has recently been given to decorative work—glorified windows and ideal dining rooms, for decorating which he receives single cheques for fifty thousand dollars—has undertaken to design the book and to make it a homogeneous artistic whole. He has chosen the paper, selected the leather for the binding, and even the silk with which it is to be

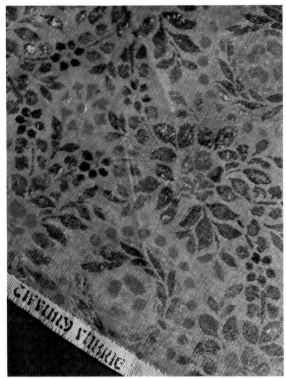

FIGURE 220 *Tiffany fabric. 1900–10. Cotton velvet with stenciled design. Signed, "Tiffany Fabric" on selvage.*

stitched. He has designed the die that is to be burned into the cover, and has drawn all the pages, each of which is to be engraved throughout, including the letterpress. It has been our good fortune to inspect his cartoons, and we think we risk nothing saying that the book will be accepted on both sides of the ocean as the most noteworthy piece of art in book form that the year has produced.

"It is Tiffany's idea to make the shape, size, and color of the pages so harmonize with the quaint lettering of the text and with the design in which the text is imbedded that the whole shall be a carrying out of a single artistic purpose. He has given as careful thought to this task as to

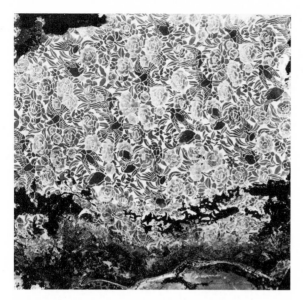

FIGURE 221   *Fabric made for the Tiffany Studios before 1910. Tiffany Studios photograph, from a damaged glass plate.*

FIGURE 222   *"Cobra" candlestick (against a background of Tiffany fabric). C. 1900. Bronze. Signed, "Tiffany Studios/New York/1203" (stamped) "TS" monogram (incised) in wax model before casting. Height 8".*

Theodore Flagg

any $10,000 window or $50,000 breakfast parlor that he has decorated, and he feels that his reputation is in a sense staked upon it. He made the engraver travel two hundred miles to receive his instructions at first hand, and stipulated that the engraver's work shall be done over as many times as he directs, resolutely insisting that no block shall be put upon the press until it produces the precise effect which he intends to produce. It is not often that a book is treated in this conscientious way; indeed, it is not often that a man like Tiffany designs a book at all, and we mistake the public mind if this work does not have a success as rare as its quality is."

Two examples of Tiffany's wallpaper were reproduced in *What Shall We Do with Our Walls?* by Clarence Cook.[2] One was black snowflakes on a gold ground; the other a design of black clover leaves and spider webs on beige. Both reveal a strong Oriental influence.

Not wanting to limit himself to traditional wall coverings in his own decorating work, Tiffany used stenciling on canvas, on paper, and sometimes directly on the walls. As early as 1878 he applied canvas painted by himself to the walls of his Bella apartment. The walls in the Fountain Court of Laurelton Hall were covered with canvas stenciled in a cypress tree design taken from tiles in the Topkapi Palace in Istanbul, Turkey (Figures 113 and 114).

It must be remembered, however, that the Tiffany Studios, always ready to satisfy the whims of all clients who could afford whims, carried a large stock of wallpapers (and other decorating materials) made by other firms here and abroad.

When Tiffany began to design fabrics is not known for certain. The curtains made by the Associated Artists for the Madison Square Theater in 1880 must have whetted his appetite for more. A set of green silk plush portieres with a gold geometric-pattern appliqué designed by Tiffany is reproduced in *Woman's Handiwork in Modern Homes*, published in 1881.[3] He displayed an assortment of fabrics in the Columbian Exposition Chapel.

Tiffany fabrics were run off in commercial mills (he had no mill of his own). One (Figure 220), a silk velvet in golden tones stenciled with pale green leaves and pink wild roses, is signed on the selvage: TIFFANY FABRIC. The dining-room chairs at Laurelton Hall, were covered with a beige cotton velvet stenciled with a small pattern in the dark mazarin blue of the rug.

The Tiffany furniture shop made handsome traditional pieces as well as those from Tiffany's own designs. The dining-room furniture from Laurelton Hall is a good example of the latter. Both tables and chairs (Figure 119) show his fascination with the Orient, but more important, they demonstrate the simplicity that marks so much of his personal work. Chairs made for his painting gallery at Laurelton Hall were, however, a version of the Louis XVI style, except for the slender vertical supports that are reminiscent of chairs he made for the Havemeyers.

Tiffany's buttons were pressed (opalescent glass glued to metal mounts). The price of twelve stitched to black cards stamped "The Tiffany Glass and Decorating Company" would have been minimal, and they are one more bit of evidence of Tiffany's desire to place at least some of his beauty within the reach of every American.

Tiffany's metalwares evolved from such things as the leads in the Kemp windows (Figures 42 and 43), which are 1.5″ wide in places and treated to look like heavy vines, and also from the door to the tabernacle (Figure 131), the candlesticks (Figure 137), and the electrolier (Figure 136) in the Columbian Exposition Chapel.

In 1898 he added a metal department to his glass furnace at Corona and placed designer Alvin J. Tuck in charge. The enamels were begun in the same year. Preparing exhibits for the Exposition Universelle scheduled for 1900, and for the other fairs soon to follow in various parts of the Western world, may have had something to do with Tiffany's expansion. The importance of the fairs' dazzling displays of turn-of-the-century progress, confidence, and optimism can hardly be overstated.

Tiffany's first metalwares were stands for vases and bases for lamps. The "Nautilus" lamp (Figure 182) was made around 1900, and therefore, in addition to being one of his earliest leaded lamps, is also an early example of his metalwork. The illustration of the shade in the patent application filed on May 2, 1899, shows that it was of a natural shell. The adjustable shade and the simple down-to-earth look of the lamp are typical of his personal work. So is the way its design was adapted to the electric light bulb (an open flame would have destroyed it).

The "Wisteria" lamp (Figure 186) is of special interest as an example both of his lamps and also of his metalwares. It is discussed here because its metalwork is as impressive as the leaded glass.

The story persists that it was designed by Mrs. Curtis Freshell who approached Tiffany about making it for her, that he offered her a special price if she would let him market it commercially, and that she agreed. This story may be true, but it is not the whole truth. The lamp is, in fact, an elegant piece of three-dimensional art made of bronze, lead, glass, and light bulbs. The imaginative quality of its design, the creative use of materials, the skill in its engineering are of especial interest. The roots fan out to make the base. Heavy leads spread out over the top both to give strength to the dome shape and to suggest a network of limbs and branches. (Open spaces between them serve as vents.) All this is reminiscent of the leading in the transoms of the Kemp house and of those in the "Butterfly" window (Figure 72). The wisteria motif may have been suggested by Mrs. Freshell, but the complete lamp was designed by a skillful hand, which could well have been Tiffany's.

Two other lamps have particularly fine metal components, the "Spider" lamp (Figure 189), and the "Spider Web" lamp (Figure 187). The spider web was a favorite Tiffany motif. He used it in a fire screen in the Bella apartment, in one of his designs for wallpaper, and in an overhead wire trellis near the main entrance at Laurelton Hall. The spider in the "Spider" lamp sits resolutely on his web. He makes a good pattern, and his legs give strength to the shade. The designer was obviously fascinated with a spider's engineering know-how. It sounds like Tiffany.

The "Spider Web" lamp is ornamented with mosaic daffodils. The shade rests on the base in a way that makes the joint invisible and the effect is that of a piece of sculpture made of metal, leaded glass, electric light, and mosaic. It is Art Nouveau, but a solid American kind. The cost could help explain the fact that few were made. So could the style. Not many interiors could "digest" anything so explosive. The big lamp could not have been planned as a moneymaker—it has the look of a work someone wanted to make regardless of the cost. It could also be an expression of the pleasure of walking in a garden early in the morning when spider webs are still strung with dew drops. It also suggests satisfaction in doing things in ways others had never thought of. Who designed the great lamp may never be known for certain, but Tiffany is one good possibility.

The best known of Tiffany's metalwares are the famous desk sets. All pieces were sold individ-

FIGURE 223 *Favrile glass scarab and floral buttons. C. 1910. Display card reads, "Tiffany Favrile Glass/Tiffany Furnaces/Sole Makers/Corona, L.I., N.Y."*

ually at prices ranging in 1904 from $4.00 to $50. In the Edwardian era letters were important. People wrote their own letters with pens dipped in their own ink. Blotters prevented blurring and saved time.

Some patterns were made in as many as thirty-one pieces including rocking blotters, blotter ends, lamps, magnifying glasses, stamp boxes, penholders, pen cleaners, scissors, letter openers, inkwells, letter scales, clocks, calendars, picture frames, paper clips, and paperweights.

The first (and also the favorite desk sets for many years) were the "Pine Bough" and "Grape" designs. In these a copper silhouette is contrasted with a sheet of Favrile glass usually green or yel-

low. The "Pine Bough" might have been suggested by the "Winter" design of the "Four Seasons" window. The "Abalone" design is reminiscent of the vine in the niche in the chapel (Figure 224). In each, an equal role was assigned to metal and to glass. In later patterns, the metal is stressed and glass was used only to add touches of color.

"Bookmark," "Byzantine," and "Zodiac" were being made by 1904. By 1918 the line included "Ninth Century," "Venetian," "Abalone," "American Indian," "Chinese," "Graduate," "Royal Copper," "Louis XVI," "Nautical," and "Modeled." "Abalone" derives, obviously, from the abalone circles in the tabernacle door of the

FIGURE 224 *Desk set. "Abalone" pattern. 1902–18. The model numbers of this set range from 1151 to 1178, and all the pieces are signed, "Tiffany Studios/New York" (stamped).*

chapel's altar. "Louis XVI" and "Adam" have the quality of Tiffany's products but none of the characteristics of his personal style.

Hundreds of individual pieces (boxes, inkwells, trays, candlesticks, paperweights, etc.) with no matching pieces were also made. Some of the finest bronzes were candlesticks (Figures 225 and 226) which added a touch of slender elegance to many a turn-of-the-century mantelpiece and dining table. A particularly tall, slender, and graceful candlestick which stood on a base in the form of a "Wild Carrot" (Queen Anne's lace) was probably among those designed by Tiffany.

A combination inkwell, penholder and stamp box, made of green iridescent Favrile glass set in

silver-plated metal (Figure 227) also suggests Tiffany's personal involvement, not only because of the iridescent turtlebacks of which he was so fond, but because of a typical mechanical feature. The handle on its one small drawer, when turned to the right, brings out a second and smaller drawer inserted in the first drawer at right angles to its long axis.

One handsome paperweight, a figure of a lioness is a good example of a Tiffany Studios piece that could not be Tiffany's personal work. The lioness (Figure 229) has a relaxed quality that reveals a knowledge Tiffany did not have. The fact that he never studied the nude shows up, one way or another, in every Tiffany figure,

FIGURE 225 *Left: Candlestick. After 1902. Bronze and Favrile glass. Signed, "Tiffany Studios/New York/1223"
(stamped). Height 16¼". Center and right: Pair of candlesticks. After 1902. Bronze with reticulated blown-glass
cups. Signed, "Tiffany Studios/New York/5393" (stamped). Height 20¾".*

FIGURE 226   *Left: Candlestick, Queen Anne's lace motif. After 1902. Bronze. Signed, "Tiffany Studios/New York/D884" (stamped); metal insert "33" (stamped). Height 19½". Center: Candlestick, bamboo motif. After 1902. Bronze. Signed, "Tiffany Studios/New York, 1205." Height 10½". Right: Candlestick. After 1902. Bronze. Signed, "Tiffany Studios/New York/1308" (metal insert not marked). Height 20½".*

FIGURE 227   Pen-and-ink stand. C. 1910. Bronze, silver-plated. Favrile glass turtlebacks and inkwell cups. Signed, Base—"Tiffany Studios/New York/10388"/"TIFFANY STUDIOS/NEW YORK/3664" (stamped); Inkwell cups—"L.C.T." (engraved); Lid—"3664" (incised). Height 4¼".

FIGURE 229   "Lioness" paperweight. After 1902. Doré bronze. Signed, "Tiffany Studios/New York/932" (stamped). Length 5".

FIGURE 228   Octagonal box. 1902–20. Silver and enamel. Signed, Base—"Tiffany Furnaces/Sterling/239" (stamped) "9/289" (incised); Inside cover—"239" (stamped) "239"—(incised). Diameter 4⅛".

FIGURE 230 *Loving cup. After 1902. Gold-plated bronze set with Favrile glass jewels. Signed, "Tiffany Studios/New York" (stamped). Height 7".*

FIGURE 231   *Inkwell. C. 1897. Favrile glass and silver. Signed, Glass—"L.C.T.o8476" (engraved); Silver—"Tiffany & Co/Maker/Sterling Silver" (stamped). Height 4¾".*

Theodore Flagg

FIGURE 232 *Pitcher. After 1902. Repoussé copper with silver and gold plating, ebony handle. Signed, "Tiffany Studios/New York" (stamped). Height 3¼".*

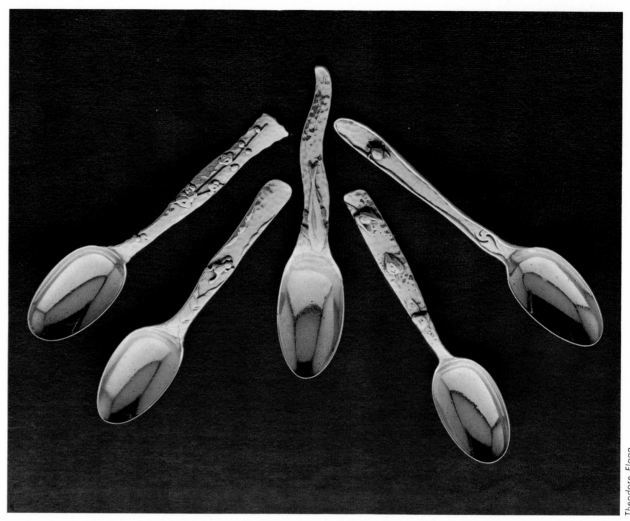

Theodore Flagg

FIGURE 233   *Spoons. Sterling silver. C. 1878. Tiffany & Co. Signed (left to right):"M Tiffany & Co Sterling 376–770"; "M Tiffany & Co Sterling 372–766"; "M Tiffany & Co Sterling/375/769"; "Tiffany & Co/Sterling/377/771"; "M Tiffany & Co Sterling 368 762."*

human or animal. The handsome animal was made by a sculptor who had studied the anatomy of man and beast for many years, and its courtly elegance suggests an influence of either Rome or Paris.

After the furnaces at Corona were reorganized in 1920, the metalwares changed in character. A new line featuring trays, bowls, and serving pieces was introduced. Small touches of highly colored enamels replaced the abalone shell and glass jewel ornaments. Patricia Gay, who had worked

in the Tiffany Studios twenty years before, was brought back to do the enameling. She continued on until 1928. The new signature was "Louis C. Tiffany Furnaces Inc. Favrile."

The previous signatures, "Tiffany Furnaces" or "Tiffany Studios" (on one line) with "New York" underneath, were discontinued. (See Appendix B for more information on the numbers and signatures.)

Silver attributable to Tiffany is not common. A large Favrile glass inkwell (Figure 231) is signed

"L.C.T. o8476," but the silver top is signed "Tiffany & Co. Maker/Sterling Silver." The cream pitcher in Figure 232 is signed "Tiffany Studios/New York." The floral patterns are inlaid silver and gold, and the handle is ebony. The use of natural forms, the richness, and the mixture of mediums are suggestive of Art Nouveau, but the simple, no-nonsense shape of the vessel's body might reflect a closeness of the society and the designer who produced it to the source of the healthy liquid it was made to contain. It may, therefore, be the personal work of Tiffany.

In 1878 S. Bing commented, on seeing some silver flatware by Tiffany & Company in the Paris Exposition of that year, that while the influence was Oriental, the style could be called a new art (Art Nouveau). The spoons in Figure 233 are signed "Tiffany & Company" or "Tiffany & Co." Most have the "M" which indicates they were made during the period Edward Moore was serving as vice-president in charge of the silver department at Tiffany & Company. That suggests the spoons were made before 1891.

Moore encouraged Tiffany in his collecting of Japanese sword guards (discs, usually of iron, often decorated with sensitive designs of inlaid gold and featuring such fragments of nature as a bee, a dragonfly, or a single sprig of flowers). His doing so points to the interesting possibility that these spoons may have been partly responsible for the most durable of the names now attached to the once again fashionable art style that sprang from the elegant turmoil of the closing years of the last century.

How many lives Tiffany touched with his "little art" is one statistic we must forever do without. But surely many Belle Époque letters might have had more lilt if the writer had gotten the message in the blotter on the desk.

NOTES

1 DeKay, op. cit., pp. 27–28.
2 Published in 1880 by Warren Fuller & Co., New York.
3 Charles Scribner's Sons, p. 58.

Chapter 14

ENAMELS

*Enamel is a strong, active force for color, which requires great care in use....
It is, by nature, assertive and capricious.*

SAMUEL HOWE

Anyone with a glass furnace and a driving urge to try new techniques would be fascinated with enamels. Tiffany, who in addition to these had a great desire to make color a more important factor in everyday life, found them irresistible.

The Tiffany metal furnaces were established in the Corona glasshouse quietly in 1898, and secret experiments in enamels went on for some time before anyone got wind of them. The public had its first view of the results in 1900 when Tiffany exhibited enamel on *repoussé* copper lamp bases at the Paris Exposition Universelle. The Tiffany Studios' exhibit in Buffalo's Pan-American Exposition, held in 1901, include "iridescent enamels" fired "upon metals" and, according to one reviewer, "In one or two instances the enamel has been fired over *repoussé* silver, which has given an interesting and most artistic effect."[1] Samuel Howe, writing at length about Tiffany's enamels in *The Craftsman* in 1902,[2] reflected Tiffany's enthusiasm for the iridescent luster effect. A dozen

pieces were shown at the St. Louis Exposition in 1904.

Enamels were not a totally new experience for Tiffany since the process is essentially fusing powdered glass to metal. And the ingredients are practically the same as those of glass: silica, lime, potash, soda, lead oxide and/or borax, depending on the aims of the enameler. Metallic oxides are, of course, added for color. The batch is melted and cooled to solid lumps (called frit) which are ground to a fine powder. This powder is then fused to the surface of a metal. When the powder is applied dry, the metal surface is treated with a binder (such as gum tragacanth) which holds the particles in place. When mixed with water and gum tragacanth, the powder is applied with a brush.

The metal to be enameled can be prepared in various ways. In *champlevé* (raised planes), depressions are etched, scraped, or gouged out of it and then filled with enamels. *Cloisonné* is made by creating little cups with flat wires set on their side and filling them with enamels. Another method calls for piercing a sheet of metal in a pattern of small openings and covering it with wet enamel (which fills in all the openings). This method is called *"plique á jour,"* and the effect is that of a miniature glass window. Enamels can also be applied to sheets of metal that have previously been embedded in warm pitch (a sticky mixture of pitch, plaster of paris, and tallow) and ornamented with a design hammered out with punches. (The pitch gives under pressure. To make a vase with this technique the sheet of metal is rounded and supplied with a bottom.) In another method, *"limoges,"* enamels are applied wet with a brush to a flat surface as in a painting. The name refers to the French town famous for work of this kind. Tiffany's favorite method was enameling on copper with a *repoussé* design.

Regardless of how the enamels are applied, all are heated (either in a kiln or over an open flame) to a temperature somewhere between 1,500° F. and 1,800° F., depending on many variables, including whether the layer is the first, second, or one of many.

Tiffany, of course, gave his enamels other little "twists." He embedded sheets of pure gold or silver foil in clear enamels to give them added brilliance. The raised parts in a *repoussé* design were often covered with opaque enamels which were then glazed with colored layers. Thick enamels were heated so they would run into the "controlled accident" designs he loved. As one might expect, any rules he followed were of his own making.

What was Tiffany's role in making the enamels?

DeKay, in describing the process leading to the creation of both jewelry and enamels, mentions "a sketch by the master," "a second watercolor cartoon," a model, consultations "with the master," and finally a work that was "the result of many consultations and many expert hands."[3] (One set of "expert hands" belonged to Julia Munson, who was in charge of the enameling department until 1903, after which she was moved to jewelry. Another belonged to Alice Goovey; another to Patricia Gay.) That is the answer. The original idea was his. Sometimes Tiffany translated it into a detailed rendering himself. More

often he handed it to his staff in the form of a quick sketch, and they did the rest.[4]

The result was a body of work all of which had his personal stamp. The motifs are often the wild flowers, grasses, and weeds he enjoyed partly because of their beauty and partly because he liked to call attention to beauty others ignored. The shapes have the organic look of much of his work, in other mediums. The lines have a quiet flow different from the hurried swirls of European Art Nouveau.

Tiffany's tendency to draw on many sources is also evident. A pin tray may be a fragment of nature (possibly one leaf) done in the spirit of a Japanese print (Figure 234, left). The raised motif on a *repoussé* bowl may suggest enamels made in the Near East. Fern tendrils on a *repoussé* copper vase may suggest something one might find by a boulder in the woods. His designs range from single entities to fragments of nature complete with light and air. He is still Tiffany the painter recording his love of the beauty around him, but instead of paint he is now using a thin coat of glass melted over a sheet of metal.

Tiffany's enamels are marked in various ways. The usual "L.C.T." is engraved on many. Some are signed with his personal signature. An occasional "E.L." stands, some think, for enamel, although one might wonder why an enamel would need to be labeled and why a period should follow each initial. Other initials—"EG" and "SG" —suggest a reference to individual workmen. One plate is stamped with a monogram reading "TG." The limited output indicates the enamels were no great financial success even though they were carried by Marshall Field in Chicago as well as by Tiffany & Company in New York.

The enameled vase in Figure 235 is from Tiffany's personal collection. The marks impressed on the bottom are "162 A-Coll." together with "SG 123" and a script signature very much like his own. The metal is heavy copper ornamented with a stylized *repoussé* floral pattern. The raised parts are moss-green enamel over gold leaf. The background is a purple-green, and the whole is slightly iridescent. All objects in Tiffany's personal collection were not necessarily designed by himself, and yet the simplicity, the relative quiet, and the rather bulky shape of this piece are typical of his personal work. When it is

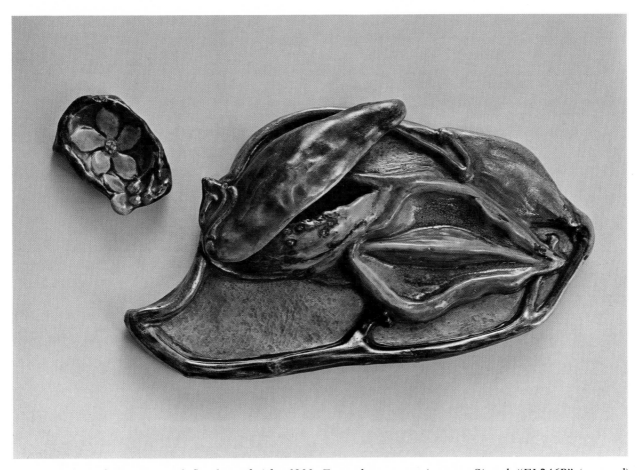

FIGURE 234 *Left: Pin tray with floral motif. After 1900. Enamel on* repoussé *copper. Signed, "EL246B" (stamped) "mL.C.T." (engraved script). Length 3". Right: Desk tray with milkweed pod motif. After 1900. Enamel on* repoussé *copper. Signed, "Louis C. Tiffany" (engraved) "EL169" (stamped). Length 11¼".*

compared with others it is easy to see that the appeal of the vase is due to the way the materials are used, not in its similarity to a familiar shape such as that of a flower.

The tray in Figure 234, right, is a milkweed pod, but without any atmosphere, as is the case with the early glass vases blown in the shape of flowers. The border is an organic shape, perhaps a vine. The main element in the design is the seedpod with a cover that swings aside to reveal the little "fish" complete with all his scales. The intervening parts, which serve as a background for the design, are beaten gold covered with clear enamel, one section being yellow gold, and another

a very orange gold. There is no suggestion of space or air.

This tray shows Tiffany's love of natural forms and of rich materials, as well as his interest in designing objects large and small with movable parts. The mark is "Louis C. Tiffany" (in script) and "EL 169."

The theme of the enameled *repoussé* copper vase in Figure 236 is fern tendrils in the spring. It calls attention to the rhythm of the unfolding shapes which push even beyond the boundaries of the vase. The blue-green ferns are set against iridescent purple-blues in a way that suggests a fragment of some pleasant woods complete with

FIGURE 235   *Vase with floral design. After 1904. Enamel on repoussé copper. Signed, "L.C. Tiffany 162A-Coll."*
(engraved script)/"SG123" (stamped). Height 7½".

FIGURE 236 *"Fern Tendril" vase. After 1904. Enamel on* repoussé *copper. Signed "Louis C. Tiffany" (engraved script)/"SG 80)) (stamped/"SC" (incised)/"249." Height 9".*

light, air, and even a little mist. The hammer marks on the metal break up the colors in a way that makes one think of the Impressionism of Tiffany's later paintings. This vase is, in a way, a circular picture by Tiffany the painter. The inside is enameled a dark blue. The marks on its gold bottom are "SG 80" and a script "Louis C. Tiffany" which bears only a faint resemblance to his personal signature. "SC" and "249" are also incised faintly.

Tiffany's enamels may relate in a fascinating way to his personal life. A sheet of metal (especially gold) covered with a layer of colored glass does have a jewel-like quality not found in metal alone, and not always in glass alone. This fact may have led to a rather curious experiment he once conducted in one of the windows in his father's store that is described by his friend Samuel Howe in *The Craftsman*. It seems Tiffany surrounded one of his small enamel vases with unmounted, polished, and partly cut gems; such as lapis lazuli, sapphire, topaz, golden beryl, Mexican fire-opal, Siberian amethyst, pink tourmaline, aquamarine, and other valuable gems corresponding to the shades of color of the vase. "In the results of the test, the enamels proved equally fine in quality and tone of color with the gems; due allowance being made for the scintillation and counter lights cast by the latter."[5]

This experiment recalls his many comparisons between Favrile glass and jewels. It may also recall his fascination as a very young boy with "the colored stones in his father's shop," and his apparent compulsion to demonstrate that glass offers the same beauty as that of gem stones. In addition to all that, it may have been one more effort, conscious or not, to prove he could measure up to an image that challenged him all his life, that of a successful, impressive, and sometimes skeptical father.

NOTES

[1] *Keramic Studio*, Vol. III, No. 2, June 1901.
[2] Vol. II, 1902, pp. 61–68.
[3] DeKay, op. cit., p. 23.
[4] Koch, Robert, *Louis C. Tiffany's Glass-Bronzes-Lamps* (New York: Crown Publishers, 1971), p. 153.
[5] Vol. II, 1902, pp. 61–68.

Chapter 15

JEWELRY-
LITTLE MISSIONARIES
OF ART

Articles of personal adornment are wont to be rated low . . . in contradistinction to objects of the fine arts. . . . One must not forget, however, that they appeal to the very widest imaginable circle of buyers. . . . It is well, therefore, that objects of the sort should be beautiful or at any rate exhibit some taste. One may say that the quality, the artistic quality, of the jewelry which is found among a people goes far to measure that people's level in art. Hence the importance of having artists instead of untrained artisans to supply jewelers with designs; hence the value to the people . . . to supply a class of jewelry not only original and individual, but often very beautiful. Each piece acts as a little missionary of art and tries in its own dumb way to convert the Philistine.

CHARLES DEKAY, *The Art Work of Louis C. Tiffany*

Louis Tiffany himself has given at least one reason why he made his jewelry. It was to go out into the world as missionaries "to convert the Philistine." That thinking is consistent with his dream of making the world more responsive to art and beauty, and consistent with his conviction that art need not always be something one goes somewhere to see. Paintings, mosaics, vases, and pots tend to settle down and stay put. Jewelry gets around.

Another reason he did not mention was that French designers—Lalique, Colona, and Feuillatre—were attracting a lot of attention with their new jewelry which delighted cafe society, actresses, and sophisticates with its smart lines, nude women, multi-legged sea creatures with a deadly grip on a baroque pearl. Tiffany wanted some of the same kind of attention.

Another possible reason may have been Louis' father, jeweler to the Queen of England, the Czar of Russia, the Emperor of Germany, the Khedive of Egypt, and a glittering host of other royal personages. Charles Tiffany had made a fortune selling jewelry distinguished more for its splendor than for the sensitivity of its design. (At the Columbian Exposition one of the eye-catchers in the Tiffany & Company exhibit was a life-size rattlesnake coiled around a life-size duck. The entire surface was encrusted with diamonds, emeralds, opals, and other gemstones. And it also served as an incense burner.) Louis Tiffany's refreshing jewelry, whether intentionally so or not, may have been a gentle response to his father's unabashed commercialism. Instead of spectacular diamonds, rubies, and emeralds, Louis used semiprecious stones chosen solely for color and char-

FIGURE 237   *Original Tiffany Studios photograph of jewelry.*

acter, and the stones are usually part of a well-integrated design. An opal will nestle among gold coils in a way that underscores the beauty of both. A tourmaline will rest in a cluster of gold not so much as a gemstone set in something, but as part of a unified design. A ring made for Miss Hanley held a piece of glass which he considered "the most beautiful gem of all."

Louis Tiffany's jewelry has the organic character of his other work. Curves do not swing back on themselves solely for sake of swinging back. Motifs such as dandelions, wild carrots, and blackberries are used with genteel enthusiasm. His jewelry has a chunky, casual quality reminiscent of jewelry worn by the Celts. Each piece is beautifully made. None has the fluttery look of European Art Nouveau. It is free of the unabashed splendor of much Edwardian jewelry. It was planned to, and did, cost less than the fashionable jewelry of the time. Louis Tiffany's jewelry was one more effort to make less-expen-

FIGURE 238 *Left: Bar pin, after a design by Louis Tiffany. 1902–1915. Lapis lazuli set in gold. Signed, "Tiffany & Co." Right: Lady's ring, after a design by Louis Tiffany. 1902–1915. Lapis lazuli set in gold. Signed, "Tiffany & Co."*

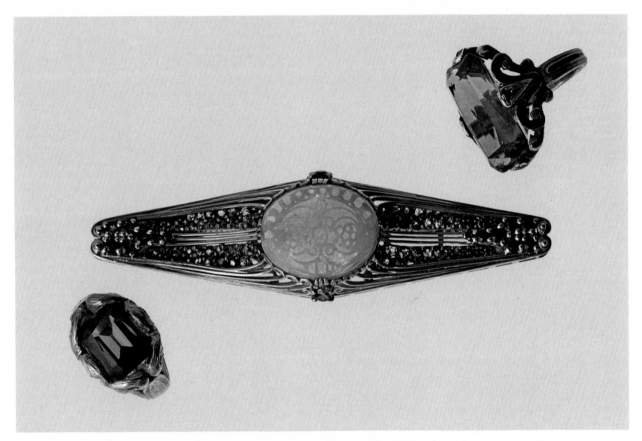

FIGURE 239 *Left: Lady's ring, after a design by Louis Tiffany. 1902–1915. Gem topaz set in gold and enamel. Signed, "14K Tiffany & Co." Center: Bar pin, after a design by Louis Tiffany. 1902–1915. Opal, demantoids, and sapphires set in gold filigree. Signed, "Tiffany & Co." Length 2 ¹³/₁₆". Right: Lady's ring, after a design by Louis Tiffany. 1902–1915. Tourmaline set in gold. Signed, "18K Tiffany & Co."*

FIGURES 240, 241   *"Peacock" necklace. Designed by Louis C. Tiffany. Made by Julia Sherman. C. 1906. Obverse: opals, amethysts, sapphires, demantoids, rubies, emeralds. Reverse: cloissoné enamel on gold. Unsigned.*

sive quality available to more Americans. These may be some of the reasons why Tiffany & Company was not very keen about his jewelry department and why it lasted not much longer than a decade.

A necklace with a grape motif exhibited in the Paris Salon in 1905 and published in the *International Studio*[1] was designed to call attention to the delicacy of some Edwardian belle's throat, but also to show anyone around who might not have realized it that quality of workmanship and good taste are very real, and in spite of all its romanticism, the turn-of-the-century world had a full measure of clods who needed such a reminder. The "Grape" necklace also called attention to a rare form of beauty found in the arbors of New England in the fall.

A gold hair ornament with a blackberry motif, published in the same issue, had enameled leaves and berries made of garnets set so closely their mountings are scarcely visible. One message this little missionary had for Philistines was that while hair piled high on the head of a beautiful woman *is* lovely to see, a walk along a country road or even through a bramble patch is a wonderful thing too.

In one ring set with lapis lazuli (Figure 238), the leaf design extends over the inside as well as the outside of the band, reminding at least the wearer that even non-visible quality can serve the human soul.

Louis Tiffany went into jewelry in a serious way in 1902. His father had died; he had inherited a large block of Tiffany & Company stock, was made vice-president and art director, and was taking a more active part in the company's affairs. His jewelry, along with his enamels, metalwork, pottery, and Favrile glass vases, was displayed and sold in a special department on the sixth floor. Much of it was executed by the craftsmen of the company.

The "Peacock" necklace (Figure 240), shown in Paris in 1906 and reproduced in the *International Studio* in the same year, and later in *The Art Work of Louis C. Tiffany*, was Tiffany's favorite exhibition piece. When making it, because of his association with Tiffany & Company, he had access to one of the world's greatest collections of rare gems. Nevertheless, the stones he chose were light-colored (and inexpensive) cabochon emeralds and rubies. The necklace has the handmade elegance of jewelry made for the court of Charlemagne, but the intrinsic value of the materials is negligible.

The obverse of the central disc is a miniature mosaic of a peacock made of opals, opalines, amethysts, carnelians, and sapphires and encircled by a ring of cabochon amethysts. The whole is festooned with chains of small pearls and demantoids (green garnets).

The reverse is *cloisonné* enamel featuring two flamingoes, another exotic bird that had fascinated Tiffany for years. The enamels have the special brilliance enamels always have when applied to gold (Figure 241).

The "Peacock" necklace is a sophisticated work of art. There is no uncertainty in its plan, no confusion as to purpose. The mosaic is a two-dimensional design—small in scale but grandly conceived. It illustrates the meaning that can be given to shapes and colors regardless of scale. It calls attention to such basic art principles as contrast and repetition. The contrast of the gold with the depth of a colored stone makes the stones look deeper and the surface sheen of the gold much richer. The repetition of the peacock motif on the bell-shaped elements ties together many disparate parts. The delicate loops of chain and pearls emphasize the rugged quality in all the rest. The cabochon stones help relate all the other parts to the central disc. But Tiffany did not think of everything. The brilliant necklace falls wrong when it is worn. It was designed for exhibition, not for a neck.

The flamingoes on the reverse are treated in a manner well suited to the medium. Their necks are entwined to make a design, not to suggest that flamingoes stand around like that. The colors are chosen for their attractiveness, not to describe a tropical landscape. The *cloisons* hold the enamels like little dishes only partly filled. The result is an uneven surface that catches any light from any source.

Materials and scale are considered carefully. It is partly medieval, partly Edwardian. On paper its cabochons, cut, and sliced stones, its pearl and demantoid garlands, its enamels and entangled birds sound impossible. But it has a miniature charm and a disarming splendor which really might convert a Philistine if he had any sense to begin with.

The necklace was made by Mrs. Frederick Fairchild Sherman (Julia Munson Sherman), the skilled craftswoman in charge of Louis Tiffany's jewelry department. When I showed her the necklace a few years ago she turned it over and over carefully and lovingly in her hands. Her first remark was, "How nice to see this again after all the years." Then she discussed the stones, and how the piece was made. When queried as to who designed it, her answer was emphatic and colored with surprise that anyone would ask, "Why Mr. Tiffany, of course." She then added that, after the mosaic on the obverse was finished, he decided the reverse was "too bare," and proceeded to design the flamingoes. Since some of the stones would have lost their color in the heat necessary for enamels, the "Flamingo" enamel was made on a separate plate and then attached to the original disc.

The "Peacock" necklace is one piece about which a great deal is known, but it too adds a touch of mystery to the Tiffany story. It was once in a well-known collection and then sold as glass. But the ruby drop at the bottom is a replacement because the original was removed, presumably because it was recognized as a gemstone. True, the necklace bears no signature, but much of Tiffany's personal work was unsigned, and most of his jewelry was signed "Tiffany and Company," anyway.

NOTE

1 December 1906, p. xxxiv.

Chapter 16

PHOTOGRAPHS

You were one of the first to photograph forms and animals in motion.

From a statement of appreciation addressed
to the Louis Comfort Tiffany Foundation
at the annual meeting of the Foundation on
Sunday, October 4, 1931

That Louis Tiffany was a pioneer in photographing things in motion will be news to some, and the assertion raises questions. What forms and animals did he photograph in motion? Did he exhibit his photographs? If so, where? Where are his photographs now?

His interest in motion is no surprise. His favorite stone, the opal, depends on changing lights for much of its beauty, as does chipped, folded, wrinkled, and iridescent glass. Laurelton Hall's fountains and the light fountain at Buffalo were color in motion. And, of course, the motion picture camera interested Tiffany. Grandchildren were dressed in gauze for miniature fetes in the gardens, which Grandpa photographed with his movie camera to their great dissatisfaction. He once considered making a full-length motion picture.

But why would the young Tiffany, determined to become a great painter, bother with the camera? The answer lies partly in the fact that the camera was new. The principle on which it operates; namely, that light entering a dark room through a very small hole will project the complete scene outside, on the opposite wall, but in reverse, has been known for centuries. Aristotle discussed it, as did the tenth-century Arabian scholar, Alhazen of Basra. Roger Bacon, the thirteenth-century English monk, mentioned the phenomenon in *Opus Maius.* Leonardo da Vinci wrote about it in detail. In the early years of the bustling nineteenth century that ancient knowledge was paired with recent discoveries about salts of silver darkening in light. An early result was the daguerreotype (in 1839). The camera, which records the reverse image on a negative, came a decade or so later. (Daguerreotype images are recorded on a metal plate coated with salts of silver, hence each is unique. The camera was a step toward mass production. Any number of prints can be made from the negative.) The camera was new and challenging when Tiffany was young, and new things fascinated him, especially those dealing with light and motion.

All artists did not share his enthusiasm for the camera. The camera shook the art world. It put some artists in a state of shock, especially the segment that believed that fine art is synonymous with realistic painting. Some of the more aggressive French painters (including Ingres) girded for battle. They denounced the new contraption as unfair competition and asked the government to ban it. Some with more flexibility, or perhaps fewer scruples, saw the camera as a short cut, and used photographs in place of sketches or models. (Ingres was among them.) The timorous used photographs in secret. Some simply gave up, abandoning the brush for the shutter, which was "more accurate" and less trouble.

But Louis Tiffany from the start recognized the photograph as a new and welcome art form as well as a useful tool. He and his staff of designers used thousands of photographs bought from professional studios all over the world. These include African storefronts, Middle Eastern mosques, palaces and dwellings, stained-glass windows in the European cathedrals, and examples of the decorative arts from many lands and cultures. They were used freely, openly, and happily.

Tiffany also used photographs to make records of windows, furniture, lamps, and artifacts made by his Studios and to illustrate brochures published by the Tiffany Studios. He himself took

FIGURE 242-49 *Photographs by Louis C. Tiffany.*

pictures of Laurelton Hall, of his design projects, and of the countryside on his many trips abroad. These, however, would not justify the implication that he pioneered in photographing forms in motion.

A number of small ($2\frac{7}{8}'' \times 4\frac{1}{8}''$) photographs, all carefully mounted nine to a plate, recently turned up among a thousand or so photographs from the reference library of the Tiffany Studios. All the little pictures are faded and some are damaged. Even so, their special character is evident. At first glance, many might be taken for accidents or rejects, except that they were so carefully preserved. Parts of buildings and other objects appear in unusual ways. Human figures are

cropped at the chin and in the middle or at the knees. A haphazard, accidental look, as though the camera might have been jostled, should not be misleading. There is an order in them. The stern of a boat lying on its side juts into one composition for no obvious reason since it is not easily recognized as a boat. But the dark mass, by contrast, calls attention to the fragile quality in a group of children standing nearby. The incomplete parts of a human figure in some remind one of the imaginative compositions of Toulouse-Lautrec (Figures 242–49).

The effects might be due to hurry—to get something before it was too late. But more likely they indicate a plan to distribute dark and light masses for formal reasons as is done in Japanese prints, or to avoid the slick clichés of the commercial photographs; or perhaps to achieve all three. Whatever the reason, the pictures have a quality of surprise that sets them nicely apart from the commercial photographs conforming to all the rules for "good composition."

The choice of subjects is also of interest. There are no ladies in bustles, no gentlemen in top hats, no elegant carriages complete with footmen and millionaires, or naked nymphs lounging on wicker settees under potted palms. This camera captured (without their knowing it) earthy human beings going about the serious business of living their lives.

The pictures make no social comment, raise no problems. Tiffany was pointing out a beauty many overlook: that of rumpled men, plain women, and ragtag children who are, without knowing it, the tomatoes, toadstools, and fern tendrils of humanity. It was the same kind of thinking that put squashes in the Heckschers' window and eggplants in the Kemps'.

One additional quality is even more telling. The subjects are not posed. Men push, shove, and talk, dogs scratch, birds fly, and women gesture. None know the camera is there. Three or more prints taken a few seconds apart will record the launching of a boat, dogs scampering around the edge of crowds, fishermen weighing their catch. Tiffany was as determined to get what they were doing as he was to get the subjects themselves.

There is much internal evidence pointing to Tiffany as the photographer; namely, the choice of subject, the fresh approach to pictorial organization, the interest in motion and the overall look—but is there any other? Fortunately, there is. The commercial photographs are stamped in various ways identifying them as the property of the Tiffany Studios. Nearly all the little photographs are hand stamped on the mat beneath: "Louis C. Tiffany."

One other bit of evidence is even more telling: Paintings by Tiffany in other collections clearly derive from these little candid shots.

Many questions remain unanswered—when and where did Tiffany show his photographs? When did he begin to take them? These will be answered by others who learn more. The following quote from the December 1906 issue of the *International Studio* may help them: "In 1877, while abroad, he [Tiffany] shared with Edward Muybridge the honor of being one of the first to take instantaneous photographs of birds and animals in motion." (Muybridge is the famous English photographer who in 1878 took the series of pictures of Leland Stanford's horse that proved for the first time that a galloping horse's feet were all off the ground at the same time.)

Further evidence that Tiffany recognized the photograph as an art form can be found in the fact that when he planned his Foundation, he provided specifically that photographers would be among the artists invited to live and work in Laurelton Hall.

Chapter 17

HAIL TO THEE, GREAT ONES

From the invitation to the Egyptian fete.

Sigmund Freud helped the world discover, somewhat to its relief, that erotic fantasies are a common experience, and that exotic events made of the same stuff as dreams take place in the privacy of every mind. Most keep such reveries to themselves, but romantics like Sidney Lanier, Edgar Allan Poe, Richard Wagner, Sir Edward Burne-Jones, and Louis Tiffany may share theirs with us in their art. Some aspects of Tiffany's inner world were reflected in his interior decorating, his painting, and his windows. Three fetes, however, which he organized with typical concern for quality and indifference to cost, let us see it in detail.

The first, the Egyptian, was held in 1913. His friend, the artist J. Lindon Smith who had made detailed drawings of some of the recent discoveries in Egypt helped in its production.

Tiffany, a sixty-five-year-old widower, was lonely and bothered about the state of the arts. He had tried many ways to raise the world's taste level and to win it to his way of beauty, but the results were not all he had hoped for. Now he took another approach. He would give a great masque—with an Egyptian theme—and his guests would join a cast of professionals in making a beautiful evening. Several hundred guests were invited for Tuesday evening, February 4, at 10 o'clock. All were asked to wear appropriate costumes and all were told where costumes could be rented for as little as $10. The place was the Tiffany Studios, 345 Madison Avenue, New York. To help set the proper mood, each invitee received a scroll in hieroglyphics, accompanied by an English translation as follows:

Hail to thee, Great ones—Happy Friends (both)
Men and Women, saith the Lord (Mistress)
of the Throne of the World
Come to Me and Make Glad Thyself
at the Sight of My Beauty
Queen.

Arriving guests were whisked, by a "modern elevator," to the fourth floor where time had been rolled back to the day in the ancient city of Alexandria, Egypt, when Cleopatra VII was awaiting Mark Anthony's return from "distant lands." A stage had been built to simulate a terrace overlooking the harbor. The royal palace stood on the right. Beyond were tropical plants, and masts and sails of ships. Guests were seated in a circle before the stage. The program began with music written for the occasion by Theodore Steinway and played by members of the New York Philharmonic Orchestra. Then a dazzling procession made its way to the stage, which had been appropriately strewn with lotus petals by Robert W. de Forest's children in Egyptian costumes. A "water sprinkler" with a sheepskin bag on his hip came first. Then women with jugs on their heads, and soldiers and merchants "from far and distant lands"[1] attended by porters bearing bundles of "treasures." These included gold from the South, textiles from the East, rare glass and golden vessels from Syria, and Favrile glass from the Tiffany Studios. The merchants asked for and received permission from the chief eunuch to display their wares in the hope the queen would be tempted to buy. With their riches spread on the stage, it assumed the character of a Far Eastern Thieves' Market. Fakirs added a note of romantic unreality by performing their magic. "Jugglers, fortune-tellers, sellers of fruit and copper" plied their trade. Slave dealers ordered their lovely merchandise to sing and dance for "prospective purchasers." One buffoon was "punished for his too ardent interest in the slave dealer's wares."

At this point Cleopatra, played by Hedwig Reicher, the famous actress, arrived by palanquin complete with throne. She was preceded by the chief eunuch, priests, and an assortment of attendants, including Negroes whose nearly naked bodies shone (according to the New York Times) "like ebony."

As the queen descended from her palanquin, the entire company prostrated themselves before her. The chief eunuch explained the presence of the wares, and she made lavish "purchases."

Then "Mark Anthony" (played by actor Pedro de Cordoba), arrived along with an assortment of Roman generals and their wives. Anthony and Cleopatra seated themselves on a crimson divan which had been brought in by slaves. The crowd drew aside to give them privacy while he told her of his journey and they exchanged caresses. Anthony had, among other gifts, brought along a beautiful youth (Mr. Paul Swan) who danced before the queen. Cleopatra in return gave Anthony wine and "a wonderful gift," a carpet borne by "four Ethiopian chairbearers." When the carpet was unrolled, Miss Ruth St. Denis, done up in brown gauze (which, according to "Town Topics," left little to the imagination), rolled out. Her specialty was Oriental dancing and she promptly launched into what the press described as "a ravishing dance of the Nile clad in the bronze costume given her by nature" to music played by the orchestra.

After Mark Anthony had recited appropriate verses from Arrgi's *Nuits Egyptiennes*, the spectators were marshaled to the stage by Roman lictors and each in turn made proper obeisance to the queen. A champagne supper (served by Delmonico's) followed, and then the livelier contingent of the gathering danced the night away to music not written for the occasion.

John W. Alexander, the distinguished portrait painter, fascinated both press and guests with his part in it all. He was wrapped so realistically as a mummy, according to one reporter obviously *not* an Egyptologist, that "he appeared to have stepped out of a case from the Metropolitan Museum of Art." (His legs and arms were bound individually which, as any Egyptologist knows, is not the way with the real thing.) Mr. Alexander did, however, manage to remain as motionless as a mummy during the entire performance and was restored to life by "a miracle just before suppertime."

Society reporters singled some guests out for special mention, among them Mrs. John D. Rockefeller, Jr., dressed as Minerva in an Athenian headdress; Mr. Rockefeller as a Persian; Cass Gilbert, the architect of the Woolworth Building, dressed as a Persian merchant in a blue robe set off with a dull crimson silk scarf and wearing a headdress banded with jewels; Mrs. Cass Gilbert, resplendent in orange-colored robes and veils of shaded orange and purple; Miss Dorothy Roosevelt dressed as a Persian; Mr. and Mrs.

FIGURE 250 *The Egyptian fete.*

FIGURE 251 *Left to right: Mrs. Charles Tiffany (Katrina Ely), Tiffany's daughter-in-law, and Julia Tiffany Parker and Dorothy Tiffany, Tiffany's daughters.*

Robert W. de Forest (he was president of the Metropolitan Museum of Art) dressed as a Maharajah and Maharanee of Punjab; and Ellwood Hendrick who played the part of chief eunuch.

Mrs. Allen E. Whitman, one of the slave girls, bore a jug of rosewater; Mrs. Hiram Bingham was an "Arabian"; and Mrs. Edward Harkness, dressed in blue and gold, represented Potiphar's wife.

Others referred to, but not by name, were a bevy of "stunning Egyptian beauties, some with gigantic scarab wings, veiled women of the Orient, bare-legged youths in leopard skins," and a goodly number of "tanned Egyptians" who were, in fact, "Pinkerton men appropriately disguised for the occasion as Orientals." Louis Tiffany, dressed in a turban with robes and jewelry, was described as an Oriental potentate.

The Egyptian Fete has been variously misinterpreted as a "bash" staged to dazzle New York's

FIGURE 252 *A mock fight between centurions Langdon Geer and Austin Strong before Cleopatra, played by Hedwig Reicher.*

"400"; as an attempt to hold the center of the stage at a time when Tiffany's art was beginning to look dated and his place as a leader in the arts was being pre-empted by younger men; and as a classic example of his proclivity to spend lavishly. The New York *Times* described it as a "social spectacle of wonderful brilliancy" which "in point of grandeur in costume art, eclipsed any fancy dress function ever presented in New York,"[2] Albeit, the Fete may have had more substance than these observations would indicate.

It was, of course, an expression of Tiffany's fascination with the current "Egyptianism." The groundwork for this movement, which influenced the arts of all the North Atlantic countries, had been laid more than a century before by archaeologists traveling with Napoleon in North Africa, and especially by the finding of the Rosetta Stone in 1799. It was given additional impetus by the work of Flinders Petrie in the middle of the nineteenth century and by the opening of the Suez Canal in 1869. Verdi's new opera, *Aida*, written to celebrate that event and performed in Cairo in 1871 in the presence of his majesty the Khedive and a brilliant assembly of world figures, gave it another push. Sarah Bernhardt's brilliant performance in *Cleopatra*, written by Victorien Sardou and presented in Paris in 1890, added to the fervor. The arrival of Cleopatra's Needle in New York, in 1880, a present to the city from the Khedive (transported at a cost of nearly $100,000 paid by W. H. Vanderbilt), undoubtedly added to the general interest in Egypt. And, of course, one of Tiffany's many visits to North Africa had included a cruise up the Nile (in 1908) in a chartered yacht (he kept his crew and friends in a

FIGURE 253 *Dressed as Romans, left to right, Attilio Piccirilli, Langdon Geer, an unidentified man, Pedro de Cordoba (who played Mark Anthony), Austin Strong, Howard Greenley, and Theodore Steinway.*

constant state of apprehension by vanishing on solitary sketching trips among the ruins ashore).

The Egyptian Fete was also one more way of saying that art is more than rare objects displayed in dull rows; that it can involve the ear, the ego, the taste buds, and the mind as well as the eye, and that space, color, people, texture, food, wine, sound, motion, light bulbs, and time can be used effectively by an artist who makes his own rules. Today, it might be called "a happening."

Tiffany, never fond of those talkative gatherings where an intelligent remark is rare and sensible conversation impossible, was pointing out that social events can have beauty.

One society reporter (who had not been invited) raised his hands in mock dismay because the guests sat on oriental rugs which, incidentally, happened to be for sale. The implication

that this was not by chance is correct. Tiffany the businessman, Tiffany the artist, and Tiffany the protagonist for beauty and good taste worked well together.

The symbolism in the Egyptian Fete gives at least a glimpse into the restricted areas of Tiffany's mind. Two aspects in particular have intriguing implications—the power of the rulers and the submission of the beautiful slaves. The Fete might have been telling of Tiffany's suppressed desire to force the world to submit to beauty as a way of life. It might have been spelling out his frustrations at not being able to win the world to the way of beauty.

The Egyptian Fete may also throw some light on the complications in Tiffany's relationships with his family. They loved him and he loved them, but they also saw him as the loving autocrat, which he obviously was. He may have unconsciously longed for absolute power because even the little world of his family did not accept his formula for adding quality to life as completely as he would have liked. One can only speculate on such matters.

Of course, to a perfectionist nothing is satisfactory. The Egyptian Fete was dazzling, but its message was probably not grasped by as many of his guests as Tiffany had hoped, and some may have been a little puzzled by it all. Then, too, the host and some guests as well had a little too much champagne. What the Fete really accomplished would be difficult to assess. The world went bumbling right along. The German Emperor, determined to find new markets for his expanding industrial establishment, continued to prepare for war, and an alliance was lining up to contain him. The world which took pride in royal families, luxury liners, posh sleeping cars, fast express trains, wisteria lamps, and public buildings adorned with classic columns, domes, and nude statues, was beginning to tilt.

And less than two weeks after the Egyptian Fete, another event, the famous Armory Show, shook the art world to its unstable foundations. It was organized by Tiffany's friend the American painter Arthur B. Davies, and opened in the 69th Regiment Armory at Lexington Avenue and Twenty-fifth Street in New York on February 17. This historic event presented abstract painting to the American public as a serious development in the history of easel pictures. The pictures were more a window on the mind than a window on the world. Colors were used to create an effect, not to describe an object. The shapes might suggest natural objects but were not intended to look exactly like them. Colors were laid out in ways that called attention to the surface of the canvas (in contrast to the broken color of the impressionists who wanted to paint the picture surface away). The paintings were of ideas, not things. They were experiments in "form," in organizing shapes and colors, not in how to represent nature. If the viewer could not make them out, that was the viewer's problem. They were made for the person who could understand, not for the average person.

Even though Tiffany had been snubbed by its organizers, he went to see the show anyway, and he hit the ceiling. More than thirty years pre-

viously, he had made a window as abstract as anything it had to offer. Perhaps ten or so years previously, he had made windows for the Brown-Renfrew mansion in Newcastle, Pennsylvania (Figure 36), which were as "wild" as anything in the Armory Show. He believed in every artist's finding his own kind of beauty. He was convinced that art is basically creating shapes and organizing colors. He should have liked these pictures because these painters were practicing what he had preached. But he was not objective enough to see the Renaissance tradition of realism embedded in his thinking. In spite of all his convictions, he wanted everything in a frame to resemble *something* in nature. It was strange.

One of the pictures, Marcel Duchamp's "Nude Descending a Staircase," suggested the action but not the image of a nude female. This bothered Tiffany. If anyone called a picture a "Nude Descending a Staircase," he wanted a nude, not something a wag could call "an explosion in a shingle factory." Tiffany believed in everyone's doing his own thing, but not *that*. He thought the viewer should be able to enjoy a picture, whether he had studied art appreciation or not.

If Tiffany had attended a course in art appreciation as it is taught in any good college, he might have seen that many pictures in the Armory Show were the result of applying principles he endorsed. He denounced the new painters as "modernists." This probably pleased them if they bothered to read his statements. He condemned them as seeking chance technical effects they hoped would make them famous—a curious statement from someone who had been glorifying the chance effects of glass for years.

But Tiffany never gave up. He organized another fete, but of a different kind. On May 15, 1914, one hundred and fifty prominent men were invited to "inspect the Spring flowers at Laurelton Hall." This was no pageant. He would *show* them what he meant. He would surround them with beauty. Laurelton Hall would speak for him. A private train provided for their convenience left New York's Pennsylvania Station at 4 P.M. It was met at the Oyster Bay Station by a fleet of cars which approached the mansion along a drive lined with blooming laurel. Tiffany's thirty-five gardeners had seen to it that the grounds were aglow with blooming phlox, tulips, and pansies. Wisteria dripped from the terraces and surrounding trees. The fruit trees were in bloom. Yellow orchids (Tiffany's favorite color) were banked around the fountain in the court. Flowers and branches of apple blossoms literally filled the house.

When the guests were seated, young Tiffanys appeared in Grecian costumes bearing salvers of roast peafowl (dressed with their own feathers) suckling pigs, ducklings, frog legs, and turtles. It had all been rehearsed the day before under the careful supervision of Miss Hanley. Delmonico's of New York had prepared the dinner with vegetables, animals, and fowl from the grounds and farm of Laurelton Hall. Music by Brahms, Beethoven, Wagner, and Bach was played on the pipe organ. A bevy of grandchildren bearing lighted braziers and scattering rose petals led the guests through the court and out to the hanging gardens for coffee and intelligent conversation. By eleven o'clock, it was all over. As the guests wound down the drive to board their train back to the city, they were treated to a breathtaking view of the great place swept by colored floodlights.

The dream had changed. The servants in ancient costumes were still there, but Tiffany, no longer an oriental potentate, was a benign benefactor enriching the lives of others with a kind of beauty they could never forget. There was less interest in power and the past, and more interest in America on May 15, 1914.

It must have been a gratifying experience. Laurelton Hall was not built as a retreat. It was built with others in mind, others who would let its beauty become a part of their thinking and their lives. For this one time, at least, the people were real and there were a lot of them.

As dramatic as the party was, Tiffany probably found it lacking in some respects. It lasted only a few hours. The guests were carefully selected, but some must have missed the fine points of the message. Anyway, before long he was planning another art event, different from its predecessors. This one would have a carefully prepared prologue, it would be staged in his Tiffany Studios, ostensibly to celebrate his sixty-eighth birthday, and it would make its points in a way *no* one could miss. It was given February 19, probably because Saturday was a better day than Friday for a party. As the Egyptian Fete had been, it was prepared by J. Lindon Smith, but it was pro-

duced by a cast of forty-two professional actors. The lighting effects alone (worked out by a German technician) cost $15,000. ($15,000 is an impressive figure by itself. When multiplied by 10—to make it comparable to today's dollar—it is even more so.) Nothing like it had ever been seen before in this country.

What transpired cannot be reconstructed with absolute accuracy. According to the New York *Times*,[3] "Poetry, music, splendor of costumes, and wonderful light effects" made the "spectacle a triumph." The stage was hung with a green screen in which a sixteen-foot circular opening provided a view of a half dome which, in the course of the evening, changed from a cold white to a series of glowing colors. The theme was the "story of the awakening impulses which at last find expression in the skill of human hands." The first scene presented human beings of aeons ago, clad in skins and bearing slain beasts. Trudging along with them were women of the tribe, an old man walking with the aid of a "gnarled staff," and trailing along at the end of the procession a buoyant and eager-eyed youth fired with a yearning to create beauty. He held a bowl on which he had drawn a crude design, but all was not exactly well with him. He would not take part in the violence of the "chase," and was "despised" by everyone except the women and the decrepit old man with the gnarled staff, who, being a seer, recognized the youth as the first artist, and as such the bearer of a message that could recast the world.

The situation deteriorated rapidly. At one point, prompted by the leaders of the chase who pointed out how useless the young artist was, the chief of the tribe decided to break his neck. He was dissuaded only by the women—who had better sense.

A fortuitous clap of thunder and a flash of lightning brought flames leaping from the ground. This terrified the tribe which departed forthwith. The young artist, who had no fear of fire, subdued the flames with his flint knife, and promptly dropped off to sleep under a jasper sky studded with stars. At this development the fire spirits danced happily around the sleeping youth. Actually, they were fascinated by the profane hands that had dared to touch them.

As the dawn came the stars faded and the clear morning light revealed Beauty as well as Youth sound asleep. The light awakened them both, and as he gazed on her, he was transported. Here was "the radiant goal of his aspirations."[4]

He promptly pledged himself, his life, and all the work of his hands, to her service, and in return, Beauty gave the starry-eyed youth dominion over all the earth's metals, minerals, and wood.

Now the masque became a dreamy idyll. As Beauty (played by a young lady with many charms) took command of the earth, the accompanying music lilted into a "softer sweeter" melody. She called out the resources of the earth who appeared as spirits from the air. Iron was first. It was black and untamed by fire. Then came Copper, followed by Wood crowned by leaves and in a "garb of living greens." Then came Alabaster, Lapis-lazuli, Glass (in shining robes), Clay (yellow and grim), Gold and Silver "with faces and forms covered with shining leaf." These were followed by the colors in a "prismatic train," and last of all "flashing beneath the ever-changing lights, tall and graceful figures adorned in wondrous garments—moonstone, amethyst, emerald, topaz, diamond, ruby, and opal."

In the next sequence, a blown-glass globe thirty-six inches in diameter moved across the stage. It contained a lovely little girl, J. Lindon Smith's daughter, who represented the Pearl. Beauty, understandably fascinated by this development, stooped to study it at close range and the Pearl responded with a winning smile. (Complications attendant on getting the little Pearl out of her blown-glass shell were not covered by the New York Times.) Glass and Clay danced as they were dissolved by the fire spirits only to reappear in a new guise—Glass, in transparent veils with an "opalescent glow," and Clay, "glazed in crystaline overlay."

In the final scene, Genius, the artist, renewed his fealty to Beauty as she stood surrounded by her hand-maidens—Painting, Sculpture, Music, and Architecture—and with this the masque came to an end.

The Quest of Beauty made two interesting points. Tiffany may never have defined beauty in words, but in this masque he leaves no doubt about what he considered its role in the world to be. It was to widen the gap between man and animal, to make man a more attractive thing himself, to civilize him. Tiffany's sympathies were not with the caveman whose sole interest was the chase. He is equally clear about the role of art. It is to serve the cause of beauty.

The Quest of Beauty is more autobiographical than the other fetes. To be sure, even in daydreams all images are the dreamer's. The seer, the man who looks down through the centuries to discern what beauty can do for the world, is as much Tiffany as the young artist, who was despised because he abhorred violence and refused to "run with the pack." It is a tale of being misunderstood and considered expendable, and a description of that pain and loneliness.

To make the point more obvious, at the sumptuous breakfast-luncheon that followed (served by Delmonico's with a menu that included terrapin), Tiffany spoke a few elegant words, which included, "What is The Quest of Beauty? Who can give the formula for it? Are there not as many definitions of Beauty as there are artists? And yet I wish to express what I have found in art. How can I say in a few words what I have been striving to express in art all my life? Art starts from an instinct in all, stronger one than another, and that instinct leads to the fixing of beauty in one of a hundred ways. If I may be forgiven a word about my own work, I have always striven to fix beauty in wood or stone or glass or pottery, in oils or watercolor, by using whatever seemed fittest for the expression of Beauty: that has been my creed." He then quoted the English poet and lawyer Philip James Bailey, author of Festus, 1839; "Art is man's nature; nature is God's art." Tiffany spoke in a setting hung with a retrospective exhibition of his paintings which included "Sow with Piglets."

His audience of several hundred included, as one might expect, many influential personages, among them Cecilia Beaux, the American painter; Mr. and Mrs. Daniel Chester French (he was the sculptor); Mr. and Mrs. Cass Gilbert; Mr. and Mrs. Will H. Low (he was the painter and designer, see Figure 69); Mr. and Mrs. Frederick MacMonnies (he was the sculptor); Mr. and Mrs. William J. Glackens (he was the painter); J. Francis Murphy (the painter); Professor and Mrs. Henry Fairfield; Mr. and Mrs. Ernest Pioxotto (he was the painter); Mr. and Mrs. Herbert F. Pratt; Mr. and Mrs. Arthur H. Scribner; Charles Scribner; Mrs. Henry O.

Havemeyer; Mrs. Walter Damrosch; Mrs. Thomas Edison; George Gardner Symons (the painter); Mr. and Mrs. Harry Willson Watrous (he was the painter).

The Quest of Beauty was the last of the great staged events. The issue of the New York *Times* that reported on it carried a story of an address by Admiral Robert E. Peary to members of the Association of Commercial Travelers of America. They were holding their Annual Dinner at the Waldorf Astoria Hotel. The Admiral cautioned the country that even though submarines might be effective in the North Sea, they could not defend America's long coast lines, and he called for more dreadnoughts. Not long afterward America was at war, and beauty, as a way of life, at least within Tiffany's frame of reference, seemed less likely than ever.

Peace came to a changed world. Tiffany's name still carried prestige, but he was no longer a force in art. Many would have given up. He made a new plan. This time it would be a kind of fete that would go on and on, down through the years. Surely someone, sometime, somehow, would get the point.

NOTES

1 From the synopsis for the fete.
2 Wednesday, February 5, 1913, p. 8.
3 Sunday, February 20, 1916.
4 Speenburgh, Gertrude, *The Arts of the Tiffanys* (Chicago: Lightner, 1956), p. 109.

works, among them signed prints by Utamaro, Hokusai and Hiroshigi. In addition, there were four thousand Tsubi (Japanese sword guards), each made like a piece of iron jewelry inlaid with gold and silver. The Chinese collection consisted of 327 items including the two turquoise-blue Kang-hsi dogs dated 1684, signed by their maker and dedicated to "our teacher and elder brother," which stood at the garden entrance to Laurelton Hall. The rare oriental and Chinese rugs catalogued by John Kimberly Mumford and Dana H. Carroll numbered over one hundred. Not catalogued were a collection of American Indian totem poles and baskets; numerous Favrile glass vases, pottery and lamps, and a collection of Roman, second century A.D., glass. Tiffany was one of the first great American collectors. If Laurelton Hall and all its collections, including the Tiffany windows and mosaics, were put on the market today, they would bring many many millions of dollars.

The first action taken by the board was to appoint Stanley Lothrop, a strange little man with oversized teeth, as director. Lothrop's record was no more impressive than he was. He had completed two years of graduate work at Harvard, and served later as assistant curator of paintings in the Boston Museum of Art. Later, he was assistant librarian and subsequently lecturer in Medieval and Renaissance Art at the American Academy in Rome. During World War I, he served with the American Red Cross, for which service he was given the title of Cavaliere by Italy's pocket-sized king. A book on Renaissance architecture in Rome which seemed to commend him especially to the trustees never got beyond the talking stage.

The Foundation was launched in an atmosphere of euphoria with one sobering note—a letter from Robert W. de Forest, Tiffany's attorney and close personal friend, a power in himself whose opinions were not to be taken lightly, written to the newly constituted board on September 12, 1918. It contained these observations:

"The institution founded by Mr. Tiffany involves, according to his ideas, many new and untried problems. In many respects its procedure must be experimental. While the general purposes which he wishes to attain are fairly clear, the definite means by which he expects to attain these purposes are not assured. It is only by experiment that means can be adapted to the end.

". . . In following his decision to carry out his plans at once so far as legal organization was concerned, I have recommended that form of legal organization which still leaves control to him to whatever extent he may care to execute it.

". . . No one can predict the continuance of income hitherto received and hitherto deemed reasonably certain. No one can predict the extent to which that income will be diminished by taxation."

The Foundation opened on May 1, 1920, with eight "students" (two silversmiths, one sculptor, one designer, and four painters), all men. The first few years were happy ones for all concerned. The plan was more clear in Tiffany's mind than Robert de Forest had realized. Students were invited for definite periods—one month, at first, then for six weeks, and later, for two months—during the warm months (from May 1 to October 30). They were housed in what had been stables—each "stall" was furnished simply but well. All opened on a courtyard complete with fountain. In 1922 women were included and Tiffany set aside five sleeping quarters and a sitting room in the main part of the residence for them. Originally, the students contributed $10 a week for board, but after 1927 even this modest charge was discontinued. The term "student," always used by Tiffany and his board, is misleading. Invitations to "study" at the Foundation were issued on the basis of work submitted and only to candidates who had advanced beyond the student stage. Formal instruction was not part of the plan, but distinguished artists were invited to visit and criticize students' work from time to time. In addition, members of an advisory board, which included such art personages as Daniel Garber, Charles Hawthorne, and Cecilia Beaux, came to visit and to talk with students about their work. Tiffany visited the gallery every Saturday to see the students and their work. The plan was founded on Tiffany's faith in Laurelton Hall, which, he declared many times, was the cornerstone of his plan. He believed that anyone who lived in its atmosphere would gain something which would help him all his life.

"Students" included interior designers, potters, jewelers, photographers, etchers, and sculptors, as well as painters. Presses, kilns, studios, workshops, and a darkroom were at their disposal, and they had complete freedom to do anything except loaf. They were there for business. The Foundation was rooted in Tiffany's puritanism as well as his desire to improve in the world. The following letter turned up in his papers after his death and was read to the Trustees in 1933:

To my Trustees of the
                                        July 28, 1922
Louis Comfort Tiffany Foundation

After three years' work of the Foundation, I find certain directions of vital importance for the Trustees to follow, that the Foundation may grow and develop as I want.

It is my wish that the Director carry out my ideas and that the Trustees see that they are followed.

To keep the Foundation a working body, all intercourse and intimate relations with the surrounding neighbors and families, which would prevent this, must be forbidden. The Director of the Foundation must not become intimate with or engaged or married to any one in the neighborhood; otherwise he must resign.

People living nearby become interested in the students, inviting them and visiting them, and it has already been proved that allowing this neighborhood social activity has interfered with the work of the students.

I did not intend this to be a social Foundation, but a place to work in and develop the students and not only make them see beauty in painting pictures, but to broaden them through the collection and books which I have given.

No man or woman should be accepted who plans to come here for any reason except hard work. Many art students are apt not to believe in hard work and such I do not wish to be allowed in this Foundation.

                        Yours very truly,
              (signed)   LOUIS C. TIFFANY

The written message never went to the "students," but they got it anyway.

The guild concept developed early. It was founded in Tiffany's belief that the artists would learn from and help each other. Eventually, outstanding students elected to membership in the guild were free to spend a month or so at the Foundation when vacancies occurred. The plan was imaginative and complete, and the Foundation was probably more expressive of Tiffany's personality than any of his other creations.

The first trouble appeared in the winter of 1923 when a heavy snow, on January 17, brought the hanging gardens (which were supported by locust posts) crashing down. Tiffany and his sister, Louise H. Tiffany, each contributed $10,000 to restore it. The stock market crash in 1929 was the next catastrophe. The Foundation's portfolio, which had stood at $1,475,292.83 in 1928, was reduced to $964,140 in 1931, and many companies stopped paying dividends.

Complications of another sort also developed. Stanley Lothrop, uncommunicative, uninspired, and singularly free of any qualities of leadership, had endless opportunities at meals and on other occasions to discuss the importance of the collections, the work of Tiffany himself, and the purpose of the Foundation, but he never did. Thus, the plan was not as effective as it could have been.

Then, too, the "students" themselves did not all react positively to the opportunities Tiffany created for them. Some had a genuine appreciation for the spirit, art, and beauty of Laurelton Hall. Some did not. A few formal statements of gratitude had been made in former years. By 1930 a minimum of gratitude for the kindness and character of their benefactor was evident, and he must have noticed this. Of course, the students were "another generation," and their views about art and society differed from his. He was convinced that Laurelton Hall, with its built-in eagerness to reach, to intrigue, and to please, would inspire young people to emulate its spirit. This is not the way it worked out. The new generation tended to equate charm with an absence of intellectual content. They were more interested in finding new forms than in trying to please anyone, except the critics.

Nevertheless, if Tiffany ever became discouraged because he liked the world more than it liked him, it did not show. With his young protégés, he was the personification of grace and friendliness.

Tiffany's reaction to the financial difficulties that clouded his last few years was one of confusion and some petulance. By 1932 his personal fortune had almost vanished, the Tiffany Furnaces had been shut down, and the Tiffany Studios owed him large amounts he could never collect. Apparently he was unable or unwilling to face the realities of the situation because he continued to travel to Florida in a private railroad car and, generally, to live on a scale unsuited to his new economic status. At a special meeting of his board held on October 28, 1932, Miss Hanley, at his behest, read a letter written the previous January 12:

To the President and Trustees of the Foundation:

I first wish to say to you all that the financial condition of the Foundation has been a great shock to me, something which would never have occurred even with bad times, had I been given to understand the full condition of things.

The only thing through which at the present time I can help the Foundation, is to give it a certain amount of land, which it can either sell now or in the future. This gift I wish to make immediately.

I have been more than pleased with what the Foundation has done in helping worthy and talented artists to get established in various parts of the country, and this as you all know is what I created my Foundation for: *the progress and development of America's Young Artists, helping them in every way to gain a foothold in the world of art.* My own life has been completely devoted to the betterment of art in all its phases for the country. Each year I want the Foundation to progress a step further, increasing its members slowly and selectively, and inviting back those who have continued to show progress. Under no conditions must the Foundation School ever close; that is the fundamental part of the Foundation, and for which it was established. Without the School there could be no Foundation.

The Guild formed from the best artists in the Foundation, I expect to increase yearly. This Guild will, I feel, in future be the most helpful thing that has been done for artists in this country, and will eventually form the governing body of the Foundation. The Exhibitions I wish held yearly for the purpose of helping to get the artists' work before the public.

I hope you all realize this fully and that each one of you will take a keen interest in the development of the Foundation. I wish to say here, which means for the present time and for the future, that I never want an officer or trustee to have any connection whatever with the Foundation who is not deeply interested and who will not work for its continued progress.

I wish to thank the president and all of you who have given me your help and sympathy in trying to better art conditions in America.

(signed) Louis C. Tiffany.

The reply from his old friend and counselor who was serving as secretary-treasurer of the Foundation was itself a little testy:

Louis C. Tiffany, Esq.
Laurelton Hall
Oyster Bay, N.Y.

Dear Mr. Tiffany:

After the reading of your letter at the Trustees' Meeting, in which the following paragraph occurs

"I first wish to say to you all that the financial condition of the Foundation has been a great shock to me, something which would never have occurred even with bad times, had I been given to understand the full condition of things"

the Executive Committee requested me to reply to your implication that the full financial condition of the Foundation has been withheld from you. The fact that your letter opens with this thought uppermost in your mind reveals your misconception of the matter.

I can readily understand, in the multiplicity of affairs which have engrossed your attention these past two very trying years, that the Foundation's problems did not loom so large and immediately threatening as the others you had to meet. This, perhaps, is one reason why the statements presented did not impress you so seriously as at present, when you are freer to give them more deliberate thought.

Throughout the fourteen years since the Foundation was established in 1918, nothing has ever been withheld from you whatever that had any relation to its finances, investments, income, disbursements and monthly cash position. The figures have been brought to you by me personally and continually in the form of monthly reports, giving the source of the income, a monthly analysis of the disbursements, and comprehensive statements showing the finances and expenditures compared with the previous year. If there was a marked increase in money spent, or a notable loss in income, the reason for these differences, I have explained to you and to Mr. Robert W. de Forest. This is a practice which I initiated at the beginning, and it has been adhered to month after month over this long span of years.

In addition to these reports, full annual statements and many quarterly and semi-annual statements were prepared and have been submitted to you personally by me, giving complete lists of the Foundation's investments, their market values, and tabulated figures showing income, disbursements, etc.,—all these likewise in comparison with previous years. The record will show that practically all such statements and reports bear your signature of approval. Furthermore, no bill has been paid or moneys expended for the Foundation without first receiving your O.K.

Up to the time of Mr. Robert W. de Forest's

passing, I consulted him very freely in connection with all these matters, especially in regard to all investments and changes relating thereto, and his recommendations were likewise reported to you as they were made. Upon Mr. de Forest's decease, it became necessary to have someone with adequate financial experience to take his place on the committee having the finances of the Foundation in charge, and we were fortunate in inducing your son, Mr. Charles L. Tiffany, who has had wide banking and financial experience, to accept the post of chairman of the Executive Committee. Since Mr. Watrous became President and a member of the Executive Committee, he too has been kept fully informed of the financial affairs of the Foundation.

Recently, it has been our good fortune to have Mr. Johnston de Forest elected a member of the Executive Committee. Mr. de Forest has made a most intensive and far-reaching study of the Foundation's finances and condition. His legal and financial experience has been an invaluable aid to the Committee in reviewing the situation as it stands and in planning to meet the problems of the Foundation's future—in which he is retaining his father's interest—in a prudent, conservative and constructive manner.

In conclusion, dear Mr. Tiffany, all the reports referred to are on file and I will be happy to bring any of them and go over them with you, or prepare any supplementary data that you may think will be helpful.

Faithfully
(Signed)   George F. Heydt
Secretary-Treasurer

Even the private little island of common sense and kindness which he had established in a world that needed both had put him down. On January 17, 1933, the gentle, troubled, eighty-five-year-old, nice little man died in his house on Seventy-second Street. He was not even to be buried from his chapel as he had wished. It was winter, the chapel was far away, and it was not heated.

With Tiffany gone the changes came swiftly. Miss Hanley asked the trustees to heat and winterize Laurelton Hall so she could live there. They refused and she resigned. Mr. Lothrop's resignation followed. Hobart Nichols, a well-known painter who had been president of the National Academy for ten years, was elected director. "Students" continued to be invited to "study" at the Foundation, but the hall itself was closed in 1938, a move that ended the Foundation as Tiffany had envisioned it. For a brief period,

Laurelton Hall had been "open to the public," but the public always seemed to go somewhere else.

When this country became involved in World War II, the trustees seized an opportunity both to serve the war effort and to close the "school." They continued, however, to plan. Clearly (to them) maintaining Laurelton Hall, the chapel, and all the other structures owned by the Foundation required money that should be used in other ways. The solution was obvious: Sell everything and invest the money in income-bearing securities. The courts were asked to and did shatter Tiffany's plans. By the end of 1946 the art collections had been sold at auction (for a total of $84,468.31). Laurelton Hall and four acres of land "after prolonged efforts" had brought less than $10,000. According to William Fielding, Tiffany's long-time friend and treasurer of the Foundation, the buildings (and they held nearly every one of his masterpieces in leaded windows) "were a liability."

Since then the Foundation has followed a course that bears no resemblance to Tiffany's wishes. Approximately $100,000 is granted each year to individual artists, but its influence on the arts of America has not been the kind of which Tiffany dreamed.

It is easy to second guess those who recast Tiffany's Foundation, but not necessarily fair. The original plan was founded on Tiffany's conviction that artists should be leaders in the battle to civilize the world and in his belief that Laurelton Hall would guide young people toward that end. It was also colored by his total lack of objectivity about himself and his views. The plan was not quite as new as Robert de Forest had stated because it was, in fact, an extension of the occasion on which he invited friends "to inspect the spring flowers" at Laurelton Hall so they could come under its spell. There was, of course, this difference: The fete was a one-shot affair; the Foundation would go on forever.

Tiffany had not taken into account the tendency of every "next generation" to question and to re-evaluate its cultural inheritance. The next generation giggled at him, rejected his art, reorganized his Foundation, and took it off in a new direction. Anyone in a hurry to condemn, however, should remember that the handsome, brown-haired, blue-eyed young Louis Tiffany was once a leader in a "let's get this all straightened out movement" himself.

Epilogue

Why was Tiffany's art rejected for so many years? What is his rightful place in the history of American art? Why the interest in his work now? How will future generations regard him? Answers to such questions must necessarily be our personal opinions.

Whatever else art is, it is communication. People tell a lot about themselves in what they make and like. The first world war with its machine guns, flying machines, tanks, and U-boats made it clear that man was well into a new age. Not only had he become dependent on the machine, but he seemed inclined to pattern society itself on the machine. One result was an increasing demand for the modern, the useful, and the new. As is always the case, the changes in ways of thinking were accompanied by changes in the arts. The new art forms had "sensible," "clean" lines, and simple, geometric, "no-nonsense" shapes. They were as functional and as free from furbelows as the parts of a rocket engine.

In this intellectual climate Laurelton Hall with its fountains, glass flowers set in cement capitals, hanging gardens, and leaded windows began to look about as relevant as a merry-go-round. Its message about the importance of being yourself, and its implication that independence is the handmaiden of beauty seemed terribly beside the point, to some, at least.

Buildings in the smart new style were as heart-warming as a cement block, as "clean" as a plumbing fixture, as logical as a computer, and as dull as all get out. Their interiors were often a glittering display of plywood, plastic, and chrome appointments, all shiny, all useful. Everybody was getting happier with each passing decade and each bright new bit of progress—well, almost everybody.

America, as it does every so often, began to think. Do we really want an environment patterned after the implacable resolve of a machine or the calculated bleakness of a factory? What does standardized art do for the human spirit? Should life turn like a wheel in a clock? Do we not need something personal, warm, and human in our architecture and in the other arts?

This kind of thinking resulted in some young people looking around for art that reflects it. The choice was not unlimited.

One discovery was Tiffany's glass and lamps which could be bought for a song, or less. They were like the touch of a friendly hand. The interest grew. New critics took an unbiased look. Museums dusted off the few pieces they had neglected to discard, and before long Tiffany was "in" again. This was all the more significant because his most important work is still unknown.

Does this mean art is good when and only when it is popular? Not at all. Popularity has nothing to do with artistic value. But like good conversation, art should add momentum and meaning to life. Tiffany's art has something vital to say, whether anyone listens or not.

Tiffany will surely fascinate many generations of Americans. He was the first American to brighten the eyes of European artists with so much envy and admiration that they studied his work and tried to imitate it for years. He dedicated a fortune to helping other artists. (Nearly every famous artist has become wealthy from his of her art, but I know of no other who did anything of this sort.) Most important of all, Tiffany's art has aesthetic vitality. When it is understood, it leads to discovery of new facets of one's own mind. Art capable of enriching the viewer's mind *must* be good whether anyone likes it or not.

Nevertheless, interest in Tiffany's work will ebb and flow. That is the way with art. The world is always interested in the "latest." And we will always have new art.

Tiffany the man will probably continue as something of an elegant enigma. Apocryphal stories will always have him "broad-shouldered, tall, handsome," or "so shy he was unable to utter a word in the presence of guests," or a spendthrift who squandered his inheritance on high life and perhaps an actress or two, or on carefully planned activities intended to keep himself in the public eye. (One tale has him giving a dinner at Sherry's at which each guest sat astride a horse. Such a dinner *was* given at Sherry's in 1903—by C. K. G. Billings.)

I have talked at length with his children, nephews, grandchildren, and great grandchildren, with William Fielding, his confidential secretary, with many close friends and associates, and with those who worked at Laurelton Hall and at the Tiffany Furnaces and Studios. I have seen the love and admiration his family and associates had for him. I have read his letters, diaries, comments in the minutes of the Tiffany Foundation. I remember his as a courtly, medium-sized (5′6″) eighty-two-year-old man, whose blue eyes twinkled with kindness and who was busy at his own work and at presiding graciously over a Foundation he had established to help young people make their way in the arts. I heard him talk with charm about the need for creative art and for imaginative thinking. I know this is an imperfect world, but I would discount the tales of his eccentricities and irresponsibilities as pretty much the standard fare we all welcome and enjoy about public figures.

All of which leads me to conclude that when, on that cold winter day in 1933, they covered him with a blanket of pink carnations and quietly laid him away in the rolling hills of Brooklyn, they marked the end of a good life and closed the career of a great man.

Appendix A

THE OLD PLATES

The following prints were made from Tiffany Studios glass photographic plates. Although the plates were partially destroyed, they may, nonetheless, be of interest to collectors and students.

FIGURE 254 *Antependium made for the Columbian Exposition Chapel in 1893.*

FIGURE 255 *Desk set. "Bookmark" pattern.*

FIGURE 256 *Inkstand. Bronze and Favrile glass.*

FIGURE 257   *Inkwells. Marble set with Favrile glass mosaic.*

FIGURE 260   *Side table. Wood and bronze.*

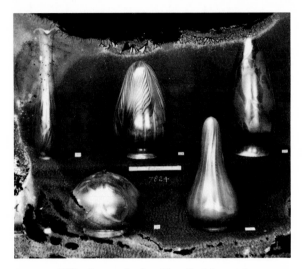

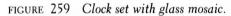

FIGURE 258   *Lampshades. Favrile blown glass.*

FIGURE 259   *Clock set with glass mosaic.*

FIGURE 261   *Desk lamp. Blown glass and bronze. Note the unexplained number 7228.*

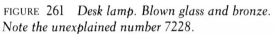

FIGURE 262   *Lamp base. Bronze.*

FIGURE 264   *Unidentified lamp with a base of Tiffany pottery.*

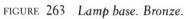
FIGURE 263   *Lamp base. Bronze.*

FIGURE 265   *Table lamp.*

FIGURE 266   *Table lamp. "Woodbine" pattern. Bronze base.*

FIGURE 268   *Table lamp. Geometric pattern with iridescent Favrile balls. Bronze base.*

FIGURE 267   *Design for a table lamp with silk shade.*

FIGURE 269   *Table lamp. Fruit design.*

FIGURE 270   *Table lamp. Pine needle filigree with Favrile glass mosaic dragonfly base.*

FIGURE 271   *Table lamp. Grapevine design.*

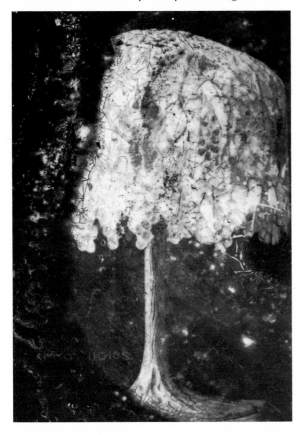

FIGURE 272   *Lamp. Floral globe with bronze base.*

FIGURE 273   *Wall sconce.*

FIGURE 274   *Wall sconce.*

FIGURE 276   *Hanging lamp. Trellis design.*

FIGURE 275   *Hanging lantern, bronze and Favrile glass.*

FIGURE 277   *Hanging lamp.*

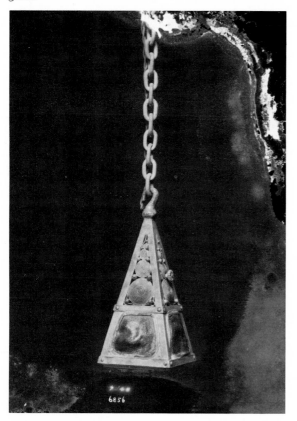

Appendix B

THE MARKS

Tiffany's marks and marking systems changed over the years. Some are clear, but others are obscure and may remain so since exceptions seem to abound for every proposed explanation. Marks are of two kinds, those cut, impressed, or stamped into or on the material, whatever it is, and those printed on paper labels. With very few exceptions, marks are in or on the most inconspicuous places, on the bottoms of vessels, for example, and on the inside of lamp shades.

This outline is not definitive. It is intended to help anyone wishing to study the matter further.

The marks listed below are mostly from pieces not illustrated in this work. Slash marks indicate that what follows is on another line. The small "o" used as a prefix to a number indicates the piece was a special order (Figure 278). "X" before a number means that the piece was an experiment (Figure 279); "EX" in a signature marks it as an exhibition piece. Numbers described as "canceled" have been scratched over with a sharp tool. "A-Coll." indicates that the piece was part of the artist's (Tiffany's) collection.

I. MARKS ON PAINTINGS

The earliest known work, a Christmas card dated 1864, is signed "L.T." Pencil and watercolor sketches made in 1866 are signed "L. Tiffany 66." Later watercolors were signed "L.C.T." in block letters. Most paintings are signed "Louis C. Tiffany" (Figure 280).

II. MARKS ON LEADED WINDOWS

Marks are acid-etched or enamel, usually in the lower right-hand corner of windows made for public buildings and mausoleums. Exhibition windows and those in private homes are rarely signed.

FIGURE 278

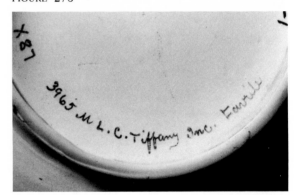

FIGURE 279

FIGURE 280

Between 1886 and 1892

The mark would presumably be "TIFFANY GLASS COMPANY."

Between 1892 and 1902

"TIFFANY GLASS & DECORATING COMPANY" is commonly used, often with the address 333–341 4th Avenue, New York.

FIGURE 281

After 1902

"TIFFANY STUDIOS NEW YORK" or "LOUIS C. TIFFANY" in block letters is common.

Some exceptions
"The Scholar," shown in the World's Columbian Exposition in 1893, is signed "TIFFANY STUDIOS/NEW YORK" in block letters, acid-etched on a small section of clear glass flashed with red (Figure 281).
"Feeding the Flamingoes" is signed in enamel "TIFFANY GLASS & DEC. CO./333–341 4th Ave. N.Y."

III. MARKS ON FABRICS

Fabric marks may be stenciled on the selvage or written on paper tags.
One velvet bears a tag: "Tiffany Studios/Fabrics/No. 978C/width 22″ x 36½″/price 144—" (Figure 282).

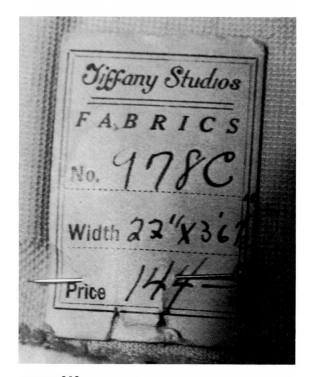

IV. MARKS ON ART GLASS

In 1926 an unsigned letter from the Louis C. Tiffany Furnaces, Inc., to the "Question and Answer" section of the December issue of *Antiques* magazine states that "all unusual pieces bear a number, the letters of the alphabet being used first as a prefix, later as a suffix to the numbers." Dr. Robert Koch in *Glass-Bronzes-Lamps* offers this plausible explanation, but also suggests caution in accepting it as the complete answer: Early pieces bore numbers only. When 10,000 was reached the next unusual piece was A1. A and B were used as a prefix in 1894. Two letters were so used each following year, the last being "Y" in 1905. Beginning in 1906 one letter was used as a suffix each year, the last being "W" for 1928.
Exceptions, as one might expect, cloud the picture. For example, pieces made for the Panama Pacific Exposition in 1915 bear "M" as a suffix (Figures 279 and 283), and

FIGURE 282

FIGURE 283

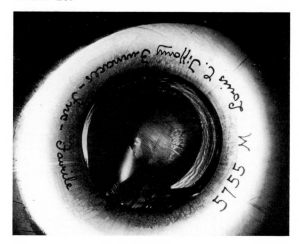

"M" on the schedule would date them 1918. Possibly the numbers relate to production totals, not to the calendar, and therefore give the order in which the pieces were made, not the year. This theory, however, would not explain why some late numbers appear on glass of an early type.

Some blown glass light fixtures in Laurelton Hall bore an engraved "Favrilite."

Before 1892

The monogram "TGC" (Figure 284) acid-etched on the pontil mark (assuming it stands for Tiffany Glass Company [1886–92]) indicates the piece was made before Tiffany's Corona Glasshouse was operating. This runs counter to Tiffany's own statements, however.

Between 1892 and 1900

Paper Labels
Some early pieces bear only numbered paper labels or simple paper labels reading "Tiffany Favrile (or Fabrile) Glass."
Paper labels bearing the "TGDCo" monogram for Tiffany Glass & Decorating Co. (registered November 13, 1894) may have been used as early as 1892 (Figure 285).

Engraved
Engraved marks include numbers, Tiffany's initials, the trade name "Favrile," and sometimes a script signature resembling Tiffany's hand. One vase is engraved on the bottom "1460" and bears a paper label with the same number (Figure 286).

Incised
Letters and/or numbers incised with a stylus may relate to inventory control.

After 1902

Paper labels
In 1902 the curvilinear "LCT" monogram (applied for May 29, 1903, and registered February 9, 1904), embossed in green and gold or printed in black and white, came into use, and the "TGDCo" label was discontinued (Figure 287).

Incised numbers
These vary in character and number of digits. In one set of six finger bowls, each is incised "610."

Examples:
Vase. Engraved script, "1535 9281 M Louis C. Tiffany Furnaces Inc. Favrile"; incised, "44655"/"544-655."
Matching sherbet glasses:
(a) Engraved script, "2336K L.C.T. Favrile."
(b) Engraved script, "L.C.T. Favrile."
(c) Engraved script, "2339K L.C.T. Favrile."
(d) Engraved script, "2340K L.C.T. Favrile."
Vase. Engraved, "X204 3772G L.C. Tiffany-Favrile."
Vase. Engraved, "L.C.T. 01276."

FIGURE 284

FIGURE 285

FIGURE 286

Vase. Engraved script, "Ex1024-Louis C. Tiffany-Favrile";
    block letters in red paint, "PARIS SALON/1st
    AWARD/L.C. Tiffany/oooC"; on the side in the
    same red paint, "24."
Bowl. Engraved script, "✗5 L.C. Tiffany-Inc. Favrile."
Vase. Engraved, "5-L.C.T. Favrile."
Vase. Engraved script, "L.C. Tiffany-Favrile"; incised,
    "7203"; curvilinear "LCT" monogram paper label; en-
    graved, "4193A."
Vase. Engraved script, "5540 M L.C. Tiffany Inc.-
    Favrile Exhibition Piece."

FIGURE 287

V. MARKS ON LEADED LAMP SHADES

Before 1902

Impressed
"TIFFANY STUDIOS NEW YORK" is often stamped
    on a tab or thin sheet of copper soldered to the inside
    of the shade. Marks on a thin ribbon of copper sol-
    dered to the leading often include numbers (Figure
    288).

After 1902

Impressed
Numbers change in character—may refer to the pattern.
    The tabs continue (Figure 289).

FIGURE 288

FIGURE 289

VI. MARKS ON LAMP BASES

Before 1900

Impressed
The "TGDCo" monogram is often used along with what
    may be serial numbers.

Between 1900 and 1902

Impressed
"TIFFANY STUDIOS/NEW YORK" and the
    "TGDCo" monogram often appear on the same piece
    along with what seem to be serial numbers (Figure
    290).

Between 1902 and 1919

Impressed
The "TGDCo" monogram was discontinued. "Tiffany
    Studios/New York" is common. Pattern numbers
    beginning with 100 replace serial numbers (Figure
    291).

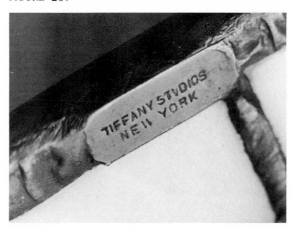

Between 1919 and 1928

Impressed
"LOUIS C. TIFFANY FURNACES INC. FAVRILE" is often used together with the curvilinear "LCT" monogram.

Incised
Incised numbers are common.

Examples:

Amber "Dragonfly" table lamp. Base stamped, "TIF-FANY STUDIOS/NEW YORK/360"; incised, "4478." Shade stamped, "TIFFANY STUDIOS NEW YORK 1495-36."

Blue "Dragonfly" table lamp. Base stamped, "TIFFANY STUDIOS/NEW YORK/363"; incised, "174" (canceled)/"392." Shade stamped, "TIFFANY STUDIOS NEW YORK."

"Black-eyed Susan" table lamp. Base stamped, "TIF-FANY STUDIOS/NEW YORK/6839"; incised, "4810." Shade stamped, "TIFFANY STUDIOS/NEW YORK."

Lamp base (blown glass) with metal fuel canister. Base engraved, "L.C.T." Canister stamped, "TIFFANY G. & D. Co/N.Y./S1362/1."

Miniature "Wisteria" lamp. Base stamped, "TIFFANY STUDIOS/NEW YORK/10001." Shade unsigned.

"Acorn" table lamp. Base stamped, "TIFFANY STUDIOS/NEW YORK/25878"/"TGDCo" monogram. Shade stamped, "TIFFANY STUDIOS, NEW YORK."

FIGURE 290

FIGURE 291

FIGURE 292

VII. MARKS ON POTTERY

Incised before firing
A common signature is the conjoined "LCT" monogram with a symbol that can be read either as "L" or as "7" (Figure 292).

Engraved after firing
The engraved marks are usually "L.C. Tiffany Favrile/Pottery" combined with pertinent information such as "A-Coll." or "Exhibition Piece."

Examples:

Vase. Incised, conjoined "LCT" monogram; engraved script, "P1304 L.C. Tiffany-Favrile Pottery."

Vase. Incised, conjoined "LCT" monogram/"7" or an "L"; engraved script, "82 A-Coll. L.C. Tiffany-Favrile Pottery."

Vase. Engraved script, "L.C. Tiffany Favrile Pottery P 1182"/conjoined "LCT" monogram/"7" (incised).

Vase. Engraved script, "Tiffany Favrile Pottery P 301"/"7"/conjoined "LCT" monogram (incised).

VIII. MARKS ON BRONZE POTTERY

Impressed or engraved
"BP" in addition to other pottery marks. Sometimes it is spelled out. Some pieces bear either Tiffany's signature or a facsimile of it (Figure 293).

Examples:
Vase. Incised, conjoined "LCT" monogram; engraved script, "L.C. Tiffany-Favrile Bronze Pottery"; engraved, "B.P.392"; incised, "4"/"7."
Vase. Incised, conjoined "LCT" monogram; engraved, "B.P346"; engraved script, "L.C. Tiffany-Favrile Bronze Pottery"; stamped, "BP190."

FIGURE 293

IX. MARKS ON CARVED ROCK CRYSTAL

Wheel cut
"L.C. TIFFANY" is often wheel engraved in block letters.
One vase is marked "115 L.C. TIFFANY" in block letters (Figure 294).

FIGURE 294

FIGURE 295

X. MARKS ON METALWARE
(DESK SETS, CANDLESTICKS, ETC.)

Before 1900

Impressed
The "TGDCo" monogram is common. Many pieces also bear individual numbers which run into the thousands.

Between 1900 and 1902

Impressed
"TIFFANY STUDIOS/NEW YORK" appears sometimes above, sometimes below the "TGDCo" monogram. Individual numbers continue (Figure 295).

Between 1902 and 1919

Impressed

"TIFFANY STUDIOS/NEW YORK" is used together with a monogram (either a curvilinear "L.C.T." or a curvilinear "TS" for Tiffany Studios), along with numbers apparently related to models (Figure 296). Fancywares (including desk sets) begin at "800," candlesticks begin at "1200." "TIFFANY FURNACES" is also used but not with "TIFFANY STUDIOS."

Between 1920 and 1928

Impressed

After 1920 "LOUIS C. TIFFANY FURNACES, INC. FAVRILE" accompanied by the curvilinear monogram "LCT" came into general use (Figure 297). "TIFFANY STUDIOS" was discontinued.

Examples:

Inkwell with enamel. Stamped, curvilinear "LCT" monogram/"LOUIS C. TIFFANY FURNACES, INC./357"; incised, "3510."

Pen tray. Stamped, "TIFFANY STUDIOS/NEW YORK/1763."

Stamp box. Stamped, "TIFFANY STUDIOS/NEW YORK/1645"; incised, "10037."

Favrile glass vase with a metal base. Base stamped, curvilinear "LCT" monogram/"LOUIS C. TIFFANY FURNACES, INC./FAVRILE/151"; incised, "6103." Glass engraved, "L.C.T."

Desk calendar. Stamped, "TIFFANY STUDIOS/NEW YORK/1118"; incised, "5803."

XI. MARKS ON SILVER

Impressed

Silver marked "TIFFANY STUDIOS" is not common. A silver-plated copper pitcher ornamented with silver and gold (Figure 232) is stamped "TIFFANY STUDIOS/NEW YORK."

Incised

A small silver box (Figure 228) is stamped "TIFFANY FURNACES/STERLING/239" and incised "9/289" on the bottom, and incised "239" on the lid (Figure 298).

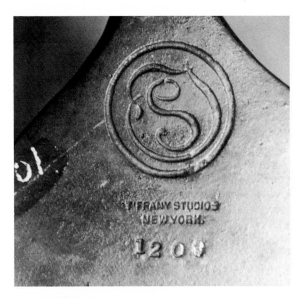

FIGURE 296

FIGURE 297

FIGURE 298

XII. MARKS ON ENAMELS

Marks on a single piece may be stamped, engraved, and/or incised.

"EL," "SG" and "EG" are the most common letters. No periods are used (Figure 299). "EL" appears (in pencil) on some photographs in the Tiffany Studios collection.

Numbers on enamels have a system all their own (Figure 300). Examples: One tray is marked "SG 123" (stamped) "162 A-Coll." (engraved). Another tray is marked "EL 169" (stamped) "34 9" (incised).

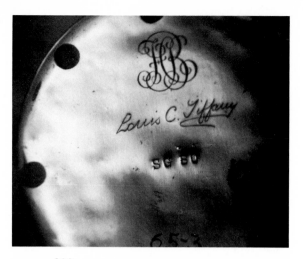

FIGURE 299

XIII. MARKS ON GLAZED CERAMIC TILES

Tiles from the dining room fireplace in Laurelton Hall are stamped: "TIFFAИY (*sic*) B 1325"
  "TIFFAИY (*sic*) B 13250"

FIGURE 300

XIV. MARKS ON GLASS TILES

Embossed
Early opalescent goldleaf-backed press-molded tiles carry "Pat. FEB. 8th 1881" and "L.C.T. & Co." on the back (Figure 301).

Engraved
One blue iridescent tile is marked "Sample H 1" on its face.

FIGURE 301

XV. MARKS ON JEWELRY

Most pieces are marked "Tiffany & Co." Some are marked "Tiffany Studios."

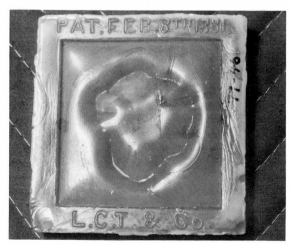

XVI. MARKS ON PHOTOGRAPHS

Tiffany photographs are stamped in the lower right-hand corner of the mat, "LOUIS C. TIFFANY."

NOTE: Photographs of the marks were made by Theodore Flagg and David Donaldson.

Bibliography

BOOKS

ALEXANDER, JAMES W.
A History of the University Club of New York, 1865–1915 New York: Charles Scribner's Sons, 1915.

AMAYA, MARIO.
Tiffany Glass. New York: Walker and Sons, 1966.

ANDREWS, WAYNE.
Architecture, Ambition and Americans. New York: Harper & Brothers, 1955.

ARMITAGE, E. L.
Stained Glass. Newton, Mass.: Charles T. Branford Co., 1959.

ARMSTRONG, D. MAITLAND.
Day Before Yesterday. New York: Privately printed, 1922.

ARMSTRONG, HAMILTON FISH.
Those Days. New York: Harper & Brothers, 1963.

Art Gallery, Illustrated, World's Columbian Exposition. Charles M. Kurtz, Ed. Philadelphia: George Barrie.

ARWAS, VICTOR.
Glass Art Nouveau to Art Deco. New York: Rizzoli International Publications, Inc., 1977.

BALDWIN, CHARLES C.
Stanford White. New York: Dodd, Mead & Co., 1931.

BANCROFT, HUBERT HOWE.
The Book of the Fair. New York: Bounty Book, 1894.

BARKER, VIRGIL.
American Painting. New York: The Macmillan Company, 1950.

BATTERSBY, MARTIN.
Art Nouveau. Middlesex, Eng.: The Colour Library of Art. The Hamlyn Publishing Group Ltd., 1969.

———.
The World of Art Nouveau. New York: Funk & Wagnalls Co., Inc., 1968.

BAUR, JOHN I. H.
Revolution and Tradition in Modern American Art. Cambridge: Harvard University Press, 1951.

———.
American Painting in the Nineteenth Century: Main Trends and Movements. New York: Frederick H. Praeger, Inc., 1953.

BEER, THOMAS.
The Mauve Decade. New York: Alfred A. Knopf, 1926.

BENJAMIN, S. G. W.
Art in America. New York: Harper & Brothers, 1880.

BING, S.
La Culture Artistique en Amerique. Paris: Privately printed, 1896.

BLASHFIELD, EDWIN HOWLAND.
Mural Painting in America. New York: Charles Scribner's Sons, 1913.

BOK, EDWARD.
The Americanization of Edward Bok. New York: Charles Scribner's Sons, 1922.

BOSSAGLIA, ROSSANA.
Art Nouveau. New York: Crescent Books, 1971.

BRINE, MARY D.
On The Road to Slumberland, or My Boy and I. Boston: G. W. Harlan, 1881.

BROWN, MILTON W.
Story of the Armory Show. New York: The Joseph H. Hirshhorn Foundation, 1963.

BURNHAM, ALAN.
New York Landmarks. Middletown, Conn.: Wesleyan University Press, 1963.

CASSOU, JEAN; LANGUI, EMIL; PEVSNER, NIKOLAUS.
Gateway to the Twentieth Century: Art and Culture in A Changing World. New York: McGraw-Hill Book Company, 1961.

Charles L. Tiffany and the House of Tiffany & Co. New York: Tiffany & Company. Union Square, 1893.

CLARK, COL. EMMONS.
   History of the Seventh Regiment (2 vols.). New
   York: Privately printed, 1890.
COAD AND MIMS.
   "The American Stage." *The Pageant of America.*
   Vol. 14. New Haven: Yale University Press, 1929.
CONNICK, CHARLES J.
   Adventures in Light and Color. New York: Random
   House, 1937.
COOK, CLARENCE.
   Art and Artists of Our Time. New York: S. Hess,
   1888.
———.
   The House Beautiful. New York: Scribner, Armstrong
   & Co., 1878.
———.
   What Shall We Do with Our Walls? New York:
   Warren Fuller & Co., 1880.
CORTISSOZ, ROYAL.
   John La Farge, A Memoir and a Study. Boston:
   Houghton, Mifflin Co., 1911.
CRAM, RALPH ADAMS.
   My Life in Architecture. Boston: Little, Brown &
   Co., 1936.
———.
   The Gothic Quest. New York: The Baker & Taylor
   Co., 1907.
DAVIS AND MIDDLEMAS.
   Colored Glass. New York: Clarkson N. Potter, Inc.,
   1968.
DAY, LEWIS F.
   Windows. London: B. T. Batsford Ltd., 1909.
DE FOREST, LOCKWOOD.
   Indian Architecture and Ornament. Boston: G. H.
   Polley & Co., 1887.
———.
   Indian Domestic Architecture. Boston: Heliotype
   Printing Co., 1885.
DEKAY, CHARLES (anonymous author).
   The Art Work of Louis C. Tiffany. New York:
   Doubleday, Page & Co., 1914.
DESMOND, HARRY W. and CROLY, HERBERT.
   Stately Homes In America. New York: D. Appleton,
   1903.
DIAMOND, FRIEDA.
   The Story of Glass. New York: Harcourt, Brace &
   Co., 1953.
DICKASON, DAVID HOWARD.
   The Daring Young Men. Bloomington, Ind.: Indiana
   University Press, 1953.
DOWNING, A. J.
   Cottage Residences. New York: John Wiley, 1860.
DREXLER, ARTHUR, and DANIEL, GRETA.
   Introduction to Twentieth Century Design. New
   York: Museum of Modern Art, 1959.
DUFFUS, ROBERT L.
   The American Renaissance. New York: Albert A.
   Knopf, 1928.
DUNN, WALDO H.
   The Life of Donald G. Mitchell. New York: Charles
   Scribner's Sons, 1922.

DUTTON, RALPH.
   The Victorian Home. London: B. T. Batsford Ltd.,
   1954.
ELLIOTT, CHARLES W.
   The Book of American Interiors. Boston: Privately
   printed, 1876.
ERICSON, ERIC E.
   A Guide to Colored Steuben Glass, 1903–1933.
   Denver: The Lithographic Press, 1963.
EVANS, PAUL.
   *Art Pottery of the United States, an Encyclopedia of
   Producers and Their Marks.* New York: Charles
   Scribner's Sons, 1974.
FIELDING, WILLIAM J.
   *Recollections of My Association With Louis Comfort
   Tiffany and His Art Foundation—The First 50 Years.*
   New York: Tiffany Foundation, 1974. Privately dis-
   tributed.
FROHMAN, DANIEL.
   Daniel Frohman Presents New York. New York:
   C. Kendall and W. Sharp, 1935.
———.
   Memoirs of a Manager. New York: Doubleday, Page
   & Co., 1911.
FURST, HERBERT.
   The Decorative Art of Frank Brangwyn. Great Brit-
   ain: Geo. Gibbons & Co., 1924.
GARDENER, PAUL V.
   The Glass of Frederick Carder. New York: Crown
   Publishers, Inc., 1971.
———.
   Glass. The Smithsonian Illustrated Library of An-
   tiques. Prepared by the Cooper-Hewitt Museum in
   association with the Book of the Month Club, Camp
   Hill, Pa., 1979.
Great Interiors. Ian Grant, Ed. New York: E. P. Dut-
   ton & Co., Inc., 1967.
HAMLIN, TALBOT F.
   "The American Spirit in Architecture." *The Pageant
   of America.* Vol. 13. New Haven: Yale University
   Press, 1926.
HARRISON, CONSTANCE CARY.
   Woman's Handiwork in Modern Homes. New York:
   Charles Scribner's Sons, 1881.
HARTMANN, SADAKICHI.
   A History of American Art. Boston: L. C. Page &
   Co., 1901.
HENZKE, LUCILE.
   American Art Pottery. Camden, N.J.: Thomas Nelson
   Inc., 1970.
HITCHCOCK, HENRY RUSSELL.
   Architecture, Nineteenth and Twentieth Centuries.
   Baltimore: Penguin Books, 1959.
HOOPES, DONELSON.
   The American Impressionists. New York: Watson-
   Guptil Publications, 1978.
HOWE, WINIFRED E.
   A History of the Metropolitan Museum of Art. New
   York: 1913.
HUETHER, ANNE.
   Glass and Man. Philadelphia: J. B. Lippincott, 1963.
HUGHES, GRAHAM.
   Modern Jewelry. New York: Crown Publishers, Inc.,
   1963.

HUTTER, HERIBERT.
   Art Nouveau. New York: Crown Publishers, Inc., 1965.
IRWIN, WILLIAM H.
   A History of the Union League Club of New York City. New York: Dodd, Mead & Co., 1952.
ISHAM, SAMUEL.
   The History of American Painting. New York: The Macmillan Company, 1927.
ITTEN, JOHANNES.
   Um 1900. Zurick: Kunstgewerbemuseum, 1952.
JACKMAN, RILL E.
   American Arts. Chicago: Rand, McNally & Co., 1928.
JACKSON, HOLBROOK.
   The Eighteen Nineties. London: Penguin Books, 1913.
JULLIAN, PHILLIPPE.
   The Triumph of Art Nouveau. Paris Exhibition 1900. New York: Larousse & Co., Inc., 1974.
KAUFMANN, EDGAR, JR.
   What Is Modern Design? New York: Museum of Modern Art, 1950.
KEMPTON, RICHARD.
   Art Nouveau, an Annotated Bibliography. Los Angeles: Hennessey & Ingalls, Inc., 1977.
KING, MOSES.
   King's Handbook of New York City, 1893. (Second Ed.) New York: Benjamin Blom, Inc., 1972.
————.
   King's Photographic Views of New York. Boston: 1895.
KOCH, ROBERT.
   Louis C. Tiffany's Glass—Bronzes—Lamps. New York: Crown Publishers, Inc., 1971.
————.
   Louis C. Tiffany, Rebel in Glass. New York: Crown Publishers, Inc., 1964.
————.
   Louis C. Tiffany's Art Glass. New York: Crown Publishers, Inc., 1977.
KOLB, H.
   Der Ornamentenschatz, Ein Musterbuch, Stilvoller Ornamente. Stuttgart, Germany: Julius Hoffman, 1883.
LARKIN, OLIVER W.
   Art and Life in America. New York: Rinehart & Co., 1949.
Late Nineteenth-Century Art. Hans Jürgen Hansen, Ed. New York: McGraw-Hill Book Company, 1972.
LEE, LAWRENCE; SEDDON, GEORGE; STEPHENS, FRANCIS.
   Stained Glass. New York: Crown Publishers, Inc., 1976.
LENNING, HENRY F.
   The Art Nouveau. The Hague: M. Nijhoff, 1951.
LIFE, EDITORS OF.
   America's Arts and Skills. New York: Time, Inc., 1957.
LLOYD, JOHN GILBERT.
   Stained Glass in America. Jenkintown, Pa.: Foundation Books, 1963.

LUCAS, E. V.
   Edwin Austin Abbey. New York: Charles Scribner's Sons, 1921.
LYNES, RUSSELL.
   The Tastemakers. New York: Harper & Brothers, 1954.
MCCABE, JAMES D.
   The Illustrated History of the Centennial Exhibition. Philadelphia: The National Publishing Co., 1876.
MCCLINTON, KATHARINE MORRISON.
   Collecting American Glass. New York: Gramercy Publishing Co., 1950.
MCKEAN, HUGH F. AND KOCH, ROBERT.
   "Looking at the World Through Colored Favrile Glass" and "Hidden Treasures in the McKean Tiffany Collection," *Revolt in the Parlor*. Winter Park, Fla.: The Parlor Press, 1969.
MCKEARIN, GEORGE S. and HELEN.
   American Glass. New York: Crown Publishers, Inc., 1941.
————.
   Two Hundred Years of American Blown Glass. New York: Crown Publishers, Inc., 1950.
MAASS, JOHN.
   The Glorious Enterprise. Watkins Glen, N. Y.: American Life Foundation, 1973.
————.
   The Victorian Home in America. New York: Hawthorn Books, 1972.
MACKAYE, PERCY.
   Epoch: The Life of Steele MacKaye. New York: Boni & Liveright, 1927.
MADSEN, STEPHEN TSCHUDI.
   Art Nouveau. New York and Toronto: World University Library, McGraw-Hill Book Company, 1967.
————.
   Sources of Art Nouveau. New York: Wittenborn & Co., 1955.
MEEKS, CARROLL L. V.
   The Railroad Station. New Haven: Yale University Press, 1956.
MENDELOWITZ, DANIEL M.
   A History of American Art. New York: Holt, Rinehart & Winston, 1960.
METROPOLITAN MUSEUM OF ART
   19th-Century America, Furniture and Other Decorative Arts. New York, 1970.
MITCHELL, LOUIS.
   The Woodbridge Record. New Haven: Tuttle, Morehouse & Taylor, 1883.
MORRIS, WILLIAM.
   The Decorative Arts. Boston: Roberts Brothers, 1878.
MORRISON, HUGH.
   Louis Sullivan Prophet of Modern Architecture. New York: W. W. Norton & Company, Inc., 1935
MUSEUM OF MODERN ART.
   Art Nouveau, Art and Design at the Turn of the Century. Garden City, N.Y.: Doubleday & Company, Inc., 1959.
NEWTON, ERIC.
   The Romantic Rebellion. New York: Schocken Books, 1962.

NORWICH, JOHN JULIUS.
  Great Architecture of the World. New York: Random House, Inc., 1975.
PAPERT, EMMA.
  The Illustrated Guide to American Glass. New York: Hawthorn Books, Inc., 1972.
PAZAUREK, GUSTAV E.
  Moderne Glaser. Leipzig: Hermann Seemann Nachfolger.
PENNELL, E. R., and J.
  The Life of James McNeill Whistler, Philadelphia: J. B. Lippincott Co., 1908.
PEVSNER, NIKOLAUS.
  Pioneers of Modern Design. New York: Museum of Modern Art, 1949.
PRIESTLEY, J. B.
  The Edwardians. New York: Harper & Row, 1970.
PURTELL, JOSEPH.
  The Tiffany Touch. Tennessee: Kingsport Press, 1971.
RAGAN, H. H.
  Art Photographs of the World & the Columbian Exposition 1893. San Francisco: Star Publishing Co., The King Publishing Company, 1893.
RALPH, JULIAN.
  Chicago and The World's Fair. New York: Harper & Brothers, 1892.
RANDEL, WILLIAM PIERCE.
  Centennial, American Life in 1876. Philadelphia: Chilton Book Company, 1969.
READE, BRIAN.
  Art Nouveau and Alphonse Mucha. London: Her Majesty's Stationery Office, 1967.
REVI, ALBERT CHRISTIAN.
  Nineteenth Century Glass. New York: Thomas Nelson & Sons, 1959.
RHEIMS, MAURICE.
  The Flowering of Art Nouveau. New York: Harry N. Abrams, Inc., not dated.
RHODES, DANIEL.
  Clay and Glazes for the Potter. Radnor, Pa.: Chilton Book Company, 1957.
ROSENTHAL, R., and RATZKA, A.
  The Story of Modern Applied Arts. New York: Harper & Brothers, 1948.
ROSS, ISHBEL.
  Taste in America, An Illustrated History. New York: Thomas Y. Crowell Company, 1967.
SAARINEN, ALINE.
  The Proud Possessors. New York: Random House, Inc., 1958.
SAINT-GAUDENS, HOMER.
  The Reminiscences of Augustus Saint-Gaudens. New York: The Century Co., 1913.
SAVAGE, GEORGE.
  Glass of the World. New York: Galahad Books. 1973-75.
SCHMUTZLER, ROBERT.
  Art Nouveau. New York: Harry N. Abrams Inc., 1962.

SELZ, PETER.
  Art Nouveau. New York: Museum of Modern Art, 1960.
SEWTER, A. CHARLES.
  The Stained Glass of William Morris and His Circle. New Haven: Yale University Press, 1974.
SHELDON, GEORGE W.
  American Painters. New York: D. Appleton & Co., 1881.
———.
  Artistic Houses. New York: D. Appleton & Co., 1882–84.
SIMON, KATE.
  Fifth Avenue. New York: Harcourt Brace Jovanovich, 1978.
SIZER, THEODORE.
  The Recollections of John Ferguson Weir. New Haven: Yale University Press, 1957.
SMITH, CORINNA LINDEN.
  Interesting People: Eighty Years with the Great and Near-Great. Norman, Okla.: University of Oklahoma Press, 1962.
SMITH, WALTER.
  "Industrial Art." *Masterpieces of the Centennial.* Vol. 2. Philadelphia: Gebbie & Barrie, 1876.
SOWERS, ROBERT.
  The Lost Art. New York: Wittenborn & Co., 1954.
SPEENBURGH, GERTRUDE.
  The Arts of the Tiffanys. Chicago: Lightner Publishing Co., 1956.
STERN, MADELINE R.
  We The Women. New York: Schulte Publishing Co., 1962.
STODDARD, WILLIAM O.
  "Charles L. Tiffany," *Men of Business, Men of Achievement.* New York: Charles Scribner's Sons, 1893.
The Story of America. Pleasantville, New York: Reader's Digest Association Inc., 1955.
The Tiffanys of America, History and Genealogy. New York: Nelson Otis Tiffany, Publisher, 1901.
TRUMAN, MAJOR BEN C.
  History of The World's Fair. Philadelphia, Pa.: Mammoth Publishing Co., 1893.
VAN TASSEL, VALENTINE.
  American Glass. New York: Gramercy Publishing Company, no date.
VEDDER, ELIHU.
  The Digressions of Elihu Vedder. Boston: Houghton, Mifflin Co., 1910.
WAERN, CECILIA.
  John LaFarge, Artist and Writer. London: The Macmillan Company, 1896.
WATKINS, LURA WOODSIDE.
  American Glass and Glassmaking. New York: Chanticleer Press, 1950.
WHALL, CHRISTOPHER W.
  Stained Glass Work. London: J. Hogg, 1905.
WHEELER, CANDACE.
  Principles of Home Decoration. New York: Doubleday, Page & Co., 1903.

————. *Yesterdays in a Busy Life.* New York: Harper & Brothers, 1918.

————. *The Development of Embroidery in America.* New York: Harper & Brothers, 1921.

WHITE, TRUMBULL and IGLEHART, WILLIAM.
World's Columbian Exposition. Boston: Standard Silverware Co., 1893.

WINTER, HENRY.
The Dynasty of Louis Comfort Tiffany. Boston: Privately printed, 1971.

————. *The Louis Comfort Tiffany Commemorative Edition,* Boston: Privately printed, 1972.

YOUNG, MAY.
Singing Windows. New York: Abingdon Press, 1962.

ARTICLES IN NEWSPAPERS AND PERIODICALS
PUBLISHED DURING L.C.T.'S LIFETIME—SIGNED

ALCOCK, SIR RUTHERFORD, K.C.B., D.C.L.
"Japanese Art," *The Art Journal,* Vol. I, 1875, pp. 101–5, 197–202, 337–39.

AVERY, MARY L.
"The Opening of the New Library Building," *Pratt Institute Monthly,* Vol. IV, No. 10, June 1896.

BEBARBIERI, ISABELLA.
"Mosaics as an Independent Art," *The Architectural Record,* Vol. 2, 1893, pp. 291–302.

BING, S.
Artistic Japan, 36 issues. Paris, 1888–91.

————. "Die Kunstglaser, von Louis C. Tiffany," *Kunst und Kunst-handwerk,* Vol. L, 1898, pp. 105–11.

————. "L'Art Nouveau," *The Architectural Record,* Vol. 12, 1902, pp. 281–85.

————. "L'Art Nouveau," *The Craftsman,* October 1903, pp. 1–15.

————. "Wohim Treiben Wir?" *Dekorative Kunst,* Vol. I, 1898, pp. 160–77.

BRECK, JOSEPH.
"Louis C. Tiffany's Window," *Metropolitan Museum of Art Bulletin,* Vol. 20, 1925, pp. 287–88.

BROWNELL, WILLIAM C.
"The Younger Painters of America," *Scribner's Monthly,* July 1881, pp. 321–34.

CAFFIN, CHARLES H.
"Decorative Windows," *The Craftsman,* Vol. III, No. 5, pp. 350–60.

COLEMAN, CARYL.
"A Sea of Glass," *The Architectural Record,* Vol. 2, 1893, pp. 264–85.

————. "The Second Spring," *The Architectural Record,* Vol. 2, 1893, pp. 473–92.

CONDER, F. R.
"Annealed Glass." *The Art Journal,* Vol. I, 1875, p. 234.

CONWAY, EDWARD HAROLD.
"Mr. Louis C. Tiffany's Laurelton Hall at Cold Spring, Long Island," *The Spur,* August 15, 1914, pp. 25–29.

COOK, CLARENCE.
"Penelope in America," *The Decorator and Furnisher,* Vol. IV (3), June 1884, p. 90.

CROSBY, ERNEST.
"The Nineteenth Century," *The Craftsman,* Vol. VI, No. 4, July 1904, pp. 409–10.

DAY, LEWIS F.
"Favrile Glass," *Magazine of Art,* Vol. 24, 1900, pp. 541–44.

————. "Modern Mosaic in England," *The Architectural Record,* Vol. 2, 1892, pp. 65–88.

DE CUERS, RENÉ.
"Domestic Stained Glass in France," *The Architectural Record,* Vol. 9, 1899, pp. 115–42.

DEKAY, CHARLES.
"A Western Setting for the Beauty of the Orient," *Arts and Decoration.* October 1911, pp. 468–71.

DE QUELIN, RENÉ.
"A Many-Sided Creator of the Beautiful," *Arts and Decoration,* Vol. 17, 1911, pp. 176–77.

————. "This Te Deum is Sung in Glass," *The International Studio,* Vol. 78, 1923, pp. 360–61.

DEWSON, EDWARD.
"Stained Glass as Applied to Transparencies," *The Decorator and Furnisher,* Vol. 3 (1), October 1881, p. 9.

DREISER, THEODORE.
"The Making of Stained Glass Windows," *Cosmopolitan,* Vol. 26, 1899, pp. 243–52.

ELLIOTT, CHARLES WILLYS.
"How to Decorate Pottery and Porcelain," *The Art Journal,* Vol. III, 1877, pp. 305–9.

FRED, A. W.
"Interieurs von L. C. Tiffany," *Dekorative Kunst,* Vol. 9, 1901, pp. 110–16.

FUCHS, GEORG.
"Eindrücke aus der amerikanischen Abteilung," *Deutsch Kunst und Dekoration,* Vol. XI, 1902, pp. 182–92.

GENSEL, WALTHER.
Tiffany-Glaser auf der Pariser Welt-Ausstellung 1900," *Deutsche Kunst und Dekoration,* Vol. 7, 1900–1, pp. 44–45, 86–93, 95–97.

GOODHUE, H. E.
"Stained Glass in Private Houses," *The Architectural Record,* Vol. 18, 1905, pp. 347–54.

GUIMARD, HECTOR.
"An Architect's Opinion of L'Art Nouveau," *The Architectural Record,* Vol. 12, 1902, pp. 126–33.

HAMLIN, A. D. F.
"L'Art Nouveau, Its Origin and Development," *The Craftsman;* Vol. III, No. 3, December 1902.

HARRISON, CONSTANCE CARY.
"Some Work of the Associated Artists," *Harper's Magazine*, Vol. 69, 1884, pp. 343–51.

HARRISON, MRS. BURTON.
"Some Work of the Associated Artists," *Household Art*, 1893, pp. 56–73.

HARVEY, JAMES L.
"Source of Beauty in Favrile Glass," *Brush and Pencil*, Vol. 9, 1901, pp. 167–76.

HEINIGKE, OTTO.
"Random Thoughts of a Glassman," *The Craftsman*, Vol. III, No. 3, December 1902, pp. 170–82.

HENDERSON, W. J.
"Some New York Theatres," *Magazine of Art*, Vol. 9, 1886, pp. 401–7.

HOWE, SAMUEL.
"A Country Home with a Human Appeal," *Long Island Home Journal*, March 1914, pp. 4–6.

———.
"An American Country House," *The International Studio*, Vol. 33, 1907–8, pp. 294–96.

———.
"The Dwelling Place as an Expression of Individuality," *Appleton's Magazine*, February 1907, pp. 156–65.

———.
"Enamel as a Decorative Agent," *The Craftsman*, Vol. 2, 1902, pp. 61–68.

———.
"The Garden of Mr. Louis C. Tiffany," *House Beautiful*, January 1914, pp. 40–42.

———.
"The Long Island Home of Mr. Louis C. Tiffany," *Town and Country*, September 6, 1913, pp. 24–26, 42.

———.
"The Making of Glass," *The Craftsman*, Vol. 3, 1903, pp. 367.

———.
"One Source of Color Values," *House and Garden*, September, 1906, pp. 104–13.

———.
"The Silent Fountains of Laurelton Hall," *Arts and Decoration*, September 1913, pp. 377–79.

———.
"The Use of Ornament in the House," *The Craftsman*, Vol. 3, 1902, p. 91.

HUMPHREYS, MARY GAY.
The Art Amateur. Vol. 5, No. 3, August 1881, pp. 47, 54.

JEWITT, LLEWELLYNN, F. S. A.
"Ancient Irish Art, A Few Words on Interlaced Metalwork," *The Art Journal*, Vol. III, 1877. pp. 174–76.

KOBBÉ, GUSTAV.
"Angel of Truth for the John G. Shedd Mausoleum," *New York Herald*, December 26, 1915.

———.
"Mr. Louis C. Tiffany, Famous Artist in Stained Glass," *New York Herald Magazine*. April 23, 1916, p. 6.

KOCH, ROBERT.
"Art Nouveau Bing," *Gazette des Beaux Arts*, March 1959, pp. 179–90.

KURTZ, CHARLES M.
"World's Columbian Exposition," *Art Gallery Illustrated*, 1893, pp. 115, 348.

LAMB, CHARLES R.
"How an American Stained Glass Window Is Made," *The Chautauquan*, Vol. 29, 1899, pp. 513–52.

LAMB, FREDERICK S.
"The Beautifying of Our Cities," *The Craftsman*, Vol. 11, No. 4, July 1902, pp. 172–88.

———.
"Modern Use of Gothic," *The Craftsman*, Vol. 8, 1905, pp. 150–70.

———.
"The Painted Window," *The Craftsman*, Vol. 3, 1903, p. 348.

———.
"Stained Glass in Relation to Church Ornamentation," *The Catholic World*, Vol. 74, 1902, pp. 661–77.

LAMPREY, B. L.
"The Yale Window," *The Decorator and Furnisher*, Vol. XIII (5), February 1889, p. 140.

LATHROP, GEORGE PARSONS.
"John LaFarge," *Scribner's Monthly*, Vol. 21, 1881, pp. 503–16.

LOCKE, JOSEPHINE C.
"Some Impressions of L'Art Nouveau," *The Craftsman*, Vol. 11, July 1902, pp. 201–4.

LOTHROP, STANLEY.
"Louis Comfort Tiffany Foundation," *American Magazine of Art*, Vol. 14, 1923, pp. 615–17.

LOUNDSBERY, ELIZABETH.
"Aquamarine Glass," *American Homes and Gardens*, December 1913, pp. 418, 441.

LOW, WILL H.
"Old Glass In New Windows," *Scribner's Magazine*, Vol. 4, 1888, pp. 675–86.

LYMAN, CLARA BROWN.
"Recent Achievements in Decorative Lighting," *Country Life in America*, October 1914, pp. 52–54.

MEIER-GRAAFE, J.
"M. Louis C. Tiffany," *L'Art Decoratif*, Vol. 1. No. 3, 1898, pp. 105, 106, 116–23.

MELANI, M.
"L'Art Nouveau at Turin," *Architectural Record*, Vol. 12, May–December 1902, pp. 734–50, 586–99.

MILLET, FRANK D.
"Some American Tiles," *The Century Magazine*, April 1882, p. 896.

MITCHELL, DONALD G.
"In and About the Fair," *Scribner's Monthly*, Vol. 12, 1876, pp. 742, 889; Vol. 13, 1877, p. 115.

MOLINIER, ÉMILE.
"Les Arts de Feu," *Art et Decoration*, Vol. 3, 1898, pp. 189–200.

MUMFORD, J. K.
"A Year at the Tiffany Foundation," *Arts and Decoration*, Vol. 14, 1921, pp. 272–73.

RIORDAN, ROGER.
"American Stained Glass," *The American Art Review*, Vol. 2, Div. 1, 1881, pp. 229–34; Div. 2, pp. 7–11, 59–64.
ROBINSON, FRANK T.
"American Art Glass," *The Decorator and Furnisher*, Vol. VI (5), August 1885, p. 150.
RUGE, CLARA.
"Amerikanische Keramik," *Dekorative Kunst*, Vol. XIV, 1906, p. 167–76.

———.
"American Ceramics—A Brief Review of Progress," *The International Studio*, Vol. XXVIII, No. 109, March 1906, pp. XXI–XXVIII.
RUNKLE, L. G.
"The Limits of Decoration," *Household Art*, 1893, pp. 125–68.
SARGENT, IRENE.
"René Lalique—His Rank Among Contemporary Artists," *The Craftsman*, Vol. III, No. 2, November 1901, pp. 65–73.

———.
"The Wavy Line," *The Craftsman*, Vol. II, No. 3, June 1902, pp. 131–42.
SAYLOR, HENRY H.
"The Country Home of Mr. Louis C. Tiffany," *Country Life in America*, December 1908, pp. 157–62.

———.
"Indoor Fountains," *Country Life in America*, August 1908, p. 366.
SCHEPFER, JEAN.
"L'Art Nouveau," *The Craftsman*, July 1903, pp. 229–38.
SCHUYLER, MONTGOMERY.
"The Romanesque Revival in America," *The Architectural Record*, Vol. 1, 1891, pp. 151–98.
SINGLETON, ESTHER.
"Glass and Glassmaking," *The Mentor*, Vol. 7, No. 5, April 15, 1919.
SMITH, MINNA CAROLINE.
"Louis C. Tiffany—The Celestial Hierarchy," *The International Studio*, Vol. 33, 1908, pp. 96–99.
STONEHOUSE, AUGUSTUS.
"A Glance at New York Theatres," *Art Review*, April 1887, pp. 6–8.
SULLIVAN, LOUIS H.
"Reply to Mr. Frederick S. Lamb on 'Modern Use of the Gothic,'" *The Craftsman*, Vol. 8, 1905.
THARP, EZRA.
"Iridescent Art," *The New Republic*, April 1, 1916.
THOMAS, W. H.
"Glass Mosaic: An Old Art with a New Distinction," *The International Studio*, Vol. 28, 1906, pp. 73–78.
TOWNSEND, HORACE.
"American and French Applied Art at the Grafton Galleries," *The Studio*, Vol. 17, 1899, pp. 39–46.
VIVIAN, H. L.
"Pictures in Mosaic," *Harper's Bazaar*, May 1914.
WAERN, CECILIA.
"The Industrial Arts of America: I, The Tiffany Glass and Decorating Co.," *The Studio*, Vol. XI, 1897, pp. 156–65.

———.
"The Industrial Arts of America: II, The Tiffany or 'Favrile' Glass," *The Studio*, Vol. XIV, No. 63, June 1898, pp. 15–21.
WEIR, HUGH.
"Through the Rooking Glass—An Interview with Louis C. Tiffany," *Collier's*, May 23, 1925.
WEST, MAX.
"The Revival of Handicrafts in America," *Bulletin of The Bureau of Labor*, No. 55, November 1904, pp. 1573–1622.
ZUEBLIN, RHOFISK.
"The Production of Industrial Art in America," *The Chautauquan*, March 1903, pp. 622–27.

ARTICLES IN NEWSPAPERS AND PERIODICALS
PUBLISHED DURING L.C.T.'S LIFETME—UNSIGNED

AMERICAN ARCHITECT AND BUILDING NEWS.
"On the Exhibit of Stained Glass at the Fair." November 11, 1893, pp. 74–75.
AMERICAN ART ANNUAL.
"Mural Paintings in Public Buildings in the United States." Vol. 19, 1922, pp. 407–38.
AMERICAN MAGAZINE OF ART.
"Watercolors by Louis C. Tiffany," Vol. 13, 1922, pp. 258–59.
ANTIQUES.
"Questions and Answers," December 1926, pp. 478.
ARCHITECTURAL RECORD.
"How the Rich Are Buried," Vol. 10, 1900, pp. 23–51.
ART DIGEST.
"Tiffany Studios Bankrupt," May 1, 1932.
ART ET DECORATION.
"La Varrerie au Musée Galliera," July 1910, pp. 21–28.
THE ART INTERCHANGE.
"Art Notes,"   Vol. XX (1), 1887, pp. 2–3.
                  Vol. XX (4), 1888, pp. 49–50.
                  Vol. XXI (9), 1888, pp. 129–30.
                  Vol. XXII (2), 1889, pp. 17–20.
                  Vol. XXVII (6), 1891, pp. 170–1.
THE ART INTERCHANGE.
"Stained Glass for Interior Decoration," Vol. XXVII (3), 1891, pp. 91–94.
THE ART JOURNAL.
"American Artwork in Silver," Vol. I, 1875, pp. 371–74.
"Art Work in Glass," Vol. I, 1875, p. 365.
"The Boston Exhibition," Vol. V, 1879, p. 190.
"Notes," Vol. V, 1879, p. 192.
"Some Examples of Ceramic Art," Vol. I, 1875, pp. 273–75.
"Tiffany's Among the Weeds," Vol. V, 1879, p. 213.
"The Watercolor Exhibition, New York," Vol. II, 1876, pp. 92–93.

BUFFALO COMMERCIAL.
"Great Display by Tiffany," evening ed., March 26, 1901.

BULLETIN OF THE STAINED GLASS ASSOCIATION OF AMERICA.
"Louis Comfort Tiffany," Vol. 23 (11), December 1928, pp. 6–12.
"A Tribute to Mr. Louis Comfort Tiffany," December 1928, pp. 8–12.

CENTURY MAGAZINE.
"Some of the Union League Decorations," Vol. 23, 1882, pp. 745–52.

DECORATOR AND FURNISHER.
"Artistic American Homes," Vol. XXIII (4), January 1894, pp. 128–29.
"Artistic Wallpaper," Vol. III (5), February 1884, pp. 30, 180.
"Editorial," Vol. III (4), January 1884, p. 121.
"High Class American Decoration: Mr. George Kemp's Salon," Vol. XXIII (6), March 1894, pp. 209–10.
"Memorial Windows," Vol. XIV (3), June 1889, pp. 73–75.
"Mr. Louis C. Tiffany's Hall," Vol. XXV (3), December 1894, p. 94.
No title, Vol. IX (1), October 1886, p. 11.
No title, Vol. X (5), August 1887, p. 164.
"The Seventh Regiment Armory," Vol. VI (2), May 1885, pp. 42–46.
"Tiffany Glass and Decorating Company's Exhibit at the Columbian Exposition," Vol. XXIII (1), October 1893, pp. 9–12.
"The Vanderbilt Houses," Vol. XII (1), April 1888, pp. 53–56.

DEKORATIVE KUNST.
"Die Sektion Amerika auf der Turiner Ausstellung," Vol. VI, November 1902, pp. 36–58.
"L. C. Tiffany," Vol. 3, 1899, pp. 108–20.
"Moderne Beleuchtungskorper," Vol. I, 1898, pp. 10–14.
"Moderne Kunst in der Französischen Architektur: das Pariser Haus," Vol. I, 1898, p. 177.
No title, Vol. XI, 1903, pp. 48–49.

DER MODERNE STIL.
Vol. VII, June 1905, p. 70.

DEUTSCH KUNST UND DEKORATION.
"Eindrucke aus der amerikanischen Abteilung," Vol. XI, 1902–3, pp. 182–92.
No title, Vol. VI, April–September 1900, pp. 549–72.
No title, Vol. VII, October 1900–March 1901, p. 86.
No title, Vol. XV, October 1904–March 1905, p. 225.
No title, Vol. XIX, October 1906–March 1907, pp. 359–61.
"Pariser Welt-Ausstellung 1900", "Art Nouveau Bing", "A. Bing's Art Nouveau Auf Der Welt-Ausstellung," Vol. VI, April–September, 1900, pp. 549–72.

DIE KUNST.
"Die Sektion Amerika auf der Turiner Ausstellung," Vol. VIII, 1903, pp. 56–58.

HARPER'S MAGAZINE.
"A Piece of Glass," Vol. 79, 1889, pp. 245–64.

INNEN-DEKORATION.
Mein Heim—Mein Stolz, Vol. XIII, Tahrgang, Darmftadt 1902.

INTERNATIONAL STUDIO.
"A Theatre Curtain of Glass Mosaic," Vol. XLIV (173), July 1911, pp. XVIII.

THE JEWELERS' CIRCULAR.
"Louis C. Tiffany and His Work in Artistic Jewelry". Vol. 30, December, 1906, pp. 33–42.

KERAMIC STUDIO.
"Exhibition of French Pottery at the Tiffany Studios," Vol. III (4), August 1901, pp. 81–82.
"French Pottery," Vol. IV (2), June 1902, pp. 30–31.
"The National Arts Club Exhibit of Porcelain and Pottery at the Pan-American," Vol. III (7), November 1901, p. 1.
No title, Vol. II (8), December 1900.
"Tiffany Glass at the Pan American," Vol. III (2), June 1901.

KUNST UND KUNSTHANDWERK.
"Ausstellung in Turin," Vol. 5, 1902, pp. 443–49.

L'ARTE DECORITIVA ALL ÉSPOSIZIONE DI TORINO.
"La Sezione Degli Stati Uniti," Chapter III, 1902, pp. 59–69.

NEW YORK TIMES.
"A Chapel on Exhibit," February 15, 1894.
"Art Notes," February 19, 1916, p. 10.
"Art Notes," October 17, 1895, p. 20.
"The Bathers Will Stay," December 13, 1914, p. 11.
"Bethlehem Day Nursery," April 8, 1894.
"Egyptian Fete a Fine Spectacle," February 5, 1913, p. 8.
"Exhibition at Tiffany Studios," May 16, 1921.
"First Club, Then Art Shop," October 21, 1905, p. 9.
"Gives a Million for Art Institute," October 20, 1919, p. 1.
"Glass Mosaic Masterpiece," February 17, 1920, p. 8.
"Gorgeous Masque in Tiffany Studio," February 20, 1916, p. 7.
"Keramics and Textiles," April 20, 1905, p. 9.
"L. C. Tiffany Gives a Dance for Daughter," January 21, 1911.
"Louis C. Tiffany Enjoined," June 9, 1916.
"Louis C. Tiffany Wins," May 22, 1904.
"Medal Awarded to L. C. Tiffany," November 24, 1927.
"Miss Tiffany, Bride of Dr. Burlingham," September 25, 1914.
(No title available) November 13, 1880.
(No title available) February 18, 1892.
"Outing of Tiffany Studio Employees," June 14, 1901.
"Paasch-Feest for Charity," April 8, 1888.
"Stained Glass at the Tiffany Galleries," February 27, 1897.
"Stained Windows for Yale," May 24, 1889, p. 4.
"Three Handsome Glass Windows," December 12, 1895.

"Tiffany Foundation Exhibit," November 13, 1921, p. 8.

"Tiffany Studios to Remove from Present Quarters at Twenty-fifth Street," March 7, 1905.

"Tiffany Studios Files as Bankrupt," April 17, 1932.

"Tiffany Sues Oyster Bay," June 25, 1916.

"Will of Charles L. Tiffany," February 16, 1902, and February 26, 1902.

SCRIBNER'S MONTHLY.

"American Progress in the Manufacture of Stained Glass," January, 1881, pp. 485–86.

"Dr. Schliemann at Mycenae," January, 1878, pp. 307–20.

"The Society of Decorative Art," Vol. 22, 1881, pp. 697–709.

TOWN AND COUNTRY.

"Modern Art in Glassware" (signed A.T.A.), December 2, 1905, pp. 15–16.

ARTICLES IN NEWSPAPERS AND PERIODICALS PUBLISHED AFTER TIFFANY'S DEATH—SIGNED

ABRAMS, HARRY N.

"A Long, Sensitive, Sinuous Line," New York Times, August 23, 1964, p. 322.

AMAYA, MARIO.

"The Taste for Tiffany," Apollo, February 1965.

AYTES, BARBARA.

"Iridescent Art Glass," Treasure Chest, May–June 1961, pp. 10–15.

BUECHNER, THOMAS S.

"Art in Glass," Art News Annual, 1955, pp. 136–50, 172–74.

——.

"The Glass of Frederick Carder," Connoisseur Year-Book, 1961, pp. 52–53.

BUTLER, JOSEPH T.

"America," Connoisseur, Vol. 189 (760), June 1975, p. 161.

CARPENTER, CHARLES H., JR.

"Tiffany Silver in the Japanese Style," Connoisseur, January 1979, pp. 42–47.

CLAY, LANCASTER.

"Japanese Buildings in the United States Before 1900," The Art Bulletin, Vol. 35, 1953, pp. 217–25.

——.

"Oriental Contributions to Art Nouveau," The Art Bulletin, Vol. 34, 1952, pp. 297–310.

DAVIDSON, R. B.

"Tiffany Glass and Bristol Glass at the Metropolitan Museum of Art," Antiques, December 1956, p. 582.

DAVIS, FELICE.

"Art Nouveau a Long Time Reviving," New York World-Telegram and Sun, September 6, 1963, p. 20.

FARRER, SAMUEL.

"Durand Glass," Antiques Journal, August 1960, pp. 12–16; May 1961, pp. 8–12.

FELD, STUART P.

"Nature in Her Most Seductive Aspects," Bulletin of the Metropolitan Museum of Art, November 1962, pp. 100–12.

FOX, DOROTHEA M.

"Tiffany Glass," Antiques, Vol. 44, 1943, pp. 240–41, 295–96.

GARRETT, WENDELL.

"The Flowering of Art Nouveau," Antiques, April 1977, pp. 1288–89.

GRANT, MARENA.

"Treasures from Laurelton Hall," Antiques, April 1977, pp. 752–59.

HANDLER, FREDERICK JOHN.

"Louis Comfort Tiffany's Pursuit of Beauty," Great Neck Newsmagazine Group, Ltd., April 1976, pp. 11–17.

HAWLEY, HENRY H.

"Tiffany's Silver in the Japanese Taste," Bulletin of the Cleveland Museum of Art, Vol. LXIII (7), October 1976, pp. 236–43.

KAUFMANN, EDGAR, JR.

"At Home with Louis C. Tiffany," Interiors, December 1957, pp. 118–25, 183.

——.

"Tiffany, Then and Now," Interiors, February 1955, pp. 82–85.

KELLOGG, CYNTHIA.

"Designs by Mr. Tiffany," The New York Times Magazine, January 26, 1958, pp. 50–51.

KOCH, ROBERT.

"Tiffany-Byzantine Inkwell," The Brooklyn Museum Bulletin, Spring 1960, pp. 5–8.

KUH, KATHARINE.

"Tiffany and the Good Life," Saturday Review, June 14, 1975, pp. 43–45.

LA COSSITT, HENRY.

"Treasure House on Fifth Avenue," The Saturday Evening Post, January 24, 1953, pp. 30–31, 102–6; January 31, 1953, pp. 30, 108–10.

LOCKWOOD, HOWARD J.

"The Metalware Productions of Tiffany Studios," Spinning Wheel, July–August 1971, pp. 22–24.

LORING, JOHN.

"American Art Glass," Architectural Digest, July/August 1975, p. 84.

MCKEAN, HUGH F.

"A Study of Louis Comfort Tiffany," The Flamingo, Rollins College, Winter Park, Florida, Winter 1955, pp. 3–4.

MESSANELLE, RAY.

"Art Glass Signed Nash," Spinning Wheel, February 1962, pp. 12–13.

O'NEAL, WILLIAM B.

"Three Art Nouveau Glass Makers," Journal of Glass Studies, Vol. 2, 1960, pp. 125–37.

PADDOCK, JOHN.

"Tiffany Windows in Searsport," Down East, Vol. XXIII (5), January 1977, pp. 36–39.

PEPIS, BETTY.

"Revival of Tiffany Lamps," The New York Times, July 9, 1956, p. 28.

PERROT, PAUL.
"Frederick Carder's Legacy to Glass," *Craft Horizons,*
May/June 1961.

POLAK, ADA.
"Gallé Glass," *Journal of Glass Studies,* Vol. V,
1963, pp. 105–15.

————.
"Tiffany 'Favrile' Glass," *Antique Dealer And Collector's Guide,* January 1962, pp. 39–41.

QUIMBY, IAN M. G.
"Oriental Influence on American Decorative Arts,"
Journal of the Society of Architectural Historians, December 1976, p. 300–8.

SAARINEN, ALINE B.
"Famous, Derided and Revived," *The New York
Times,* March 13, 1955, p. 9.

SAKS, JUDITH.
"Tiffany's Household Decoration–A Landscape Window," *Bulletin of the Cleveland Museum of Art,* Vol.
LXIII (7), October 1976, pp. 227–35.

SCHAEFER, HERWIN.
"Tiffany's Fame in Europe," *The Art Bulletin,* December 1962, pp. 309–28.

TUCCI, DOUGLASS, SHAND.
"Ralph Adams Cram: America's Gothic Scholar-Architect," *American Art Review,* Vol. 3, No. 3,
May–June 1976, pp. 125–36.

VAN TASSEL, VALENTINE.
"Louis Comfort Tiffany," *The Antiques Journal,* Vol.
7, No. 7, 1952, pp. 19–21, 42; No. 8, pp. 13–15, 42.

WALKER, DOROTHY.
"Dark Mansions," *New York World-Telegram,* December 29, 1939, 2nd Sec., p. 11.

WEISSBERGER, HERBERT.
"After Many Years: Tiffany Glass," *Carnegie Magazine,* October 1956, pp. 265–68, 279.

ARTICLES IN NEWSPAPERS AND PERIODICALS
PUBLISHED AFTER TIFFANY'S DEATH—UNSIGNED

ART AND ARCHAEOLOGY.
"Tiffany Studios Active," May 1933.

ART DIGEST.
"Tiffany Foundation: Note on the Founder," October 15, 1949.
"Louis C. Tiffany" (obituary), February 1, 1933.
"Tiffany's Great Curtain," October 15, 1934.

ART NEWS.
"Favrile Glass, from the Private Collection of Its
Designer, Louis C. Tiffany," April 4, 1936.

HARPER'S MAGAZINE.
"Revival of the Fanciest: Tiffany Glass," September
1956, p. 80.

HOUSE BEAUTIFUL.
"Iridescence, the New Dimension in Decorating," October 1956, pp. 176–81.

MEDICAL NEWSMAGAZINE.
"A World of Art Nouveau," Vol. 21 (2), February
1977, pp. 67–70.

MIAMI HERALD.
"Tiffany's Houses Odd—But Then So Was He," April
14, 1968, p. 6B.

NEW YORK HERALD TRIBUNE.
"Tiffany Home and Art Works Will Go on Sale,"
September 8, 1946.
"Long Island Landmark Burns," March 6, 1957.

NEW YORK TIMES.
"Louis C. Tiffany, Noted Artist, Dies," January 18,
1933.
"Family Gets Bulk of Estate," January 29, 1933.
"Old Tiffany Home Made City History," April 26,
1936.

NEW YORK WORLD-TELEGRAM.
"Louis Comfort Tiffany Made Laurelton Hall a
World's Museum," December 29, 1939.

NORTH SHORE JOURNAL.
Locust Valley, Long Island, Vol. 3, No. 3. March 4,
1971. (Included as a special supplement in *The
Leader.*)

OCCASIONAL NEWSLETTERS TO MEMBERS OF CHICAGO
HISTORICAL SOCIETY.
May 1973.

SOUTHERN LIVING.
"In Light of Tiffany's Work," Vol. 12 (6), June
1977, p. 61.

TIME MAGAZINE.
"New Art Nouveau," March 10, 1958, pp. 74–77.

ARTICLES BY LOUIS C. TIFFANY

"American Art Supreme in Colored Glass," *The Forum,*
Vol. XV, 1893, pp. 621–28.
"Color and Its Kinship to Sound," *The Art World,* Vol. 2,
1917, pp. 142–43.
"The Dream Garden," *Curtis Publishing Company,*
Philadelphia, Pa.
"The Gospel of Good Taste," *Country Life in America,*
Vol. XIX, No. 2, November 1910, p. 105.
"The Quest of Beauty," *Harper's Bazaar,* December 1917,
pp. 43–44.
"The Tasteful Use of Light and Color in Artificial Illumination," *Scientific American,* Vol. 104, April 1911,
p. 373.
"What Is The Quest of Beauty?" *The International
Studio,* Vol. 58, April 1916, p. lxiii.

BROCHURES AND PUBLICATIONS ISSUED
BY TIFFANY'S CORPORATIONS

A COLLECTION OF ENGLISH FURNITURE by Luke V. Lockwood. Tiffany Studios, 1907.

ANTIQUE TEXTILES.
Tiffany Studios.

THE ART OF AMERICAN INDIANS.
Tiffany Studios, 1909.

BRONZE LAMPS.
Tiffany Studios, 1904.

CHARACTER AND INDIVIDUALITY IN DECORATIONS AND
FURNISHINGS.
    Tiffany Studios, 1913.
COLLECTION OF ANTIQUE CHINESE RUGS.
    Tiffany Studios, 1908.
ECCLESIASTICAL DEPARTMENT.
    Tiffany Studios (c. 1900–5).
EXAMPLES OF RECENT WORK FROM THE STUDIO OF
LOUIS C. TIFFANY by Ethel Syford.
    with Tiffany Studios, 1911.
GOD'S ACRE by James Burrell.
    Tiffany Studios, 1906.
A LIST OF WINDOWS AND EXTRACTS FROM LETTERS AND
NEWSPAPERS.
    Tiffany Glass and Decorating Company, 1897.
MAUSOLEUMS.
    Tiffany Studios, 1914.
MEMORIALS IN GLASS AND STONE.
    Tiffany Studios, 1913.
MEMORIAL TABLETS.
    Tiffany Glass and Decorating Company, 1896.
MEMORIAL WINDOWS.
    Tiffany Glass and Decorating Company, 1896.
THE MOSAIC CURTAIN FOR THE NATIONAL THEATER OF
MEXICO.
    Tiffany Studios, 1911.
NOTABLE ANTIQUE ORIENTAL RUGS, THE TIFFANY STUDIOS
    COLLECTION OF. University Press, 1906, Cambridge.
A PARTIAL LIST OF WINDOWS.
    Tiffany Studios, 1910.
PORTFOLIO OF WORK OF THE TIFFANY STUDIOS.
    Tiffany Studios, 1901.
A SYNOPSIS OF THE EXHIBIT AT THE WORLD'S FAIR,
CHICAGO.
    Tiffany Glass and Decorating Company, 1893.
TIFFANY DOMESTIC WINDOWS.
    Tiffany Studios.
TIFFANY FAVRILE GLASS.
    Tiffany Glass and Decorating Company, 1896.
TIFFANY FAVRILE GLASS.
    Tiffany Studios.
TIFFANY GLASS MOSAICS.
    Tiffany Glass and Decorating Company, 1896.
TRIBUTES TO HONOR.
    Tiffany Studios.
THE ZODIAC DESK SET.
    Tiffany Studios.

EXHIBITION CATALOGUES

ART NOUVEAU.
    Lyman Allyn Museum. Robert Koch and Jane Hay-
    ward, New London, Conn., 1963.
ART NOUVEAU.
    Virginia Museum of Art, November 22–December
    26, 1971.
ART NOUVEAU BELGIUM/FRANCE.
    Institute for the Arts, Rice University, Houston, Tex.,
    1976.

ART NOUVEAU, THE RISEMAN COLLECTION OF TIFFANY
GLASS.
    Auction Catalogue. Sotheby Parke Bernet Inc., New
    York.
THE ARTS AND CRAFTS MOVEMENT IN AMERICA
1877–1916.
    Catalogue of exhibition organized by the Art Mu-
    seum, Princeton University, and the Art Institute of
    Chicago, 1972.
THE ARTS OF LOUIS COMFORT TIFFANY AND HIS TIMES.
    John and Mable Ringling Museum of Art, Sarasota,
    Florida. February 7–June 1, 1975.
AUCTION CATALOGUE.
    The Louis C. Tiffany Studios of New York. Lester
    Dutt Associates. Washington, D.C., March 14–19,
    1938.
CATALOGUE OF THE 23RD ANNUAL EXHIBITION.
    The Architectural League of New York, Samuel
    Howe, 1907.
CATALOGUES OF THE SECOND–TWELFTH ANNUAL
EXHIBITION(S).
    The Architectural League of New York, 1887–98.
EXHIBITION OF L'ART NOUVEAU.
    Introduction by S. Bing, the Grafton Galleries, Lon-
    don, 1899.
LOUIS COMFORT TIFFANY.
    Museum of Contemporary Crafts. New York, 1958.
NINETEENTH-CENTURY AMERICA—FURNITURE AND OTHER
DECORATIVE ARTS.
    Metropolitan Museum of Art, 1970.
SALON DE L'ART NOUVEAU.
    Catalogue Premier. S. Bing, Paris, 1895.
THE STAINED GLASS WINDOWS OF SAINT JOSEPH.
    Photographs by James Enyeart. Albrecht Art Mu-
    seum, St. Joseph, Missouri, 1976.
WINTER 1975/76.
    Metropolitan Museum of Art. Vol. XXXIII (4),
    Figure 85.
WORKS OF ART BY LOUIS COMFORT TIFFANY.
    The Morse Gallery of Art, Rollins College, Winter
    Park, Florida, February 21–March 31, 1955.

ARTICLES BY LOUIS COMFORT TIFFANY FOUNDATION

EXHIBITION OF PAINTINGS AND ORIENTAL OBJECTS OF
ART BELONGING TO THE LOUIS COMFORT TIFFANY
FOUNDATION GALLERY.
    Art Center, 65–67 East 56th Street, March 6–March
    25th, 1922.
LOUIS COMFORT TIFFANY FOUNDATION.
    Founded 1919. Oyster Bay, Long Island, 1954.
LOUIS COMFORT TIFFANY FOUNDATION, ITS
REORGANIZATION AND DISTRIBUTION OF SCHOLARSHIPS,
1954.
LOUIS COMFORT TIFFANY FOUNDATION CATALOGUE OF CHI-
NESE AND JAPANESE OBJECTS OF ART. 1920.
    Matsuki, Bunkio, and Carroll, Dana H.
CATALOGUE OF ORIENTAL & CHINESE RUGS, 1920.
    Mumford, John Kimberly and Carroll, Dana H.

Index

9727

9727